D1739573

J. S. BACH AT HIS ROYAL INSTRUMENT

J. S. Bach at His Royal Instrument

ESSAYS ON HIS ORGAN WORKS

Russell Stinson

OXFORD UNIVERSITY PRESS

2012

Oxford University Press, Inc., publishes works that further
Oxford University's objective of excellence
in research, scholarship, and education.

Oxford   New York
Auckland   Cape Town   Dar es Salaam   Hong Kong   Karachi
Kuala Lumpur   Madrid   Melbourne   Mexico City   Nairobi
New Delhi   Shanghai   Taipei   Toronto

With offices in
Argentina   Austria   Brazil   Chile   Czech Republic   France   Greece
Guatemala   Hungary   Italy   Japan   Poland   Portugal   Singapore
South Korea   Switzerland   Thailand   Turkey   Ukraine   Vietnam

© Oxford University Press 2012

Published by Oxford University Press, Inc.
198 Madison Avenue, New York, New York 10016
www.oup.com

Oxford is a registered trade mark of Oxford University Press

All rights reserved. No part of this publication may be reproduced,
stored in a retrieval system, or transmitted, in any form or by any means,
electronic, mechanical, photocopying, recording, or otherwise,
without the prior permission of Oxford University Press.

Library of Congress Cataloging-in-Publication Data
Stinson, Russell.
J.S. Bach at his royal instrument : essays on his organ works / Russell Stinson.
p. cm.
Includes bibliographical references and index.
ISBN 978-0-19-991723-5 (hardcover : alk. paper)
1. Bach, Johann Sebastian, 1685–1750. Organ music.   2. Organ music—History and criticism.
I. Title.
ML410.B1S855 2012
786.5092—dc23   2012007235

Publication of this book was supported by the Dragan Plamenac Endowment
of the American Musicological Society.

Even in his secular compositions he disdained everything common, but in his compositions for the organ he kept himself infinitely more distant from it; so that here, it seems to me, he does not appear like a man, but as a true disembodied spirit, who soars above everything mortal.

—JOHANN NIKOLAUS FORKEL, 1802

Contents

Introduction

"HOW WELL MENDELSSOHN understands the treatment of Bach's royal instrument is generally known; and yesterday he laid before us nothing but precious jewels, in the most glorious variety and gradation." Thus begins Robert Schumann's glowing review of the legendary all-Bach organ recital played by Felix Mendelssohn in 1840 at St. Thomas's Church, Leipzig, where Bach served as cantor for most of his professional life. Bach's royal instrument? This epithet surely refers less to the particular organ on which Mendelssohn performed, which by that time bore little resemblance to the instrument Bach had known, than to Bach's dominion over the organ as a musical instrument in general. Like the young Mozart ("In my eyes and ears the organ is the *king* of instruments"), Schumann also sensed something royal about the organ's towering stature and perhaps its capacity for volume as well. His sobriquet, however, is ultimately more concerned with Bach himself than any issues of—pardon the pun—organology. Just as Schumann stood in awe of Bach's reputation as the greatest organ virtuoso in music history, so he hailed his famous predecessor as "the greatest composer in the world" who had "written the majority of his most splendid pieces" for the organ (letter to J. G. Herzog).

While Johann Sebastian Bach's general supremacy as a composer can hardly be contested, not even the most ardent organ lover today would necessarily accept Schumann's pronouncement about the supremacy of Bach's organ works in relation to all of his other compositions. Still, it is undeniable that Bach dominates the field of organ music like no other composer dominates any other repertory. Not surprisingly his organ works have long attracted musicological attention, spawning a vast literature in the process. That the topic has by no means been exhausted is due to several factors. Consider, first of all, the sheer number of Bach's surviving organ compositions (close to three hundred) and the sheer size of that repertoire (the nine volumes of the relatively small Peters edition total almost nine hundred pages). The incomparable quality of the music—its stylistic diversity, which results in part from the dizzying array of compositional models involved, and its mind-boggling complexity—is yet another reason why no one will ever have the "last word" on the subject. In addition, Bach's organ works have exerted a profound and lasting influence on later generations, including many of the greatest composers, performers (organists and otherwise), conductors, critics, and scholars in the whole history of music.

Published here (and all for the first time) are seven essays that delve into various unexplored aspects of these masterpieces. The opening chapter begins with a critique of recent literature, with special emphasis on the second edition of Peter Williams's *The Organ Music of J. S. Bach,* and ends by unveiling what must be the best-kept secret in modern Bach scholarship. I then discuss a particular compositional procedure that helps us better understand not only Bach's organ chorales but also those of his predecessors and contemporaries. The next two chapters grew out of my book, published in 2006, *The Reception of Bach's Organ Works from Mendelssohn to Brahms.* I delivered preliminary versions of each as conference papers in Knoxville (14th AGO National Conference on Organ Pedagogy), Leipzig ("Die Orgel im Zeitalter der Romantik"), Rochester ("Mendelssohn and the Contrapuntal Tradition"), and Edinburgh (1st International Conference on Historical Keyboard Music). Chapter 3 deals with neglected aspects of Mendelssohn's Leipzig Bach recital and with his relationship to such fellow "receptors" of Bach's organ works as Schumann and the organists C. F. Becker and J. G. Schneider. Chapter 4 investigates how Schumann—and such colleagues of his as Becker and the Bach fanatic Eduard Krüger—promoted Bach's organ music in the *Neue Zeitschrift für Musik.* Chapters 5 and 6 represent a comprehensive inquiry into César Franck's and Edward Elgar's reception of the music. The archival data presented there shed light in particular on Franck's organ studio (where, as may also be seen in the two appendices, he taught works by Bach, Mendelssohn, Schumann, and himself) and on Elgar's interpretation of Bach's organ works both as a performer and unofficial critic. The final chapter, which surveys the reception of selected works over a period of almost three centuries, is at once the longest and the farthest-flung. Its dramatis personae include such disparate figures from the annals of music history as Wagner, Mozart, and the rock group Emerson, Lake and Palmer, but I also take into account such films as *The Godfather* and *Solaris,* a poem by Hermann Hesse, and the appropriation of certain pieces by the Nazi party.

This book would not have been possible without the assistance of a great many institutions and individuals. First and foremost, I was privileged to conduct on-site research at archives in Leipzig (Stadtgeschichtliches Museum, Städtische Bibliotheken), Lower Broadheath (Elgar Birthplace Museum), Paris (Archives Nationales), and Zwickau (Robert-Schumann-Haus). My travel to these locations was supported by grants from the American Bach Society and Lyon College. I also benefited from a visiting appointment in Bach studies at the University of Louisville, where ready access to a first-rate music library and a reduced teaching load expedited my research and writing, respectively. For answering queries, providing photocopies, and/or volunteering valuable bits of information, I would like to thank the following colleagues, friends, and family members: Catherine Bordeau; Melvin Dickinson; Pieter Dirksen; Nobuaki Ebata, Reinmar Emans; Sven Hiemke; Linda Holzer; Kevin Jackson; Wayne Leupold; Michael Maul; Kathleen McMorrow; Stephanie Poxon; Robert Shay; Rollin Smith; Birgit, Matthew, and Patrick Stinson; Thomas Synofzik; Nicholas Temperley; Yo Tomita; Melvin Unger; Katherine Wheeler; Kathy Whittenton; Christoph Wolff; Peter Wollny; Daniel Zager; and especially Wm. A. Little. Other acknowledgements appear in the footnotes. A special word of gratitude goes to Robert Bailey for help in translating French (unless otherwise indicated, all translations from the German language are mine alone); to Orphe Ochse for supplying me with her archival notes on Franck's organ studio; and to Sean Roulier for his rendering of the musical examples. My greatest debt is to my wife Laura for her patience, support, and love.

It is my hope that even the most seasoned aficionado of Bach's organ works will find in these pages much new information about and many new insights into this marvelous music.

Russell Stinson
Batesville, Arkansas
December 2011

J. S. BACH AT HIS ROYAL INSTRUMENT

1

Studies and Discoveries

IF THE PAST decade can serve as any indication, scholarly interest in Bach's organ music will continue unabatedly well into the new millennium. Many articles on the subject have already appeared, as well as books and editions. The main goal of this chapter is to review one of the most important of these publications, namely, the second edition of Peter Williams's monograph *The Organ Music of J. S. Bach*, published by Cambridge University Press in 2003, while simultaneously discussing scholarship in general on Bach's organ works over the past three decades. We will also examine a virtually unknown work by one of Bach's pupils that raises a fundamental question about one of the master's most popular organ fugues.

Williams's study was originally issued by the same press in two installments, with volumes 1 and 2, a piece-by-piece commentary on the free works and the chorale settings, respectively, appearing in 1980, and with volume 3 (*A Background*), a survey of such topics as liturgy, instruments, and performance practice, following in 1984. The thirty-two pages of additions and corrections to volumes 1 and 2 with which this third volume concludes may be interpreted as the author's first attempt to revise his book; he was able to update all three volumes when they were published in German translation between 1996 and 2000. This most recent incarnation conveniently combines the first two volumes into a single one, and with a largely rewritten text. (Williams contends in his preface that volume 3 "needs a separate revision," but none is yet forthcoming.) Our primary concern will be the abundant new material found in the second English edition, much of which involves Williams's reliance on and criticism of literature published between 1980 and 2002.

Due to various factors, Williams's new text is roughly a hundred pages shorter than the previous volumes 1 and 2, despite commentaries on almost sixty additional works—including thirty-one hitherto unknown chorales from the so-called Neumeister Collection (BWV 1090–1120) that surfaced in 1984—and despite a greatly enlarged glossary and bibliography: many of the commentaries have been drastically abbreviated, footnotes have all but been eliminated, the number of musical examples has been reduced from around six hundred to three hundred, and the number of manuscript sources listed for individual pieces has been reduced as well. Given the dramatic differences between the two editions, it is as if Williams has authored an entirely new book. The relatively impassioned (and sometimes even playful) tone of his new commentary, plus his greater willingness to speculate on such matters as rhetoric, numerology, and religious symbolism, only reinforces this impression. This is not to say that any scholarly objectivity has been lost or that the author has shed his habit of equivocating rather than taking a definite stand on the issues, whether they involve chronology, authenticity, or musical style.

Several of the changes between the two editions are explained in the preface, where Williams writes that "if the Neumeister chorales are the work of J. S. Bach, so must many another piece be." This statement both establishes some (characteristic) skepticism on his part about the authenticity of the Neumeisters and defends his inclusion of more than twenty chorale arrangements that are either listed in the appendix of the Bach-Werke-Verzeichnis (BWV Anh.) or that do not appear in that venerable catalogue. In these matters, Williams was guided by the volume of the recently completed Neue Bach-Ausgabe (NBA) titled *Organ Chorales from Miscellaneous Sources*—or at least the editor's preliminary research for that volume—which contains more than fifty such works, including a heretofore unpublished setting of "Wachet auf" for organ and trumpet (BWV Anh. 66).[1]

For detailed data on manuscript sources, Williams refers the reader to the critical commentaries of the NBA, the revised edition of the BWV, and the forthcoming organ-music volumes of the *Bach-Compendium*. (Today, however, the best and easiest way of accessing this information is through that magnificent and authoritative website known as the "Göttinger Bach-Katalog.") Williams has done an admirable job in summarizing recent scholarship in this arena, although he is not infallible. Take, for instance, his two references to the copyist formerly known as Anonymous 5, who at the time Williams was revising his book was hypothesized by Marianne Helms to be the Leipzig organist (and Bach pupil) Johann Schneider.[2] The first reference, regarding a copy of the Prelude and Fugue in E Minor, BWV 548, reads "Anon 5 = Johann Schneider?" but the second, regarding a copy of the Fantasy in G Major (*Pièce d'Orgue*), BWV 572, reads "J. Schneider, c. 1729?" which implies that only the date of the manuscript was in question. Furthermore,

---

1. The editor of this volume, published in 2008, is Reinmar Emans, whose accompanying critical commentary runs 555 pages.
2. Dürr and Helms 1981, 195.

Helms proposed that this manuscript originated at the end of 1722. Thanks to some nifty detective work by Andrew Talle, published in the 2003 *Bach-Jahrbuch*, this elusive scribe is now known to be Bernhard Christian Kayser, who evidently as a teenager studied under Bach in Cöthen and then followed his teacher to Leipzig.[3] Talle, too, dates Kayser's copy of the G-major fantasy to 1722, although the piece seems to have been composed several years earlier.

Williams's preface also states that he was "at pains to refer to other composers in relation to J. S. Bach, not least since these are now better served by editions and studies." This remark is particularly true of Bach's pupil Johann Ludwig Krebs (forty-five references) and Bach's kinsman and colleague Johann Gottfried Walther (sixty-six references). So often did Krebs "ape his master" when composing for the organ (p. 442) that he comes off here as the ultimate Bach epigone. Williams now suggests that the fughetta on "Das Jesulein soll doch mein Trost," BWV 702, with its wide voice spacing, high tessitura, and meandering tonality, is actually a composition by Krebs, despite Pieter Dirksen's compelling argument that it is an authentic—and very late—Bach work that belonged, with seven other chorale fughettas (BWV 696–99, 701, and 703–4), to a cycle of organ chorales for the seasons of Advent, Christmas, and New Year.[4] Yet Williams also now distances himself from the long-standing hypothesis that Krebs wrote the Eight Little Preludes and Fugues, BWV 553–60, despite Alfred Dürr's discovery that the watermark of their principal source is otherwise found only in three fascicles of a manuscript owned by Krebs, one of which is in Krebs's hand as well.[5] As Williams nicely puts it, "the *eminence grise* is more likely to be a southern composer such as J. K. F. Fischer."

Nor does Williams wholeheartedly accept a more recent theory that Krebs is responsible for the last forty measures of the Fugue in C Minor, BWV 537/2. This provocative hypothesis is the work of John O'Donnell, who in an article in the 1989 *Organ Yearbook* (a journal edited by Williams) noticed that the contrapuntal quality of the movement starts to deteriorate precisely at the point in the work's earliest manuscript where the handwriting switches from that of Krebs's father—the Bach pupil Johann Tobias Krebs—to Ludwig's. O'Donnell concluded, therefore, that "Ludwig Krebs's contribution was not an exercise of copying but of completing a Bach work copied by his father from an incomplete source."[6] Neither Williams nor O'Donnell mentions that only in this final section of the fugue does the subject appear, in mm. 105 and 127–28,

---

3. Talle 2003, 155–72.

4. See Dirksen 2002. Dirksen's edition of these works (*Johann Sebastian Bach: Leipziger Choralfughetten*) was published by Breitkopf & Härtel in 2007.

5. Dürr 1987, 34. These pieces were excluded from the NBA, but they are scheduled to appear in vol. 1 (*Pedagogical Works*) of the new Leupold edition of Bach's complete organ works. See Stauffer 2010b, 42–43.

6. O'Donnell 1989, 90. In this regard, Williams mistakenly refers to the "last *ninety* bars" of the fugue (p. 60). Another argument made by O'Donnell is that the subject of this fugue is based on a theme by Johann Mattheson.

respectively, with a passing tone between the fifth and sixth notes or with an immediate restatement of its third bar (see ex. 1.1, which shows that the restatement is slightly

EXAMPLE 1.1. Fugue in C Minor, BWV 537/2, mm. 124–30

embellished and transposed up an octave from the alto to the soprano voice). The latter technique, which also serves as a climactic gesture since it is reserved for the last fugal statement, would seem to be especially supportive of O'Donnell's theory, so rarely is it encountered in fugues composed by or attributed to Bach. Indeed, this may be a unique instance.

Whereas the lone bombshell in the first edition was the now famous hypothesis that the Toccata and Fugue in D Minor, BWV 565, was originally composed for solo violin and by someone other than Bach, Williams now advances several new and sometimes radical ideas. One is that the six Trio Sonatas, BWV 525–30, may at one time have been slated for publication, perhaps (before being replaced because of their technical difficulty?) as the original Part 2 of the *Clavierübung*. Williams's presentation of the admittedly circumstantial evidence in support of this attractive argument reveals a comprehensive understanding of musical as well as philological matters:

> Such a set of sonatas might have been compiled for publication, corresponding to the set of harpsichord partitas issued in 1731, matching the progressive chamber music of the late 1720s for the *Collegium musicum*, and even employing up-to-date notation (three staves, tempo marks, some slurs and dots). Both Partitas and Sonatas use the treble G-clef, although earlier versions of movements in both sets had used the soprano C-clef: a change made perhaps for the sake of publication. P 271 [Bach's autograph] has more convenient page-turns than other copies and may have been intended as printer's fair copy to be used in the engraving process itself.

In response to Forkel's report that Bach "drew up" the trio sonatas for his eldest son Wilhelm Friedemann, Williams observes that both Friedemann and the Bach pupil Heinrich Nicolaus Gerber composed the occasional organ trio, but that the seventeen by J. L. Krebs, which were "perhaps student assignments in writing both traditional and more *galant* invertible counterpoint," are more obviously modeled after Bach's. According to a recent article by Owen Jander, published in the inaugural issue of the fine new journal *Keyboard Perspectives*, Bach intended for his trio sonatas to teach Friedemann the differences between various meters and tempo markings, for each of the eighteen movements, with one exception, has its own combination of the two.[7] How could this fascinating fact have been overlooked for so long?

Continuing in BWV order, Williams also offers some interesting remarks on the two versions of the "gloriously massive" Toccata in F Major, BWV 540/1. He sees no reason why the longer version, whose pedal part famously extends all the way up to f′, must continue to be regarded as the earlier one. That distinction, he implies, could just as easily belong to the version used for the first print of the toccata (ca. 1832), one traditionally assumed to be a "reduction" by J. T. Krebs, who is the scribe of the movement's earliest source. In this version, the eleven bars in the two pedal solos of the longer version that employ notes above middle C are absent, and the main motive of the principal section of the toccata is often transposed down an octave when stated in the pedals, obviously to avoid these same high pitches.

Williams is not the only modern musicologist to question the conventional wisdom on this subject. Indeed, in his recent edition of the shorter version of the toccata, Siegbert Rampe has written that there is "no room for doubt that the shorter version is the early form of this work."[8] What leads Rampe to this conclusion are the many readings of the shorter version deemed by him to be "distinctly earlier," the relatively symmetrical form of this version, and the fact that Bach is not known ever to have significantly reduced the length of a piece while revising it. Rampe also proposes that Bach prepared the longer version either for a performance by himself at the Weissenfels court church, whose organ was one of only two in central Germany with a pedalboard to f′, or, for the sake of his pupils who had access to pedal harpsichords or clavichords with this compass, as a kind of exercise in playing high pedal notes.

With all due respect to these two scholars, musical common sense suggests that the conventional wisdom is correct. To quote from Peter Ward Jones's scalding review of Rampe's edition:

[T]hough [Krebs's manuscript] may be the earliest source, it is difficult to accept that it corresponds wholly to Bach's original conception. The octave span of the

---

7. Jander 2007, 74 and 76, respectively.
8. Rampe 2007, x–xi.

imitative arpeggio figure, which forms the principal motif of the main section of the toccata and is always introduced by pedals, is so integral to the piece that its frequent alteration in this early source to avoid pedal notes above c surely reflects an adaptation made out of necessity, and not Bach's original intention.[9]

Consider, too, how musically unconvincing the first pedal solo is without mm. 58–59 of the longer version, which strongly implies that someone other than Bach is responsible: a lopsided three-bar phrase (mm. 55–57) is combined with a similarly misshapen one of five bars (mm. 60–64), versus phrases of four and six bars in the longer version. As for the sixteen "distinctly earlier" readings enumerated by Rampe, all but one can be dismissed as copying errors by Krebs (compare mm. 270–73 of the shorter version to the more ornate reading in mm. 279–82 of the longer version). Krebs, then, was copying from an early version of the toccata that has not survived.

Williams's opening paragraph on the Prelude and Fugue in B Minor, BWV 544, contains these observations: "The work's idiom has much in common with B-minor music in the *St. Matthew Passion* and Cantata 198, Funeral Ode for the Electress of Saxony, which was performed in the university church in 1727—with an organ prelude and postlude? The elegiac B minor of the cantata's opening chorus matches BWV 544 closely, and they could well be contemporary." That the organ work and the cantata were composed at around the same time is suggested more tangibly by the autograph fair copy of the former, which dates from ca. 1727–31. From these circumstances, Williams seems to be rather coyly implying that the B-minor prelude was played as the prelude to the memorial service for the electress, and the fugue as the postlude.

Had he pursued this line of reasoning any further, Williams would have discovered that "contemporary descriptions of the service…make specific references to an organ prelude and postlude."[10] This quote is taken from Christoph Wolff's acclaimed biography *Johann Sebastian Bach: The Learned Musician*, published in 2000, in which we also read that due to the importance of the event, "only Bach" could have played the organ prelude and postlude. Wolff contends moreover that "A particularly fitting piece would be the Prelude and Fugue in B minor, BWV 544, the prelude of which would have drowned out the instrumental ensemble's tuning for BWV 198, also in B minor." An endnote in Wolff's book states that the new Scheibe organ at the university church was tuned to chamber pitch rather than choir pitch, and therefore would have sounded at the same pitch as the instruments. Thus the hypothesis that the B-minor was played at this service involves far more evidence than the general stylistic similarities alluded to by Williams.

It was Gilles Cantagrel, however, in a monograph from 1998 with the picturesque title *Le moulin et la rivière: Air et variations sur BACH*, who first posited this theory, although

9. Ward Jones 2009, 579. The arpeggio figure is "altered," that is, transposed down an octave, in mm 233–34, 245–46, 249–50, 281–82, 289–90, and 343–44 of the shorter version.

10. Wolff 2000, 316–17.

his discussion relies far too heavily on questionable melodic connections between the organ work and the cantata.[11] Cantagrel even proposes that in homage to the electress, Bach based his fugue subject on a Bohemian folk song, one that would have held special significance for her because it tells the story of an unhappily married woman, much like the electress herself was as the wife of the philandering August the Strong. An English summary of Cantagrel's argument may be found in the liner notes to the Ricercar Consort's recording of this cantata, which begins with the B-minor prelude and ends with the fugue.[12] Between the two parts of the cantata, where the memorial oration would have been delivered, is heard the mournful organ miniature "Herzlich tut mich verlangen," BWV 727, also in B minor.

The "Dorian" toccata and fugue (BWV 538) is the only one of Bach's organ compositions known to have been played by him at an organ examination, but Williams wonders whether the Toccata, Adagio, and Fugue in C Major, BWV 564, might not have been specifically composed for this purpose. He bases this conjecture on the many opportunities throughout this long work to play on two different manuals: "Short phrases, rests, gaps and little repetitions characterize all the movements...and each could be aiming to use two manuals in its own way: for echoes in the opening solos, then for alternation in a 'ritornello duologue,' for solo plus accompaniment (a melody over a realized continuo), [and, in the fugue] for contrast (entries *versus* episodes)." In addition, Williams suggests that the slurs in the pedal solo—a rare circumstance for one of Bach's pedal lines—indicate the use of the heel for the thirty-second notes in these passages and that the Adagio originated as an oboe solo, with the last three beats of m. 13 transposed up an octave. There is no comment whatsoever, though, on the extraordinarily long sequence in mm. 9–14 of this movement, which features four sequential statements of a measure-long phrase, twice as many as is normal for Bach. Surely this is just as "italianate" a trait as the pizzicato pedal, five Neapolitan sixths, and the *petite reprise* in mm. 20–22. One could also quibble with Williams's claim that the use of two manuals in the Adagio is optional rather than obligatory, since the right-hand melody encroaches on sustained notes in the left-hand accompaniment a total of eight times (mm. 9–14, 19, and 21).

In his new commentary on the Toccata and Fugue in D Minor, BWV 565, Williams summarizes how other scholars have reacted to his transcription hypothesis. He concedes that violoncello piccolo could have been the original instrumentation, but he is far more doubtful about an original version for harpsichord. Furthermore, he happily accepts either Johann Peter Kellner (a younger colleague of Bach's who evidently had a keen interest in transcription) or Johannes Ringk (one of Kellner's students and the copyist of the work's earliest source) as the transcriber. In rebuttal to Wolff's argument that the

---

11. Cantagrel 1998, 597–608.

12. *J. S. Bach: Tombeau de Sa Majesté la Reine de Pologne* (Mirare Productions 030).

piece is simply an early, albeit flamboyant, specimen of Bach's "organistic art,"[13] Williams rightly states that organists of Ringk's generation knew many of the "more approachable characteristics" of earlier organ music, and he maintains that these individuals could "fake" these characteristics in their own compositions, even to the extent of deriving most of the themes from the same few notes. Unfortunately, he chooses to ignore Wolff's intriguing idea that the unusual octave doublings in the first ten measures of the toccata were intended to compensate for the lack of 16′ manual stops on Bach's organ in Arnstadt.

The seven pages on the Passacaglia in C Minor, BWV 582, comprise one of Williams's boldest commentaries, if not one of his best. In the first edition of his book, he found it "difficult to believe that the fugue [with which the passacaglia concludes] could have been composed before J. S. Bach got to know ritornello concerto movements in 1713 or so," but he now dates this work around the time of Bach's pilgrimage to Lübeck in 1705–6, a trip made by the twenty-year-old to "comprehend one thing and another about his art" from the great Dietrich Buxtehude.[14] Williams arrives at this new dating, which is the earliest ever proposed, owing to recent research on the work's earliest source, the Leipzig manuscript known as the Andreas Bach Book. According to Hans-Joachim Schulze, the scholar who in 1984 identified Bach's older brother Johann Christoph (d. 1721) as the main scribe of this anthology, the compilation of the Andreas Bach Book may have begun in 1706,[15] and in the case of the passacaglia, Johann Christoph evidently was working from a lost autograph that had already been in existence for some time. Musical style also factors into the equation, for it has long been acknowledged that BWV 582 is heavily indebted to Buxtehude's three ostinato works for the organ.

Bach's main thematic exemplar for his passacaglia, however, is not German but French, the first half of his ostinato being melodically identical to that of a "Trio en passacaille" from André Raison's *Premier livre d'Orgue*, published in 1688. That only the first half of the theme is used as the primary subject of the concluding fugue leads Williams to speculate that Bach's passacaglia began life as a fugue on Raison's theme, to which was added a long passacaglia at the beginning, rather like Bach's addition of a toccata at the end of the Fugue in C Minor on a Theme by Legrenzi, BWV 574 (pp. 172–73).[16] Furthermore, Williams implies that these two fugues in C minor on foreign themes constituted a collection of sorts, since the passacaglia and the Legrenzi fugue were the sole contents of the lost manuscript known as the "Guhr autograph." This "Fugue in C minor on a Theme by

---

13. Wolff 2000, 72. Wolff has since fashioned his thoughts on this work into a full-length article. See Wolff 2002.

14. On the latter quote, see David and Mendel 1998, 46.

15. Schulze 1984, 50.

16. As in the first edition of his book, Williams suggests that the second half of Bach's theme is loosely modeled after another of Raison's ostinatos, that of a "Trio en chaconne" from the same collection, but the melodic resemblance there seems tenuous at best.

Raison" commences as a fairly strict permutation fugue on three subjects, but as it unfolds, "the episodes increase in length and complexity…creating a movement of broad sweep and unusually tense continuity," and "the subject appears less and less often, as in much maturer Bach fugues." Williams also neatly identifies the various musical elements that contribute to the fugue's dramatic conclusion:

> The last twenty bars are amongst the most climactic in Bach: an entry in the top voice, then a sustained sequence, a relentless pedal line, wide texture (C–c''' in m. 187), a repetitive figure (m. 281), Neapolitan sixth, pause, implied pedal point (last six bars), and a *ritardando* (last two bars). The final cadence is plagal, as it has never been in the Passacaglia variations.[17]

Best of all, this commentary ends with perhaps the finest summary of the musical and historical significance of Bach's passacaglia ever written. Confining himself to a single, vigorously rehearsed paragraph, Williams manages here to identify about every attribute of the music that makes this work such a masterpiece:

> If ever there was a work greater than the sum of its parts—a singable theme, impeccable harmonic logic, clear pedigree, imaginative response to other music, conscious manipulation of motifs, careful working-out of permutation, calculated shape—it is the Passacaglia in C minor. Its ebb-and-flow alone is hard to attribute to a young composer. So is its massive structure, sustained by an archetypal theme matched only by two other, much later, variation works, the Chaconne in D minor for violin and the *Goldberg Variations* for harpsichord.

The issue that has always surrounded the Pastorale in F Major, BWV 590, besides unwarranted doubts about the authenticity of the piece, is whether Bach ever meant for its four movements to form a single composition. George Stauffer certainly thought so when he argued in the 1983 *Organ Yearbook* that the work represents an "ingenious synthesis" of the multimovement Baroque pastorale and dance suite (pastorale–musette–air–gigue).[18] Williams admits that each movement "subtly incorporates a pastoral drone," but he implies that only the first may have anything to do with Christmas. Neither writer

---

17. Apropos of the famous Neapolitan sixth in m. 285, Williams writes, without explanation, that the chord "is no occasion for an improvised cadenza!" Another contentious performance-practice issue in this piece is whether to break between the passacaglia proper and the fugue. On this matter, Williams states that "In closing measure 168 on a weak beat and rising to the mediant, a composer of the period could not more clearly imply *attaca, senza pausa.*"

18. Stauffer 1983. Curiously enough, Stauffer interprets a wax spot on one of the manuscript sources as evidence that the piece was performed at an eighteenth-century Christmas Eve service during which "open candles were employed" (p. 58). Didn't every household at the time have a supply of candles?

mentions that the theme of the last movement evidently derives from the first phrase of the Christmas carol "Resonet in laudibus," also known as "Joseph, lieber Joseph mein," a realization that of course strengthens Stauffer's viewpoint (see ex. 1.2).[19] Moreover, Hans

EXAMPLE 1.2. Pastorale in F Major, BWV 590, fourth movement, mm. 1–3

Musch has recently shown that many instrumental and vocal composers from the late sixteenth to the late eighteenth century (including J. E. Eberlin and Michael Haydn, as well as the young Mozart) embellished the first four notes of the melody exactly as in the first measure of Bach's theme.[20] The matter, therefore, seems resolved: Bach's Pastorale is a tonally closed Christmas suite whose first movement depicts the shepherds associated with Jesus's birth and whose last movement sounds one of that season's most beloved tunes.

Receiving its own commentary for the first time in Williams's second edition is the Fantasy in C Minor, BWV 1121. This piece was initially published in the 1920s but, in accordance with its only source, without a composer attribution. It was not generally accepted as a Bach work until the early 1980s, when this manuscript—a tablature from the Andreas Bach Book—was determined to be a Bach autograph dating from 1706–10. Three editions naming Bach as the composer have since appeared,[21] and various recordings have been issued as well, by organists and harpsichordists. Williams relates this relatively early opus, which can be played as written without any pedal, to such Bach organ works as the (similarly imitative) Fantasy in B Minor, BWV 563, and to such harpsichord works by him as the Sonata in D Major, BWV 963. (Shouldn't the final chord have a Picardy third?)

Turning to Bach's approximately two hundred chorale settings for the organ, Williams's discussion of the *Orgelbüchlein* incorporates material culled from at least sixteen different publications that have appeared since the early 1980s. These items include a volume of the NBA, edited by Heinz-Harald Löhlein and published in 1984, where for the first time were printed allegedly early versions of "Heut triumphieret Gottes Sohn" and "Es ist das Heil uns kommen her," BWV 630 and 638, as preserved in copies by J. G. Walther and

---

19. This correspondence was first brought to light not in the Bach literature but, surprisingly, in an article on one of Mozart's symphonies. See Plath 1974, 95 n. 5. My thanks to Christoph Wolff for informing me about this publication.

20. Musch 2007, 239.

21. Zászkaliczky 1990; Hill 1991; and Bartels and Wollny 2003.

J. T. Krebs. Williams implies, quite justifiably, that the variant readings for "Heut trium-phieret" may be nothing more than copying mistakes by Walther. In the case of "Es ist das Heil," though, Williams misleadingly cites only the additional sixteenth-note *suspirans* motive found in m. 4 of the autograph as evidence that "the autograph version is revised from an earlier." In fact, there is another such *suspirans* in the tenor voice two bars earlier, which, like the one in m. 4, creates continuous surface motion in the rhythm one-fourth the value of the main pulse, a hallmark of *Orgelbüchlein* style.[22] What is more, the Walther-Krebs version offers a distinctly different reading for the first beat of the last measure.

An edition of the *Orgelbüchlein* that appeared too late for Williams to reference in this regard was published in 2004 as part of the Wiener Urtext Edition series. Edited by Ulrich Leisinger, this is the most authentic performing edition currently on the market: almost half of the settings are notated on two staves, as in the autograph manuscript, and *exactly* the same spellings, diacritical marks, and punctuation used by Bach in this source for work titles and headings are given in the critical notes. Leisinger includes as legitimate early versions not only that of "Es ist das Heil" as notated by Walther and Krebs but also that of "Herr Christ, der ein'ge Gottessohn," BWV 601, as preserved in the Neumeister Collection. In "Herr Christ," Bach revised for the sake of motivic unity, better counterpoint, and a change in form from bar (AAB) to binary (AABB).[23]

Williams educated himself on Bach's compositional process in the *Orgelbüchlein* by studying Löhlein's facsimile edition of the autograph, published in 1981, and by reading the critical commentary of Löhlein's NBA volume. (Anyone today interested in this line of inquiry should go immediately to the awesome new "Bach Digital" website, which features high-resolution scans of a whole host of Bach sources—including the autograph of the *Orgelbüchlein*—owned by libraries in Berlin, Leipzig, and Dresden.) Williams is usually strong in this area, but with respect to "Lobt Gott, ihr Christen, allzugleich," BWV 609, he merely asks whether Bach's "standard procedure" in composing the many melody chorales in the *Orgelbüchlein* was to notate the soprano chorale melody first, then the bass, and then the inner voices. As I demonstrated in my 1996 monograph on the collection, there is considerable documentary evidence that Bach did indeed follow this order.[24]

Compositional influence, performance practice, and biography are but three other topics touched on by Williams in covering the *Orgelbüchlein*. For example, he points out that "Wer nur den lieben Gott lässt walten," BWV 642, is apparently the model for J. L. Krebs's setting of "Ich ruf zu dir, Herr Jesu Christ." The fact that Krebs's work is marked *pro organo pleno*, therefore, suggests that Bach's should be registered likewise. We learn also that J. T. Krebs's copy of "In dir ist Freude," BWV 615, contains a rare specimen

---

22. Stinson 1996, 67–68.

23. Stinson 1993, 471–76.

24. See Stinson 1996, 37–38.

of pedal markings. Organists used to playing the fourth note of the pedal ostinato with the heel might like to know that Krebs executed this motive toes only. And in the case of "Das alte Jahr vergangen ist," BWV 614, Williams goes out on a limb to speculate that this rather melancholic essay was occasioned by the death of Bach's infant twins in 1713. Alas, this theory is supported by no evidence whatsoever.

That the six cantata transcriptions known as the Schübler chorales (BWV 645–50) are the handiwork not of Bach but of a "modestly talented pupil" (perhaps Friedemann Bach, who is alluded to on the title page of the original print) seems at first blush to be the single most radical new idea in Williams's book. He was guided in this direction by his compatriot Walter Emery, whose chapter on Baroque organ music in the *New Oxford History of Music* includes the following remark about these pieces: "The arrangements are much less effective than the originals, and it is hard to see why Bach published them."[25] Also worth citing in this regard is Christoph Wolff's belief that Bach was not closely involved in the making of the original print.[26] Williams, for his part, points out the anomalous nature of the Schüblers as they relate to other prints of Bach's music issued during his lifetime: they are the only transcriptions that were printed, and they involve a remarkably wide gap between date of composition and date of publication. More importantly, to quote Williams, "the chorales are far more literal than Bach's other transcriptions." Thus the Schüblers hardly exemplify Bach's penchant as a transcriber to improve compositionally on his models, whether the models are his own works or someone else's. Notice, too, the strange dominant-tonic appoggiatura added by the transcriber to the chorale melody in m. 20 of "Wachet auf," which succeeds only if played before the beat, like a grace note (see ex. 1.3). One is hard-pressed to locate a second occurrence of this

EXAMPLE 1.3. "Wachet auf, ruft uns die Stimme," BWV 645, mm. 20–21

particular appoggiatura type anywhere in Bach's oeuvre. Maybe, then, he really isn't the transcriber.

Did Bach intend to publish the so-called Great Eighteen chorales (BWV 651–68), as is sometimes suggested? Williams thinks not, observing that the autograph manuscript is "not clearly enough written" to have served for a facsimile etching and that, in contrast to various Bach prints from the last dozen years of the composer's life, it contains

25. Emery 1986, 677 (cited by Williams in the text of his book but missing from his bibliography).
26. Wolff 1986a, 129.

no articulation markings (p. 338). Essentially the only stone left unturned by Williams vis-à-vis this collection is a copy of "O Lamm Gottes" made by the Thuringian organist Johann Gottlieb Preller (1727–86). Williams is aware of this source, but he cites it merely as containing the same early version of the work (BWV 656a) as the copy by J. T. Krebs. In reality, as Thomas Synofzik explained roughly ten years ago in the early-music magazine *Concerto*, the situation is a bit more complicated: Preller's manuscript does often agree with the variant readings found in Krebs's copy, yet in other instances it preserves readings of greater refinement than even the autograph (particularly in verse 3, where there are added voices as well as diminutions).[27] To judge from Synofzik's findings, Bach first revised this piece while still in Weimar, where he served from 1708 to 1717, but when decades later in Leipzig he set out to revise it for inclusion in the Great Eighteen, he had access only to the version copied by Krebs. We can only hope that the exceedingly obscure version copied by Preller, which really deserves its own catalogue number (BWV 656b?), will appear in the revised edition of the NBA currently underway or in the new editions of the complete Bach organ works being issued by Wayne Leupold Editions and Breitkopf & Härtel, so that it may be widely performed and studied.[28]

Among the issues addressed by Williams with respect to the miscellaneous setting of "Wie schön leuchtet der Morgenstern," BWV 739, are authenticity, chronology, and geographical orientation. Early on in this commentary is to be found the following statement: "J. S. Bach's hand in [the Berlin manuscript] P 488 no more proves that he was the composer than does the *Plauener Orgelbuch* copy." But as I explained in my 1985 article "Bach's Earliest Autograph," P 488 contains a manifestly compositional revision by Bach revealing him to be the composer as well as the scribe.[29] I also hypothesized in that study that Bach performed this piece in 1706 when he and the Gehren organist Johann Kister tested an organ by Johann Albrecht in the village of Langewiesen (the examination took place on the first Sunday in Advent, the exact day to which this chorale is assigned in many hymnals of the period). Unfortunately, this event is mentioned nowhere in Williams's book, neither in the commentary on BWV 739 nor in the "Calendar" at the end.

---

27. Synofzik 2000.

28. According to the publisher's website (www.baerenreiter.com), the revised edition of the NBA will encompass fifteen volumes, two of which will contain organ chorales. The recently published inaugural volume of the Leupold edition, whose general editor is George Stauffer, incorporates for the first time in an edition of Part 3 of the *Clavierübung* Bach's handwritten corrections and additions to the original print. Approximately a dozen added ornaments are to be found, including a flashy trill-with-appoggiatura-and-turn for the left hand, which complements the one printed for the right hand, at the end of the E-flat fugue. On this topic, see also Stauffer 2010a and Stauffer 2010b, 42. Two volumes of the Breitkopf edition, whose editorial board consists of Werner Breig, Pieter Dirksen, and Reinmar Emans, have thus far appeared. Nine of the ten volumes will contain early and variant versions on CD-ROM, thus allowing for easy comparison with the hard-copy standard versions.

29. Stinson 1985.

Williams and I do agree that Bach may have composed "Wie schön leuchtet" in prep-aration for his stay in Lübeck during 1705–6, but Williams considers the work's form and style more Thuringian than North German, whether the alleged North German models are Buxtehude's chorale fantasies, as I set forth, or those of Johann Adam Reinken, as Christoph Wolff has proposed.[30] Williams's main ammunition here is Michael Kube's discovery, made about fifteen years after my article was published, that Bach arranged the *Stollen* of the chorale in a strikingly similar way to how Thuringian masters like Pachelbel did so.[31] I happily concede this point, but I would still maintain that in setting the cho-rale's *Abgesang*, Bach relied primarily on such North German exemplars as Buxtehude's fantasy on "Nun freut euch, lieben Christen g'mein."

Indeed, thanks to a spectacular find made about five years ago by Michael Maul and Peter Wollny, it is now certain that Bach knew this Buxtehude composition years before his Lübeck sojourn, for Maul and Wollny managed to unearth in the library of Duchess Anna Amalia of Saxe-Weimar-Eisenach a fragmentary tablature of the work penned by Bach at the tender age of thirteen or fourteen, when he was still living in Ohrdruf with his older brother Johann Christoph.[32] Uncovered along with this source was a second completely unknown tablature in Bach's hand containing Reinken's huge fantasy on "An Wasserflüssen Babylon." Bach prepared this manuscript in 1700—and under the supervi-sion of Georg Böhm—during his first year as a choral scholar at the church of St. Michael in Lüneburg. These two sources represent the earliest music manuscripts of any kind in Bach's hand, and their contents show that even in his early teens (when he was probably just tall enough to reach the pedals), he was playing the longest and most virtuosic organ works then in existence. The Reinken copy, moreover, bears remarkable implications for our understanding of one of Bach's most famous organ performances, that given in 1720 on the fifty-eight-stop instrument at St. Catherine's, Hamburg. On that occasion Bach played in front of an audience that included the elderly Reinken, and much to Reinken's delight, Bach improvised for nearly half an hour on no other chorale than "An Wasserflüssen Babylon."

If the Neumeister chorales (BWV 1090–1120) are genuine, they are presumably even earlier than the setting of "Wie schön leuchtet." Many of Williams's commentaries on these pieces touch on matters of performance practice, for example, the degree to which pedal should be employed or whether to use one or two manuals. Of particular interest is his theory that the rubric "Choral" found throughout three settings (BWV 1094, 1097, and 1109) indicates the hymn lines as they were sung by the congregation. This idea, of course, may be applied to undoubtedly authentic organ chorales by Bach that contain

30. Wolff 2000, 64.

31. Kube 2001.

32. Maul and Wollny 2007. See also the recent recording by Jean-Claude Zehnder, *J. S. Bachs früheste Notenhandschriften* (Carus 83.197).

this cue, including two ("Nun danket" and the second setting of "Jesus Christus, unser Heiland") from the Great Eighteen.

Williams sees in the Neumeisters both negative and positive "signs of youthfulness" (p. 543). On the negative side is all the "faulty grammar," which manifests itself in parallel fifths and octaves, open fifths, doubled thirds, and the like. On the positive is a rather dissonant cadence type in which a leading-tone diminished-seventh chord sounds against the tonic pitch before resolving to the tonic triad. (Williams also discerns this Bachian "fingerprint" at the close of the aforementioned Fantasy in C Minor, BWV 1121.) As I discussed about twenty years ago, this progression tends to occur in these pieces as a final cadence—with the tonic pitch doubling as the final note of the chorale tune—and within the huge body of organ chorales from around 1700 it seems to be otherwise found as a final cadence only in fifteen works by Bach.[33] These statistics strongly suggest that the Neumeisters are indeed authentic.

A host of other issues pertaining to Williams's monograph are taken up in the following list:

(1) Apropos of the Toccata in F Major, BWV 540/1, it is erroneously stated that Johann *Ludwig* Krebs in 1721 became the organist in the town of Buttstädt, giving him access to the "other" organ in central Germany with a pedalboard to f' (see discussion earlier in this chapter). Ludwig was all of eight years old at this time. It was his father Johann *Tobias* who received that appointment.

(2) Absent from the manuscripts listed for the Fantasy and Fugue in G Minor, BWV 542, is a copy of the fugue that helps to document the early transmission of this movement in the city of Hamburg. The source came to the attention of the musicological community only in 1999, and it is in the hand of one Johann Ernst Bernhard Pfeiffer (1703–74), who in 1725 competed unsuccessfully for the position of organist at the Hamburg Cathedral and ten years later was appointed organist at St. Peter's Church there.[34] According to Johann Mattheson, the cathedral's music director and the supervisor of the competition, the contestants were judged in six different areas, one being a fugal improvisation on the subject (as well as one of the countersubjects) of this very fugue.

(3) In discussing the Prelude, Trio, and Fugue in B-flat Major, BWV 545b, whose only manuscript is primarily in the hand of Benjamin Cooke, organist at Westminster Abbey from 1762 to 1793, Williams cites one of his bibliographical sources as "Knight 2000." No corresponding item, though, appears in the bibliography. The study in question, which shows that this work would have

---

33. Stinson 1993, 464–67.
34. Neubacher 1999, 403; and Neubacher 2001.

been unplayable on the rudimentary pedalboard of the Abbey's organ at this time, is David Knight, "The Pedal Organ at Westminster Abbey in the Eighteenth Century, with some Remarks on BWV 545b," published in the 2000 *Organ Yearbook* (an issue of that journal titled "Bach und die Orgel").

(4) The commentary on the Toccata, Adagio, and Fugue in C Major, BWV 564, contains the following sentence on the *grave* interlude that occurs between the Adagio and the Fugue: "This *Grave*, in its recitative link, thick chords, new harmonies and 'forbidden' bass intervals, updates a passage in Buxtehude's Praeludium BuxWV 142, itself a development of links in the capriccios of Frescobaldi's *Fiori musicali*." This historical perspective is extremely valuable. Still, as Lawrence Archbold has pointed out, Williams surely means the canzonas from Frescobaldi's collection, not the capriccios.[35]

(5) Like the setting of "Wie schön leuchtet" previously discussed, the "Jig" Fugue in G Major, BWV 577, was decades ago arbitrarily blacklisted by the NBA, only to be published there in the new millennium.[36] No doubt one reason for this change in attitude was the discovery in the 1980s of two additional eighteenth-century manuscripts naming Bach as the composer (all four of the work's sources carry this attribution). Williams should have provided all of this information, if only to encourage organists once again to perform this delightful bit of juvenilia. Its gigue-like subject is cribbed from Buxtehude's C-major fugue, BuxWV 174, but Bach regularly states his theme in the pedals as well as the manuals.[37] The result is one of his most technically demanding organ works and a classic example of the composer transcending his models.

(6) Two mistakes in Williams's coverage of the *Orgelbüchlein* bear mentioning. First, he claims that a copy of the collection stemming from the circle of the Bach pupil Johann Philipp Kirnberger contains "additions" by J. P. Kellner. Kirnberger did study under Kellner, but Kellner's hand nowhere appears in this source. Rather, Kirnberger added a title page and made revisions to a manuscript prepared by one of his scribes.[38] Second, there is a bit of confusion in the otherwise excellent discussion of "Erschienen ist der herrliche Tag." Williams argues that this setting is modeled after Buxtehude's organ chorale "Wir danken dir, Herr Jesu Christ," a similarly canonic work based on the same

---

35. For Archbold's review of Williams, see *Notes: Quarterly Journal of the Music Library Association* 61, no. 2 (December 2004): 430–32. A further error detected by Archbold in this perceptive critique is the listing of the Prelude in C Major, BWV 567 (a work presumably by J. L. Krebs), as "Prelude in G major."

36. See the discussion in Bartels and Wollny 2004, 62–70.

37. As a certain American organist once proclaimed, "When he plays the 'Jig' fugue, the tune comes one, two, three times in the hands, and the fourth time, when it comes in the feet, I dance the jig." See *Virgil Fox—Heavy Organ: Bach Live in San Francisco* (Decca DL 75323).

38. Leisinger and Wollny 1997, 416–17.

tune and to some extent the same accompanimental motive. He observes, too, that Walther set "Erschienen ist" as a canon and that a copy of Buxtehude's work in Walther's hand has survived. With such encyclopedic knowledge on display, it is unfortunate that in the first complete sentence on p. 292 the Bach work is cited only as "BWV 628," which is the catalogue number of an entirely different piece.

(7) Missing from the discussion of "Christ lag in Todesbanden," BWV 718, is any mention of the heading *Übungsstück* ("exercise piece") added by J. L. Krebs to his copy of this work.[39] As a technical study, the piece offers a profusion of ornaments and, at least in the Abgesang (marked *Allegro*), nonstop and wide-ranging figuration for both hands, which in mm. 43–53 are also required to change manuals every four beats. How many other organ chorales were adapted for this purpose, one wonders, and to what extent does the practice reflect Bach's pedagogy? "Christ lag" is a work, by the way, that has come under scrutiny as of late vis-à-vis the most recent (2008) addition to the Bach canon, the organ chorale "Wo Gott der Herr nicht bei uns hält," BWV 1128.[40] Remarkably, both constitute miniature chorale fantasies in which a phrase of the *Abgesang* is subjected to a long, modulatory series of echo effects made possible by constant manual changes.

(8) In his commentary on the Neumeister chorale "O Herre Gott, dein göttlich Wort," Williams provides erroneous measure numbers for what he identifies as three different harmonizations of the first two phrases of the hymn tune. These occur at mm. 10, 19, and 40, not mm. 2, 21, and 42.

(9) In the "Calendar" that concludes the book, the wrong year is given for the examination of the Christoph Cuntzius organ at Our Lady's Church in Halle conducted by Bach, Johann Kuhnau, and C. F. Rolle. That event took place in 1716, not 1714.

The second edition of *The Organ Music of J. S. Bach*, therefore, is not an altogether reliable reference work nor is it a completely up-to-date survey of its topic, even by the standards of 2003. But given the scope of its coverage and the sheer amount of material presented, such minor flaws are inevitable. Williams's monograph simply contains too much new information and too many new insights not to be regularly consulted by scholars and performers alike—something that may continue to be said about the first edition of his study. The author is to be congratulated on another magnificent contribution to the Bach literature.

---

39. Friedrich 2002, 8.

40. See Blaut and Schulze 2008, 26; and Morana 2008, 77. See also the recording *Johann Sebastian Bach: Wo Gott der Herr nicht bei uns hält* (Rondeau ROP6023), which includes performances by Ullrich Böhme of both of these organ chorales.

The one sentence in Williams's book that most piqued my interest occurs in the discussion of the "Little" Fugue in G Minor, BWV 578: "Perhaps because it is so catchy, J. G. Schübler (a pupil, later engraver of the *Six Chorales*) also wrote a fugue on this theme." Quite maddeningly, no reference is provided, but I subsequently managed to identify Williams's source as one of two publications by the team of Ulrich Leisinger and Peter Wollny, either their article on Carl Philipp Emanuel Bach's earliest compositional efforts, published in the 1993 *Bach-Jahrbuch*, or their 1997 catalogue of the Bach holdings of two libraries in the city of Brussels.[41] In the former study, Schübler's fugue is mentioned only because its one source, a huge manuscript-anthology at the Conservatoire royal de Bruxelles, also contains one of C. P. E. Bach's harpsichord concertos. The work is described there as "a *Fuga Lass mich gehn denn dort kommt meine Mutter her di J. G. Schübler*, which arranges the theme of BWV 578 for two voices." According to the catalogue, the source for Schübler's fugue is in the hand of an eighteenth-century musician by the name of J. C. Brückner, who, like Schübler himself, hailed from Thuringia. Schübler, who was probably born around 1725, studied with Bach in Leipzig during the early 1740s and spent the rest of his life as an organist and schoolteacher in the Thuringian village of Mehlis.[42] Like other members of his family, he was also active as a music engraver, particularly of works by Bach and his sons. His death date is unknown.

Yes, the poetic meter of the text *Lass mich gehn denn dort kommt meine Mutter her*, as inscribed by Brückner on the title page of this manuscript, perfectly matches the rhythm of the first phrase of Bach's theme (see ex. 1.4). Less obvious is whether the word *Gott*

EXAMPLE 1.4. Fugue in G Minor ("Little"), BWV 578, mm. 1–2

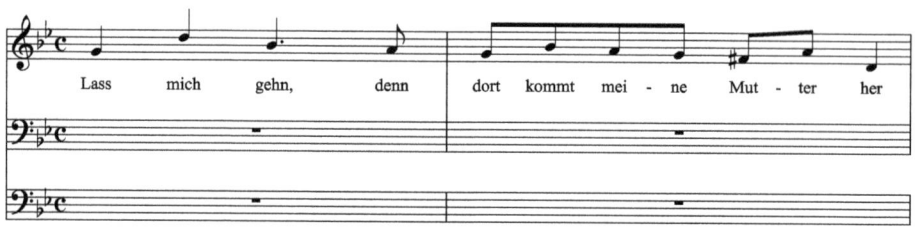

found to the left of the composer attribution is somehow meant to continue the text in conjunction with the remainder of the fugue subject. This source, minus its blank fourth page, is reproduced in figure 1.1; a complete transcription of Schübler's fugue is found in example 1.5.

The complete title entered by Brückner reads *Fuga. / Lass mich gehn denn dort kommt meine / Mutter her etc. etc. / di / J. G. Schübler*. Somewhat lower on the right side of the page appears the ownership inscription *Poss: / J. C. Brückner*. Three additional hands are

41. Leisinger and Wollny 1993, 197 n. 161; and Leisinger and Wollny 1997, 118, 462–67, and 533.
42. Boyd 1999, 441.

FIGURE 1.1a. Johann Georg Schübler, Fugue in G Minor ("Lass mich gehn, denn dort kommt meine Mutter her"), title page (Conservatoire royal / Koninklijk Conservatorium, Brussels, 25448 MSM)

FIGURE 1.1b. Johann Georg Schübler, Fugue in G Minor ("Lass mich gehn, denn dort kommt meine Mutter her"), mm. 1–26 (Conservatoire royal / Koninklijk Conservatorium, Brussels, 25448 MSM)

FIGURE 1.1C. Johann Georg Schübler, Fugue in G Minor ("Lass mich gehn, denn dort kommt meine Mutter her"), mm. 27–43 (Conservatoire royal / Koninklijk Conservatorium, Brussels, 25448 MSM)

evident as well, starting with the one responsible for the insert *Lass mich gehn, denn dort kommt / und und Gott*, which reproduces most of the original title, with *etc.* translated as *und*. Directly beneath the composer attribution someone else has written, in pencil and obviously in reference to Schübler, *J. S. Bachs Schüler.* At the very bottom of the page is found the inscription *Als ein Zeichen der innigsten Verehrung / dem Herrn Professor Zelter von / Forkel* ("As a sign of sincerest respect, to Mr. Professor Zelter, from Forkel"). Thus the manuscript went from Brückner to the early Bach biographer J. N. Forkel, who in turn donated it to his colleague and friend C. F. Zelter, the director of the Berlin Singakademie from 1800 to 1832. We know from other documentation that the source then went from Zelter to the Berlin organist A. W. Bach (no relation to Johann Sebastian), from whose estate it was purchased by the anatomy professor G. R. Wagener. It came into the possession of the library of the Conservatoire royal de Bruxelles in 1904, when the conservatory acquired Wagener's gigantic music collection. The library's stamp appears in the middle of the page.

EXAMPLE 1.5. Johann Georg Schübler, Fugue in G Minor ("Lass mich gehn, denn dort kommt meine Mutter her")

Schübler's fugue, which may be one of only two extant works by him,[43] makes for a fascinating case study in compositional borrowing, and it represents the only such adaptation of a Bach work by one of his pupils to have survived. To begin with—and in contrast to how the piece has previously been described—not only is the subject of Bach's fugue appropriated but also its main countersubject. Indeed, whenever the subject is stated in its entirety, it is accompanied by that measure-long segment of the countersubject containing a trill on its second beat (see mm. 7, 13, 20, 27, and 38). All the episodes, conversely, are of Schübler's own fashioning. The result is a work roughly half as long as its model and one lacking a pedal part. Schübler also pared down the texture of Bach's fugue, which is essentially a three-voice work, to two voices. Schübler's fugue is redolent of any number of Bach keyboard works scored for only two voices (for example, the Two-Part Inventions, various preludes from the Well-Tempered Clavier, and the Four Duets from Part 3 of the *Clavierübung*), but its closest match is provided by the Fugue in E Minor from Book 1 of the Well-Tempered Clavier, the only two-voice fugue from that collection.

For whatever reasons, Schübler chose cut time as his meter, as opposed to Bach's use of common time. His first nine bars are identical to Bach's, except for the pitch of the very last note of the upper voice. After a freely composed bridge passage (mm. 10–11), which is two beats shorter than Bach's but rhythmically very similar, the subject is restated in the tonic with the countersubject stated above it, as in Bach's fugue; the same pitch levels obtain as well, with the subject now sounding an octave lower than at the outset—and therefore giving the illusion of a third voice. Starting in m. 14, the upper voice diverges melodically from Bach's countersubject, but the sixteenth-note motion is again maintained. Because this statement of the subject is followed in mm. 16–18 by a sequential episode that modulates to B-flat major, the exposition may be said to end in m. 15.

Schübler's presentation of the subject and countersubject in the relative major (mm. 19–22) corresponds to two passages in Bach's fugue. The following episode (mm. 22–25), like the first, contains four descending stepwise sequences of a motive lasting two beats, but now the upper voice imitates the lower. After a modulation to D minor for the next statement (mm. 26–29), there is a rather different type of episode (mm. 31–34) based on the head motive of the subject and moving along the circle of fifths. Schübler may have been inspired here by the false entrance of the subject in m. 25 of Bach's fugue. The episode that follows in mm. 35–36 is the shortest and most conventional, and its descending, arpeggiated figuration recalls an episode toward the end (mm. 55–57) of the model. After a modulation back to G minor, the two themes are stated for the last time. Whereas Bach's fugue ends with this material, Schübler's contains three extra bars. The deceptive cadence in the middle of m. 42 is an especially nice touch.

The astute observer will notice that the transcription of Schübler's fugue found in example 1.5 differs from Brückner's manuscript in a number of ways. First of all, the soprano

---

43. See the discussion in Löhlein 1987, 154.

clef used by Brückner for the upper staff, which is the clef used in most of the manuscript sources for Bach's fugue, has been modernized to treble clef. His use of so-called dorian notation, however, has been retained. I refer here to the system, commonly employed by Bach in his early works, by which minor flat keys are notated one flat short of modern practice; this is also how Bach's fugue is notated in the earliest surviving manuscripts.[44] The advantage of dorian notation is not having to cancel the flat on the sixth degree of the scale when that pitch is a half step higher than in the natural minor scale. The disadvantage is forgetting to flat the pitch when it conforms to the natural minor, as happened to Brückner in mm. 13, 21, 22, and 30. These and other obvious errors of pitch have been corrected. Brückner also erred on the second beat of m. 13 by recopying the previous beat of the countersubject instead of the trill; this mistake has been rectified as well. Giving Brückner (and Schübler) the benefit of the doubt, I have resisted the temptation of changing the a′ quarter note on the second beat of m. 31 to four sixteenths in the order f#′–d′–f#′–d″, which would assimilate that measure to the three sequences in the next three bars.

At any rate, the text *Lass mich gehn, denn dort kommt meine Mutter her* translates as "Let me go, because here comes my mother," and it exemplifies trochaic hexameter, a very unusual meter in German poetry generally encountered only in children's rhymes.[45] To judge from the grammar, the speaker is being detained, though not physically, and he is informally addressing a single person as he sees his mother coming toward him. Absolutely nothing, however, is known about the text's origins or authorship. Perhaps it was the opening line of a multistanzaed children's poem, each of which began with this same line before leading into a particular situation for the child in question.

Of course, the more interesting question is whether in the early eighteenth century this text was associated with the melody used for the opening phrase of Bach's fugue subject. More specifically, when the young Bach set out to compose this work, did he intentionally begin it just like a popular children's song he knew from his native Thuringia? There is certainly nothing in the music to indicate otherwise. On the contrary, these two bars seem ideally suited to commence a folk song: they are easy to sing (unlike the remainder of the theme); they can be harmonized with just the tonic and dominant triads; and they conclude with a half cadence, suggesting the antecedent phrase of a four-bar period, which is a melodic type entirely representative of the folk music of western Europe.

Other questions arise as well. Did Bach instruct Schübler to write his fugue as a composition exercise, or did Schübler undertake the project years later on his own volition? If the latter is true, what was Schübler's source for Bach's fugue? (There is no extant manuscript of Bach's fugue in his hand, nor have any Bach copies by Schübler survived.) And was Schübler the only one of these two musicians who saw any connection whatsoever between this text and the melody that begins Bach's fugue subject? We will probably never know.

---

44. Kilian 1978–79, 545.
45. For advice on linguistic matters, I thank Wm. A. Little.

2

Bach and the Varied Stollen

AS AN ARRANGER of chorale melodies, Johann Sebastian Bach has few if any peers in the entire history of music. The sheer number of his chorale settings (around eight hundred, counting individual movements of partitas as well as independent works) attests to this fact, as does their astonishing quality and variety. As Bach set these hymns, whether for voice or keyboard, by far the most common melodic type that he encountered was bar form, a design commonly diagrammed as AAB and one characterized by an immediate restatement of the opening two or three musical phrases, known as the tune's *Stollen*. Here we will look at those organ works by Bach in which he varies the music of the Stollen on the restatement instead of repeating the material note for note. To my knowledge, the topic has never been explored.

In writing bar-form chorales for the organ, Bach employed the technique of the varied Stollen about one-fourth of the time, which is apparently a far higher percentage than in his vocal works. Just consider the roughly two hundred bar-form chorales found in the composer's *371 Four-Part Chorales*, only nine of which feature a varied Stollen,[1] or the sixteen bar-form chorales contained in the St. Matthew Passion, St. John Passion, and Christmas Oratorio, only one of which qualifies (the elaborate arrangement of "O Mensch, bewein dein Sünde gross" that concludes Part 1 of the St. Matthew Passion). The reason for this discrepancy has to do with chronology and compositional influence,

---

1. See, as printed in the standard edition by Kirnberger and C. P. E. Bach, nos. 119, 142, 216 (identical to the famous setting of "Es ist genug"), 237, 241, 297, 332, 337, and 341.

for most of Bach's organ works that include a varied Stollen seem to have been written at a very early date and in imitation of the North German organ school.

For the sake of historical context, consideration will be given first to how Bach's predecessors and contemporaries dealt with this issue in their organ chorales, beginning with two of the greatest exponents of the genre at the turn of the eighteenth century, Johann Pachelbel (1653–1706) and Dietrich Buxtehude (ca. 1637–1707). Pachelbel, who lived in southern Germany and the central German region of Thuringia, as well as in Austria, left behind roughly seventy bar-form chorales for the organ, only two of which contain a varied Stollen;[2] almost forty of these settings are movements from chorale partitas, an especially common chorale type in Thuringia. Buxtehude, conversely, who lived in Scandinavia and northern Germany, is responsible for twenty-three bar-form chorales, all of which contain a varied Stollen; most of these settings, in accordance with North German practice, are single-movement ornamental chorales. Not surprisingly, this same geographical-musical dichotomy prevails in the organ chorales of Johann Heinrich Buttstedt (1666–1727) and Andreas Nicolaus Vetter (1666–1734), both of whom were Pachelbel's pupils, and Daniel Erich (1660–1730) and Georg Dietrich Leiding (1664–1710), who were Buxtehude's pupils. Buttstedt and Vetter together produced almost fifty bar-form chorales for the organ, including numerous partita movements, none of which includes a varied Stollen; Erich and Leiding are together responsible for eight bar-form chorales, all of which qualify.

A survey of the Baroque organ chorale in general reveals much the same pattern. Take, for instance, Andreas Armsdorff (1670–99), a Thuringian, who in only one of his twenty-two bar-form chorales saw fit to vary the Stollen, or Friedrich Wilhelm Zachow (1663–1712), a resident of the central German region of Saxony, who in only three of his twenty-seven bar-form chorales adopted the procedure. About a century earlier, we find the acknowledged founder of the North German organ school, Jan Pieterszoon Sweelinck (1562–1621), employing the varied Stollen in virtually all of his bar-form chorales (thirty times out of thirty-two examples). Given the many Germans who traveled to Amsterdam to sit at the feet of this master—dubbed "the maker of Hamburg organists"—Sweelinck may well be responsible for instituting the varied Stollen as a compositional practice in organ music. He also applied the technique in ways that anticipate his successors, sometimes merely changing the figuration within the accompanimental voices (i.e., those voices not assigned the chorale melody) but at other times embellishing the chorale tune or moving the Stollen of the chorale from the soprano to

---

2. Compare mm. 2–7 and 8–13 of Pachelbel's setting of "Christ, unser Herr, zum Jordan kam," published in Matthaei 1965 (10–12), and mm. 3–13 and 16–27 of Pachelbel's newly discovered arrangement of "An Wasserflüssen Babylon," published in Maul and Wollny 2007 (38–41). My statistics here regarding the number of bar-form chorales by a given composer include only those arrangements, whether an independent work or a partita movement, in which the entire chorale tune is set. (In conducting my research, I consulted numerous modern editions, which, for the most part, will not be cited individually.)

the bass voice. A specific case of Sweelinck's influence in this respect seems to be the fifty-two bar-form chorales of his pupil Samuel Scheidt (1587–1654), forty-four of which are found in Scheidt's so-called Görlitz Tablature, a collection of more than a hundred cantionale-like settings that were intended as accompaniments to congregational singing. Even though Scheidt hailed not from northern Germany but from Saxony, all but two of his bar-form chorales (the two arrangements in the Görlitz Tablature of "Herr Jesu Christ, du höchstes Gut") feature a varied Stollen. Similarly, Matthias Weckmann (ca. 1619–74), a Thuringian, chose in all eleven of his bar-form chorales to vary the Stollen, presumably because he had studied under Sweelinck's pupil Jacob Praetorius (1586–1651).

That leaves only two other Baroque composers who wrote large numbers of bar-form chorales for the organ, Georg Böhm (1661–1733) and Johann Gottfried Walther (1684–1748). Böhm's thirty-two examples are mostly partita movements, and only once is there a varied Stollen.[3] This is entirely what one would expect from a native Thuringian, even if Böhm spent most of his career in northern Germany. Walther spent his entire life in Thuringia (and a brief portion of it as a pupil of Buttstedt's). Of his approximately one hundred bar-form chorales, about forty contain a varied Stollen, which makes him a huge exception to our paradigm. Walther's patented techniques of variation are moving the chorale tune from the soprano to the bass, transposing the accompanimental figuration up or down an octave, and inverting the accompanimental voices.

Walther notwithstanding, these statistics indicate that Baroque composers in central Germany (especially Thuringia) usually opted to restate the Stollen note for note, while those in northern Germany tended to vary it. That North Germans were so inclined bespeaks a relatively free attitude toward the Protestant chorale consistent with the two most representative chorale types of the North German organ school: the ornamental chorale, in which the chorale tune appears, normally in the soprano voice, amid profuse embellishment; and the chorale fantasy, wherein the tune is subjected to various textures, meter changes, "echo" effects (usually involving manual changes), the fragmentation of individual phrases, and—most pertinent to our concerns—the varied restatement of individual phrases, whether, in the case of bar-form chorales, from the Stollen or the *Abgesang* (the "B" section of the AAB design).

Bach wrote numerous ornamental chorales, and he left behind a handful of works that qualify as miniature chorale fantasies, evidence enough that his organ chorales betray North German influence. His tendency to vary the Stollen can be regarded as a further manifestation of this influence, whether the work involved is an ornamental chorale, chorale fantasy, or some other chorale type. For a native Thuringian, the statistics are

---

3. Compare mm. 6–17 and 24–37 of the first movement of Böhm's partita on "Aus tiefer Not schrei ich zu dir," published in Beckmann 1986 (36–39).

remarkable: of Bach's roughly eighty-five bar-form chorales for the organ, twenty-one exhibit a varied Stollen.[4] These works are given in table 2.1.[5]

According to this list, Bach's use of the varied Stollen is most pronounced early on in his career, when he was relying heavily on North German models both for chorale settings and free organ works.[6] And the trend is at its strongest in what appear to be the composer's earliest works of any kind, the organ chorales from the Neumeister Collection, BWV 1090–1120. Of the nineteen bar-form chorales in this group (counting "Du Friedefürst, Herr Jesu Christ" as two works because the entire chorale tune is set twice in succession), eight contain a varied Stollen.[7] A slightly smaller percentage obtains for Bach's "miscellaneous" organ chorales (so called because they are transmitted apart from any collection). Of the thirty-eight bar-form chorales in this group, which may be assigned to the years 1703–12, nine contain a varied Stollen.[8] Bach's later chorale collections, on the whole, yield much smaller numbers. Of the sixteen bar-form chorales from the *Orgelbüchlein*, compiled mostly during Bach's Weimar period (1708–17), only two feature a varied Stollen; of the nine bar-form chorales from the "Great Eighteen" chorales, composed mostly in Weimar and revised decades later, only one work qualifies; and of the five bar-form chorales from Part 3 of the *Clavierübung*, composed shortly before publication in 1739, only one work qualifies.[9]

If we now look more closely at how Bach varies the Stollen in these twenty-one pieces, starting with the nine Neumeister chorales, we see in each instance that he provides different accompanimental figuration on the restatement—and this is so common a practice that it is usually not indicated in table 2.1—but only in the case of "O Herre Gott, dein göttlich Wort" is this the sole variation technique used. Two other relatively simple examples are "Ach Herr, mich armen Sünder" and "Du Friedefürst, Herr Jesu Christ,"

---

4. In compiling these statistics, I have limited myself to works whose authenticity is reasonably certain, taking into account only those chorale settings included in both the Bach-Werke-Verzeichnis and—save the newly discovered setting of "Wo Gott der Herr nicht bei uns hält," BWV 1128—the organ volumes of the Neue Bach-Ausgabe. Works that because of their dubious authorship are found in the *Anhang* or appendix of the BWV were not considered.

5. Four other organ chorales by Bach technically qualify for inclusion in this table, but the differences between the original statement and restatement of the Stollen in these pieces are trivial at best. See "Hilf Gott, dass mir's gelinge," BWV 624; "Kommst du nun, Jesu, vom Himmel herunter," BWV 650; "An Wasserflüssen Babylon," BWV 653; and "Durch Adams Fall ist ganz verderbt," BWV 705.

6. The composition dates given in table 2.1 are taken from numerous sources, including Wolff 1986b, 10 (Neumeister chorales); Maul and Wollny 2007, viii and xxii (BWV 739 and 764); Blaut and Schulze 2008, 32, and Böhme 2008 (BWV 1128); Stinson 2001, 26 (BWV 656); and Stinson 1996, 15–17 (*Orgelbüchlein* chorales).

7. These works are listed in table 2.1 in the order of their appearance in the original manuscript.

8. Roughly a fourth of these thirty-eight "works" are the nine movements of the partita on "O Gott, du frommer Gott," BWV 767.

9. The Schübler chorales (BWV 645–50) are not taken into account here because they are transcriptions of cantata movements. Besides, Bach may not even be the transcriber (see chap. 1).

TABLE 2.1.

Organ Chorales by Bach Containing a Varied Stollen

Work and Location of Stollen	Approximate Composition Date	Manner in which Stollen is Varied on Restatement
"Aus tiefer Not schrei ich zu dir," BWV 1099 (Neumeister Collection), mm. 1–10 and 10–20	1695–1705	first phrase of Stollen is repeated with different accompanimental figuration and with additional statement in bass voice; second phrase is repeated with canonic voices inverted
"Ach Herr, mich armen Sünder," BWV 742, mm. 5–9 and 9–13	1695–1705	different ornamental scheme used
"Du Friedefürst, Herr Jesu Christ," BWV 1102 (Neumeister Collection), mm. 4–9 and 10–16	1695–1705	different ornamental scheme used
"Gott ist mein Heil, mein Hilf und Trost," BWV 1106 (Neumeister Collection), mm. 1–6 and 7–11	1695–1705	chorale tune migrates, with slight embellishment, from tenor to soprano
"Jesu, meines Lebens Leben," BWV 1107 (Neumeister Collection), mm. 1–4 and 5–8	1695–1705	chorale tune migrates from soprano to tenor (mm. 5–6), then to bass (mm. 7–8)
"O Herre Gott, dein göttlich Wort," BWV 1110 (Neumeister Collection), mm. 9–17 and 18–26	1695–1705	different accompanimental figuration used
"Alle Menschen müssen sterben," BWV 1117 (Neumeister Collection), mm. 1–4 and 5–8	1695–1705	chorale tune migrates, with considerable embellishment, from tenor to soprano
"Werde munter, mein Gemüte," BWV 1118 (Neumeister Collection), mm. 1–4 and 5–8	1695–1705	chorale tune migrates, in conjunction with meter change, from soprano to tenor
"Wie schön leuchtet der Morgenstern," BWV 739, mm. 3–19 and 21–35	1703–5	chorale tune migrates from soprano to bass

"Wie schön leuchtet der Morgenstern," BWV 764, mm. 3–18 and 22–23	1703–5	different accompanimental figuration used (restatement of Stollen is a two-measure fragment)
"Jesu, meine Freude," BWV 713, mm. 7–27 and 32–53	1703–12	chorale tune migrates between voices on both statements of Stollen (scheme for initial statement is soprano→tenor→bass; scheme for restatement is tenor→bass→ soprano)
"Allein Gott in der Höh sei Ehr," BWV 715, mm. 1–5 and 5–10	1703–12	different harmonization used; consequently, different interlude used between the two phrases of the Stollen
"Christ lag in Todesbanden," BWV 718, mm. 3–11 and 15–23	1703–12	different ornamental scheme used; texture increased from two to three (and sometimes four) voices
"Ein feste Burg ist unser Gott," BWV 720, mm. 4–10 and 12–19	1703–12	chorale tune migrates from the right hand to the left; different ornamental scheme also used
"Herzlich tut mich verlangen," BWV 727, mm. 1–4 and 4–8	1703–12	chorale tune is embellished; new motive in bass voice and added dissonance may symbolize lines 3–4 of chorale text
"Ach Gott vom Himmel sieh darein," BWV 741, mm. 1–18 and 18–29	1703–12	the two phrases of the Stollen are combined into a single phrase, stated in stretto

(Continued)

Table 2.1. (Continued)

Work and Location of Stollen	Approximate Composition Date	Manner in which Stollen is Varied on Restatement
"Wo Gott der Herr nicht bei uns hält," BWV 1128, mm. 1–10 and 12–21	1707–8	chorale tune migrates, with slight embellishment, from tenor and bass to soprano; countermelody migrates, with technical simplifications for the sake of pedal performance, from alto and soprano to bass; final cadence prolonged for two bars (mm. 20–21)
"O Lamm Gottes, unschuldig," BWV 656 (Great Eighteen chorales), verse 3, mm. 103–12 and 112–22	early version (BWV 656a) seems to date from 1707–8	accompanimental voices transposed up an octave (mm. 113–14) and then inverted (mm. 115–20)
"O Mensch, bewein dein Sünde gross," BWV 622 (Orgelbüchlein), mm. 1–6 and 6–12	1708–12	different ornamental scheme used
"Helft mir Gotts Güte preisen," BWV 613 (Orgelbüchlein), mm. 1–4 and 4–8	after 1726	different accompanimental figuration used
"Allein Gott in der Höh sei Ehr," BWV 676 (Clavierübung, Part 3), mm. 1–33 and 33–66	late 1730s	upper two voices inverted

where, in addition to writing different accompanimental figuration for the chorale tune, Bach merely supplies a different ornamental scheme. Generally speaking, however, his handling of the varied Stollen in these works testifies to an extraordinarily inventive musical sense. "Aus tiefer Not schrei ich zu dir," for example, begins in homophonic texture (mm. 1–3) but for the second phrase switches to canonic writing in augmentation between the soprano and bass voices (mm. 4–10). On the restatement of the Stollen, where there is an extra statement of the first phrase in the bass (mm. 12–14), the second phrase is again rendered canonically but with the parts inverted (mm. 14–20). In the four works with a migratory chorale tune, three different patterns emerge (tenor→soprano, soprano→tenor, and soprano→tenor→bass), and conspicuously absent is the conventional scheme of soprano→bass. Furthermore, in "Gott ist mein Heil, mein Hilf und Trost" and "Alle Menschen müssen sterben," Bach embellishes the restatement of the Stollen, thereby uniting the technique of a migratory cantus firmus with the Baroque practice of an ornamented repeat. In "Werde munter, mein Gemüte," he also changes meter at the point of migration, which throws the restatement into particularly bold relief.

Turning to the nine miscellaneous chorales listed next in table 2.1, the two settings of "Wie schön leuchtet der Morgenstern" are preserved together in an autograph manuscript that can be dated with relative certainty to the period 1703–5, Bach's first few years as organist in Arnstadt.[10] Both works are in G major, and each is equipped with a varied Stollen. Otherwise, though, they are a study in contrast: BWV 739 represents a miniature version of the North German chorale fantasy, and one perhaps indebted to Buxtehude's famous fantasy on this hymn,[11] while BWV 764 is a melody chorale, a Thuringian chorale type in which the chorale tune appears in the soprano voice as a continuous, unembellished melody. The latter work was composed directly into the manuscript, and it breaks off after m. 23 probably because of Bach's dissatisfaction with the "new" accompanimental motive introduced a bar earlier. This motive was to have accompanied the restatement of this unusually long Stollen, but it is nothing more than an embellished version of the motive used more or less constantly for the initial statement (mm. 1–17).

Table 2.1 continues with two more works whose styles are completely different. In the case of "Jesu, meine Freude," Bach was again dealing with a long Stollen, and he hit upon the idea this time of using a different voice for each of the three phrases, but changing the scheme on the restatement. The result is the most migratory Stollen in any of the twenty-one works under discussion, and one that is complemented by a busy fugue in the accompanimental voices. Instead of contrapuntal artifice, "Allein Gott in der Höh sei Ehr" offers a chordal rendition of the entire chorale tune, replete with daring harmonies and rhapsodic interludes between phrases. Both traits label the piece as one of the "Arnstadt Congregational Chorales," those notorious works (also including BWV 722,

---

10. For a comprehensive discussion of this source, see Stinson 1985.

11. Buxtehude, too, moves the chorale tune into a different voice on the restatement of the Stollen, but in the order bass→soprano.

726, 729, 732, and 738) alleged by modern scholars to have confused Bach's congregation in Arnstadt when he used them as hymn accompaniments. If there is any truth to this notion, the presence of a varied Stollen in the only one of these settings in bar form would only have made matters worse, especially considering how bizarrely Bach harmonizes the tune on the restatement (between mm. 8 and 9, for example, a diminished triad on D-sharp "resolves" to a dominant-seventh chord on G). Witness also the chromatic passing tone added to the melody on the second beat of m. 6 and the added arpeggiation on the last beat of m. 7. Both gestures correspond to the idea of an ornamented repeat.

The two pieces that follow are perhaps best understood in relation to works already discussed. "Christ lag in Todesbanden," for example, begins exactly like "Du Friedefürst, Herr Jesu Christ," with jaunty, quasi-ostinato figuration in the left hand followed a few measures later by the entrance of the ornamented chorale tune in the right. Both the texture and rhythmic makeup are reminiscent of the chorale *bicinia* of Georg Böhm. But for the restatement of the Stollen in "Christ lag," Bach adds a second voice for the left hand and occasionally a second one for the right hand as well, in addition to changing the ornamental scheme for the cantus firmus. In "Ein feste Burg ist unser Gott," this bicinium-like texture obtains for both statements of the Stollen, except that the chorale tune migrates between statements from the right hand to the left. Moreover, this is the only work under consideration with a migratory chorale tune in which both statements of the Stollen are ornamented.

In the case of "Herzlich tut mich verlangen," we may have our only example of a Stollen being varied to symbolize the chorale text. Buxtehude's organ setting of "Durch Adams Fall ist ganz verderbt" is a deservedly famous but also extremely rare specimen of this practice, and Bach unquestionably applies the technique himself in the final movement of Cantata 37, *Wer da gläubet und getauft wird*.[12] That he does so in this organ chorale may be suggested by comparing lines 1–2 of the first stanza of the hymn ("From my heart I am longing / for a blessed end") with lines 3–4 ("For here I am surrounded / by trouble and misery") and by comparing Bach's music for the initial statement of the Stollen (mm. 1–4) with that for the restatement (mm. 4–8).[13] Already on the second beat of the restatement, the bass voice introduces a descending motive that leads to harsh diminished sevenths with the embellished chorale tune, precisely where the affect of the text changes from beatification to gloom. Moreover, the bass motive itself incorporates this doleful interval between the last two beats of m. 5. No such dissonance is to be found during the initial statement.

---

12. See, respectively, Stinson 1996, 98; and Dürr 2005, 328. With regard to Bach's use of the varied Stollen in his cantatas, it has been claimed that in the opening movements of his so-called chorale cantatas, the composer "often makes substantial changes to the music of the second *Stollen*, while still retaining the basic *Barform* of the melody itself." See Boyd 1999, 58–59. To my knowledge, no systematic investigation of Bach's use of the varied Stollen in his cantatas has yet been undertaken.

13. On this point, see also Hull 1929, 58. Translation from Williams 2003, 468.

Concluding the series of miscellaneous chorales are two works loosely constructed along the lines of the chorale motet, a favorite Thuringian type in which each phrase of the chorale serves as a point of imitation, always using the same basic rhythms for each imitative statement (as opposed to a final statement in augmentation). Still, rarely in either piece do all four or five voices participate in the exchange. In "Ach Gott vom Himmel sieh darein," Bach begins by setting the two phrases of the Stollen as two separate points of imitation, but on the restatement, remarkably enough, he combines the two phrases to form, at least in the manual voices, one continuous phrase lasting four measures instead of two. What further differentiates the restatement is its reliance on stretto technique.

The recently unearthed setting of "Wo Gott der Herr nicht bei uns hält" poses even more exceptions to the format of the chorale motet, beginning with its layout of two manuals and pedals.[14] Both hands begin on the Oberwerk, registered *piano*, with the opening chorale phrase presented in the tenor voice along with an ornamental countermelody in the alto. When this phrase is passed to the bass voice, the right hand leaps to the Rückpositiv, registered *forte*, to blast forth the ornamental countermelody in the soprano. The second phrase of the chorale is treated likewise, except that it is fitted with dotted rhythms and a chromatic passing tone, and its countermelody is twice as long and far more ornate. On the restatement of the Stollen, the first phrase is rendered by means of a single, lightly embellished statement in the soprano. Meanwhile, the countermelody, shorn of its trill so that it can be more easily pedaled, is relegated to the feet. It is also transposed down a third, leading to a cadence in G minor instead of B-flat major, the key used on the original statement of the Stollen. Not until mm. 17–19 is the second phrase actually restated, again in the soprano (and again with slight embellishment, at least at the cadence) and supported once more by a technically simplified version of its countermelody in the bass. But the phrase is foreshadowed three different times in mm. 15–17: first, in the alto during the two-voice interlude at mm. 15–16; second, in what can only be described as a false entry in the soprano at mm. 16–17; and, third, in a corresponding false entry in the bass at m. 17, obviously meant to suggest canonic writing with the soprano. To conclude the restatement of the Stollen, the cadence of the second chorale phrase is echoed not once but twice, in the manner of the North German chorale fantasy.[15]

The last four works listed in table 2.1 come from chorale collections compiled by Bach himself. Like "Du Friedefürst, Herr Jesu Christ," "O Lamm Gottes, unschuldig" is a rare example of a "continuous" partita, one in which there are no breaks between variations. Bach writes three variations (what he calls "verses"), one for each of the three stanzas of

---

14. For an edition of this work, see Blaut and Pacholke 2008. See also Blaut and Schulze 2008.

15. One wonders if the second "echo" might be played with the right hand on the *Rückpositiv*, for the sake of a decrescendo.

the chorale text, and achieves some measure of variety by the downward migration of the chorale tune, variation to variation, in the sequence soprano→alto→bass. But verse 3 also displays a different meter, a chromatically inflected version of the chorale tune, several different accompanimental motives (two of which dramatically depict stanza 3 of the chorale text), and a thicker texture.[16] Adding further to the climactic nature of this variation is Bach's use of a varied Stollen, one characterized, à la Walther, by octave transposition and invertible counterpoint.

Turning to the two works from the *Orgelbüchlein*, as Bach drafted his holograph of this incomparable set, he tended to reserve only one tiny page per chorale title, a condition that seriously discouraged writing a varied Stollen (a note-for-note restatement obviously requires less space, since all is needed is a set of repeat signs).[17] In the case of "O Mensch, bewein dein Sünde gross," though, he set aside two facing pages for what is an unusually long chorale melody. Only because of this exceptional circumstance was Bach able to compose directly onto the first of these pages two beautifully embellished versions of the tune's Stollen.

The situation with "Helft mir Gotts Güte preisen" is a bit more complex. Only one page had been allotted for this title, and by the time the work was entered into the autograph both the preceding and following pages were filled up with works of their own. Despite these severe restrictions, however, Bach's setting of "Helft mir" contains a varied Stollen. On the restatement, a pedal scale is added to the first phrase, and surface motion in sixteenth notes is maintained for the duration. Both features suggest an ornamented repeat (the pedal line becomes even more active during the Abgesang). Most unusually, the second and third phrases of the tune's Abgesang are melodically identical, and Bach arranged them with exactly the same music, indicated in the autograph—but not in performing editions—by a set of repeat signs.[18] That he did so merely to compensate for the extra space consumed by the varied Stollen presupposes that he was again composing directly onto the autograph, but in this instance only speculation can be offered.[19]

Rather different issues are raised by the final work in table 2.1, a masterful trio on "Allein Gott in der Höh sei Ehr" included by Bach in the third installment of his *Clavierübung*, published in 1739. A few years earlier, he had examined and recommended for publication a partita by Walther on this hymn, the fifth variation of which strikingly parallels Bach's setting both in its use of invertible counterpoint to produce a varied

---

16. For particulars, see Stinson 2001, 83–84.

17. For particulars, see Stinson 1996, 11 and 44–49.

18. For a recent facsimile edition of the autograph of the *Orgelbüchlein*, see Hiemke 2004.

19. Essentially the only marking in this entry that could be construed as a compositional revision is the substitution of an eighth rest for an eighth note on e in the second complete bar of the bottom system (m. 13 in performing editions), which could indicate that Bach changed his mind here so that the pedal scale might begin, in syncopated fashion, off the beat. The two most recent editions of the *Orgelbüchlein* describe this entry as a fair copy containing no revisions whatsoever. See Löhlein 1987, 38; and Leisinger 2004, 87.

Stollen and in its use of canon to set the first two phrases of the Abgesang.[20] Characteristically, however, Bach easily outstripped his model (and greatly expanded upon it as well) by integrating into the design a lengthy fugal ritornello based on the opening phrase of the chorale and by tacking on a fugal exposition of the last phrase. It is important to note also that the ritornello theme is a fairly constant presence, sounding not only between the phrases of the chorale proper but also simultaneously with them. Another difference between the two settings is that Bach's invertible counterpoint, which begins with the ritornello statement at mm. 33–45, involves only his two manual voices, while Walther's involves all three parts. What is more, the chorale tune in Bach's setting stays in the same register—the voice assigned the ritornello is transposed down an octave, with more or less the same ornamentation—while that in Walther's migrates from the soprano to the bass voice. Considering, too, that Bach also restates the bass line note for note and in the same register, this trio constitutes the most subtle as well as the most sophisticated example of a varied Stollen in any of the pieces that have been discussed here, no doubt a reflection of its late composition date.

To sum up, in writing for the organ Bach responded to the issue of the varied Stollen— which he must have regarded as a compositional challenge of sorts—in highly diverse and imaginative ways. Such variety and innovation, of course, are symptomatic not only of Bach's organ music in general but of his compositional output as a whole.

---

20. Butler 1990, 10–15. Walther's partita, a modern edition of which may be found in Beckmann 1998, 29–41, was published in 1738.

3

Some Observations on Mendelssohn's Reception

of Bach's Organ Works

THERE CAN BE little question that Felix Mendelssohn Bartholdy was the most influential champion of Bach's organ works during the early Romantic era. As a performer, editor, composer, antiquarian, teacher, and all-around ambassador, he occupied himself with this music his entire life. In so doing, he helped to bring a historical repertory into the mainstream of musical life in the early nineteenth century. Scholars have recently paid serious attention to Mendelssohn's activities in this realm, but there is still much to be said on the subject.[1] In addition to discussing Mendelssohn's Bach reception I hope also to shed new light on how his contemporaries, including Robert Schumann and the organist Carl Ferdinand Becker, were active in their own right as "receptors" of Bach's organ works.

Most of my remarks will involve the organ recital played by Mendelssohn on August 6, 1840, at the church of St. Thomas in Leipzig.[2] On that occasion—and for the first and only time in his career as an organist—he offered the public a full-length, all-Bach program, in the same organ loft where Bach himself had often performed (the organ that Bach knew was somewhat smaller and included a Rückpositiv, and the main case was entirely different).[3] And he did so specifically to raise money for a monument to Bach, one that still stands today

---

1. See, for example, Little 2010; Little 2007; Stinson 2006, 7–75; Little 2005; Stinson 2002; and Sieling 1999, 305–13.

2. For a comprehensive discussion, see Pape 1988.

3. On the history of this instrument, see Wolff 2005, 11–18; and Wolff and Zepf 2006, 70.

just yards from the former site of St. Thomas's School.[4] The performance also represents one of the first documented examples of an all-Bach organ recital, even if it did begin and end with Mendelssohn's improvisations. These facts are well known, as are a host of others, thanks mainly to a review by Robert Schumann in the *Neue Zeitschrift für Musik* and a letter from Mendelssohn to his mother. Still, various aspects of the recital, which is without a doubt the most famous organ concert in music history, have yet to be fully investigated.

There is first of all the handbill for the event, which lists, in order, the day of the week, date, location, performer's name, repertoire, and starting time.[5] Also provided are two paragraphs explaining how the proceeds are to be used and where tickets may be purchased. The wording, layout, and typeface closely match the handbills for concerts at the Leipzig Gewandhaus during Mendelssohn's tenure there as conductor. Given in figure 3.1 is Schumann's personal copy of this document. Unfortunately, it contains no handwritten annotations whatsoever.

As indicated by the handbill, the recital began not with a prelude but a fugue, which Mendelssohn prefaced with a brief improvisation. To quote from Schumann's review, "After a short introduction, [Mendelssohn] played a very splendid Fugue in E-flat Major, containing three ideas, one built upon the other."[6] Schumann can only be describing the Fugue in E-flat Major (BWV 552/2) that closes Part 3 of the *Clavierübung*, Bach's only organ fugue in this key as well as his only double fugue with three subjects. In writing these words, Schumann may have been relying on more than just his aural analysis of the music, for his heavily annotated personal copy of Part 3 of the *Clavierübung* surfaced recently in Berea, Ohio, and in that source he made sure to mark every time that the first subject of this fugue appears in the third section of the work, where the theme is stated simultaneously with the third subject. Schumann's personal copy of this collection, incidentally, is bound together with roughly ten other Bach prints owned by him, which after his death came into the possession of his wife, Clara. These sources preserve not only numerous markings by Schumann but ones by Johannes Brahms that represent, in fragmentary form, Brahms's long lost piano transcriptions of Bach's F-major organ toccata, BWV 540/1, and G-major organ fantasy, BWV 572.[7]

To return to Mendelssohn and the E-flat fugue, he appears to have learned this work in the summer of 1837, while he and his wife, Cécile, were vacationing in and around Frankfurt. Having agreed to perform on the organ at the Birmingham Music Festival that September, he chose to play this fugue along with the Prelude in E-flat Major that opens

---

4. The original manuscript of Mendelssohn's appeal for subscribers to his concert was recently located by Wm. A. Little in the archives of the Gesellschaft der Musikfreunde, Vienna. For a facsimile reproduction, along with commentary, see Little 2010, 415–28.

5. For a complete English translation, see Stinson 2006, 59.

6. "Mendelssohn's Orgelconcert," *Neue Zeitschrift für Musik* 13, no. 14 (August 15, 1840): 56; reprinted in R. Schumann 1854, vol. 3, 256–59. Translation from David and Mendel 1998, 502–3. See also Glöckner et al. 2007, 670–72.

7. For a detailed description of these materials, see Stinson 2008.

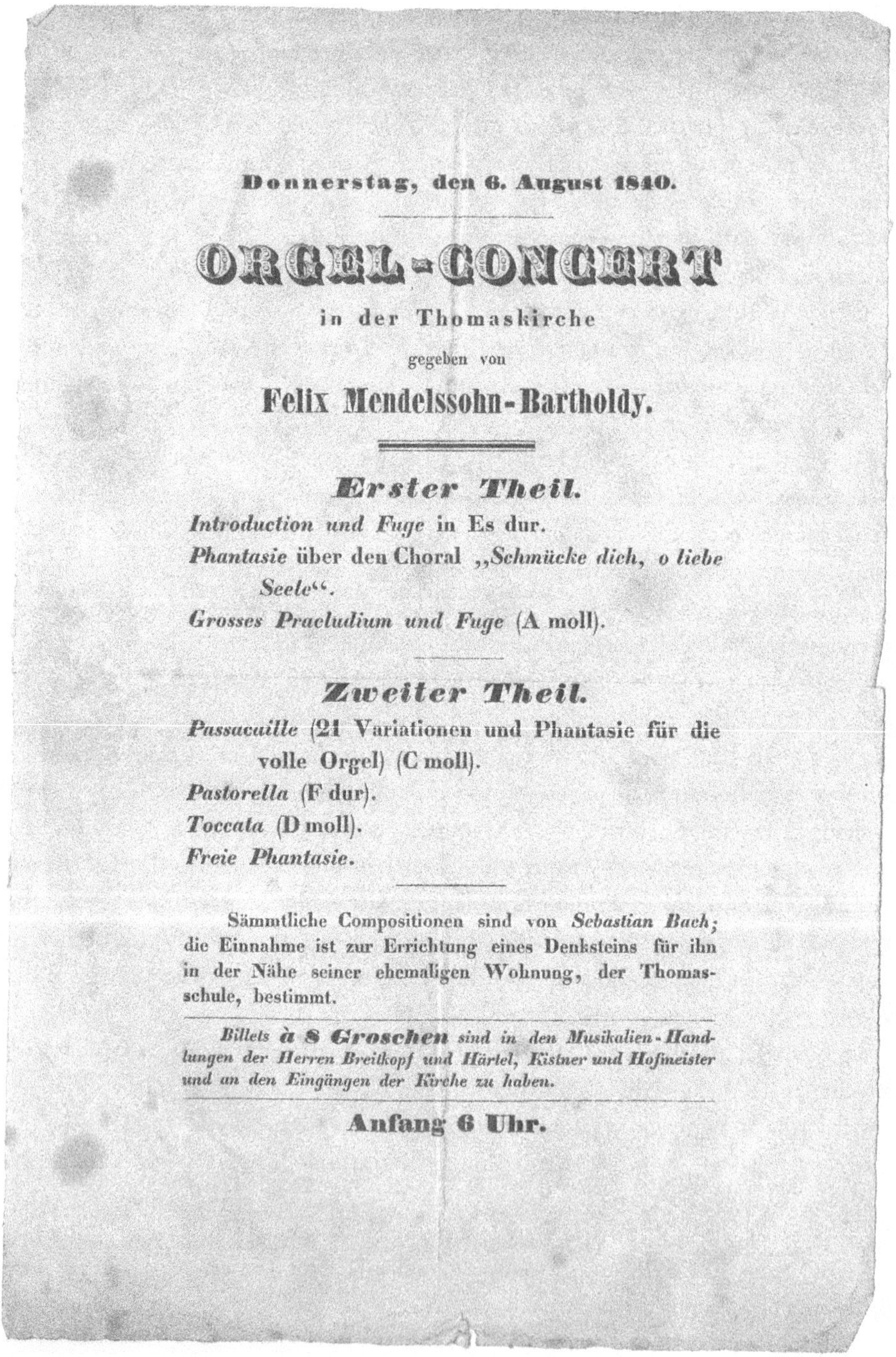

Donnerstag, den 6. August 1840.

ORGEL-CONCERT

in der Thomaskirche

gegeben von

Felix Mendelssohn-Bartholdy.

Erster Theil.

Introduction und *Fuge* in Es dur.

Phantasie über den Choral „*Schmücke dich, o liebe Seele*".

Grosses Praeludium und *Fuge* (A moll).

Zweiter Theil.

Passacaille (21 Variationen und Phantasie für die volle Orgel) (C moll).

Pastorella (F dur).

Toccata (D moll).

Freie Phantasie.

Sämmtliche Compositionen sind von *Sebastian Bach;* die Einnahme ist zur Errichtung eines Denksteins für ihn in der Nähe seiner ehemaligen Wohnung, der Thomasschule, bestimmt.

Billets à **8 Groschen** sind in den *Musikalien-Handlungen der Herren Breitkopf und Härtel, Kistner und Hofmeister und an den Eingängen der Kirche zu haben.*

Anfang 6 Uhr.

FIGURE 3.1. The handbill for Mendelssohn's Bach recital. Robert Schumann's personal copy (Robert-Schumann-Haus, Zwickau, catalogue no. 3390-C3)

Part 3 of the *Clavierübung*, reasoning that in both movements he could achieve a variety of organ colors. As he wrote to his mother, Lea, "both in the prelude and in the fugue one can show off the piano, pianissimo, and the whole range of the organ."[8] No doubt he hoped to entertain his Leipzig audience in much the same way, presumably employing registration changes at least between the three main sections of the fugue. Because the St. Thomas organ contained three manuals—as it had for most of its existence— Mendelssohn could have accomplished these registration changes merely by switching manuals.

Two months earlier, Felix and Cécile had spent a week in Heidelberg, often in the company of her cousin, the lawyer and amateur organist Fritz Schlemmer. There, Fritz entertained Felix at the organ of the Heiliggeistkirche, and one can only assume that Felix returned the favor.[9] The two men would become lifelong friends. Interestingly enough, in the summer of 1838 Schlemmer himself played the E-flat fugue at a music festival in Frankfurt—the more technically demanding prelude may have exceeded his abilities—quite possibly in imitation of Mendelssohn's performance at Birmingham. The critic Carl Kossmaly, writing for the *Neue Zeitschrift*, praised Schlemmer's playing but, in stark contrast to Mendelssohn's thinking, doubted that the work was appropriate for public consumption.[10] Kossmaly may have regarded Bach's organ music in general as too complex or anachronistic to be appreciated by lay audiences.

The second item on the Leipzig recital was an arrangement of the communion hymn "Schmücke dich, o liebe Seele." Only one authentic organ setting of this chorale by Bach has survived, that from the Great Eighteen chorales (BWV 654), and the general consensus is that Felix played this piece. Susanna Grossmann-Vendrey, however, in her study of Mendelssohn's encounter with early music, identifies the work in question as BWV 759, an organ setting of "Schmücke dich" attributed to Bach in various nineteenth-century sources but now regarded, on philological as well as stylistic grounds, as a composition by Bach's pupil Gottfried August Homilius.[11]

To support her theory, Grossmann-Vendrey might have mentioned that Mendelssohn probably owned not one but two publications containing BWV 759: *J. S. Bach's Choral-Vorspiele für die Orgel mit einem und zwey Klavieren und Pedal*, edited by Johann Gottfried Schicht and published by Breitkopf & Härtel between 1803 and 1806; and *Choral and Instrumental Fugues of John Sebastian Bach*, vol. 1, edited by Henry John Gauntlett and

---

8. Letter of July 13, 1837. See Mendelssohn Bartholdy 1863, 145; and Glöckner et al. 2007, 669.

9. Ward Jones 1997, 34–36.

10. Kossmaly 1838; and Glöckner et al. 2007, 669–70.

11. Grossmann-Vendrey 1969, 187. On the authorship of BWV 759, see Williams 2003, 495; Emans 1997, 69; and Albrecht 1988, 116–18. According to Pape 1988, 22 n. 55, BWV 759 may represent an early version of the Great Eighteen chorale, but this is obviously incorrect.

published by Lonsdale between 1838 and 1839.[12] Still, certain musical factors strongly suggest that Mendelssohn performed the setting from the Great Eighteen. For one thing, he referred throughout his life to one of Bach's settings of "Schmücke dich" as a piece he utterly adored and enjoyed playing at the organ.[13] Schumann, too, spoke glowingly of this same work, both in his critique of Mendelssohn's recital, where he described the piece as "as priceless, deep, and full of soul as any piece of music that ever sprang from a true artist's imagination," and in an earlier article published in the *Neue Zeitschrift*. In the latter essay, Schumann wrote:

> You, Felix Meritis... played one of Bach's chorale preludes; the text was "Schmücke dich, o [liebe] Seele." The *cantus firmus* was hung with wreaths of gilded leaves, and flooded with a spirituality that prompted you to confess: "If life were to deprive me of hope and faith, this single chorale would replenish me with both."[14]

That two consummate musical geniuses such as Mendelssohn and Schumann could have revered such an insubstantial work as BWV 759 seems improbable if not impossible (notwithstanding the fact that BWV 759, like the setting from the Great Eighteen, is an ornamental chorale and therefore consistent with the imagery of "wreaths of leaves"). Indeed, these two Bach experts might have taken the overtly galant style of this piece as evidence that it was composed by someone other than Bach.

In addition, Mendelssohn's description of how he once performed the work effectively removes BWV 759 from consideration because the piece is scored throughout for only two *manualiter* voices (plus a third voice for the pedals): "For the moving parts I have an eight-foot flute, and also a very soft four-foot flute, which continuously floats above the chorale tune....But there is [also] a manual with reed stops on which I can play the chorale tune, so I use a mellow oboe, a very soft four-foot clarion, and a viola."[15] By using the plural construction of "moving parts," Mendelssohn reveals that the work in question contained two or more *manualiter* accompanimental voices, which he played on a different manual from that used for the chorale tune. Still, this feature alone does not completely eliminate BWV 759 as a possibility, since the work does begin and end with two

---

12. The assertion made in Thistlethwaite 1990, 172, that Gauntlett's edition contains not BWV 759 but rather the Great Eighteen chorale should be emended accordingly. Mendelssohn, who owned one of the largest collections of Bachiana of anyone in the early nineteenth century, referred or alluded to these two publications in four different sources: a letter to Franz Hauser; a manuscript copy of the Great Eighteen chorales; a letter to Breitkopf & Härtel criticizing Schicht's edition for its bogus work headings; and the preface to Mendelssohn's own edition of the *Orgelbüchlein* (Breitkopf & Härtel, 1845). See, respectively, Little 2007, 390; Crum and Ward Jones 1980–89, vol. 2, 33; and Elvers 1968, 162. For particulars on Schicht's edition, see Klotz 1957, 53.

13. Stinson 2006, 23–25, 40–41, and 72.

14. "Monument für Beethoven," *Neue Zeitschrift für Musik* 4, no. 51 (June 24, 1836): 211–13; reprinted in R. Schumann 1854, vol. 1, 215–23. Translation based on Pleasants 1965, 93.

15. Letter to Mendelssohn's family of September 16, 1831. See Mendelssohn Bartholdy 1861, 277–78; and Glöckner et al. 2007, 278–79.

manualiter accompanimental voices. But Mendelssohn also describes how the 4′ flute that he used for these accompanimental voices regularly sounded at the same time as the chorale tune ("continuously floats above the chorale tune"), indicating a work with at least three *manualiter* voices, such as the Great Eighteen chorale.

Schumann, too, left behind evidence pointing to the Great Eighteen chorale. First, in a footnote to his review of Mendelssohn's concert, Schumann stated that, according to his knowledge, the setting of "Schmücke dich" that was played had not yet been published.[16] In making this statement, Schumann presumably cannot have meant BWV 759, because he had owned Schicht's anthology for more than three years and was intimately familiar with its contents, as the many analytical markings in his personal copy attest.[17] Second, and more definitively, in his handwritten notes for a never-completed memoir of Mendelssohn, drafted shortly after his friend's death in 1847 and titled *Erinnerungen an F. Mendelssohn*, Schumann included the following entry: "Regarding Bach's chorale prelude 'Schmücke dich, o liebe Seele' (in E-flat major) he said with the most sincere expression: 'if life had taken everything from me, this piece would again comfort me.'"[18] Relying on his memory to paraphrase what he had written several years earlier, Schumann saw fit to designate the key of the work as E-flat major, the key of the Great Eighteen chorale, and not F major, the key of BWV 759. This may have been his way of distinguishing between two settings of the same chorale attributed to the same composer.[19] It might seem odd that Mendelssohn listed the Great Eighteen chorale in his program as a "Phantasie," but compared to the hundreds of organ chorales by Bach (such as those from the *Orgelbüchlein*, a collection published by Mendelssohn himself in the mid-1840s) where the hymn tune is presented continuously and devoid of embellishment, this is an extremely free arrangement.

The first part of the recital concluded with a work reported on by Schumann to his fiancée, Clara Wieck: "Mendelssohn's concert lasted somewhat long. But you would have taken great joy in it, especially in the Prelude in A Minor (the same one that you play from the 6 Great), which assumed on the organ a very grand, unique, and brilliant character. There might have been a total of 400–500 listeners."[20] Just as Mendelssohn listed this work in his program as "*Grosses* Praeludium und Fuge," Schumann cites it here as one of the "*6 grossen*" preludes and fugues, a reference to the six organ preludes and fugues BWV 543–548, which since 1812 had been published under the title *Sechs*

16. "Dieses und die folgende Pastorella sind, wie wir glauben, noch ungedruckt."

17. Stinson 2006, 77–79.

18. "Bei dem Choralvorspiel v. Bach 'Schmücke dich, o liebe Seele' (in Es dur) sagte er mit d. innigsten Ausdruck: 'wenn mir das Leben alles genommen hätte, dies Stück würde mich wieder trösten.'" See Eismann 1948, 39.

19. Schumann's mention of the tonality of this piece also distinguishes it from BWV Anh. 74, another organ setting of "Schmücke dich" in F major. On this undoubtedly spurious work, see Emans 1997, 69.

20. Letter of August 7, 1840. See Weissweiller 1984–2001, 1062. Translation from Stinson 2006, 56–57.

Praeludien und sechs Fugen für Orgel oder Pianoforte mit Pedal von Johann Sebastian Bach.[21] As these pieces gained in popularity, having gone through five printings by 1840, they had acquired a nickname befitting their relatively large size. Another point to be made about Schumann's report is that he apparently had never heard the A-minor played on the organ.

Mendelssohn thus treated his Leipzig audience to the same A-minor prelude and fugue (BWV 543) that he had played to great acclaim in London three years earlier and doubtless at other times too.[22] Indeed, if one can trust the biography of the English organist Herbert Oakeley, Mendelssohn performed this piece so frequently in London churches that it became known there not as the "*Bach* A-minor" but the "*Mendelssohn* A-minor."[23] In particular, it was the virtuosic pedal part of the fugue that so thrilled the Londoners. According to Oakeley's biography, when Mendelssohn played the fugue at Christ Church, Newgate Street, he became so excited himself that "when he came to the great pedal solo at the end he just sat on the organ seat and tore his hair!"

The second part of the recital began with the Passacaglia, or, as Mendelssohn always called it, "Passacaille" in C Minor, BWV 582. Schumann's remark that the work was "admirably handled in the choice of registers" leaves little doubt that Mendelssohn frequently changed registrations between variations, thereby exploiting the various timbres of that rather substantial organ, which by this time had grown to around forty stops (was he aided by registrants, who might also have turned pages?). Perhaps, then, he only gradually built up to the "volle Orgel" registration cited in the program. As to the meaning of the word "Phantasie" here, the term must refer to the four-minute-long fugue that concludes the piece.[24] Strictly speaking, this fugue is prefaced not by twenty-one variations, as the program claims, but by twenty, suggesting that the initial, solo statement of the ostinato-bass theme was counted as Variation 1.

Mendelssohn's audience must have included readers of the *Neue Zeitschrift für Musik*, a periodical that was published as well as edited (by Schumann, of course) in the city of Leipzig. It is worth noting, therefore, that earlier in 1840 the *Neue Zeitschrift* had hailed Bach as a kind of culmination point in the history of variation writing and had cited the Passacaglia (whose ostinato theme was printed as a musical example) as proof of his greatness in this domain.[25] Making this proclamation was the Leipzig organist Carl Ferdinand Becker, who also commented on earlier examples of ostinato-bass variations for organ, including Dietrich Buxtehude's D-minor passacaglia and Johann Pachelbel's D-minor chaconne. Becker may or may not have sensed the extremely close relationship between these two (at the time) unpublished works and Bach's passacaglia.[26] But since he owned

21. Kilian 1978–79, 15–16 and 256–57.

22. Stinson 2006, 29–30 and 44–47.

23. Oakeley 1904, 77–79.

24. On this matter, see also Pape 1988, 24.

25. Becker 1840.

26. It has long been recognized that Bach borrowed from both works in composing his passacaglia, even if André Raison's "Trio en passacaille" is the exemplar for Bach's passacaglia theme (see chap. 1).

the primary manuscript source of all three pieces, which is the so-called Andreas Bach Book, he was uniquely equipped to make this realization.[27]

The recital continued with the Pastorale in F Major, BWV 590. Only its first movement had been published at the time (as Bach's "Pastorella"), which is evidence that it was also the only one performed.[28] To be more specific, this publication was the brainchild of Mendelssohn's erstwhile friend Adolf Bernhard Marx, who in 1825 had issued the first movement as a supplement to his journal, the *Berliner allgemeine musikalische Zeitung*.[29] In his accompanying commentary, Marx was so awed by the music that he could scarcely describe it: "We can hardly venture to say anything about this splendid Pastorale. It is so permeated by the most intimate, truly rustic feeling, and handled so expressively, richly, and charmingly in every voice from the first to the last measure…that one can only sense and marvel and be silent."[30] Marx also considered the movement to be an independent work, and he regarded it as merely a torso due to the way it concludes in A minor, rather like a da capo aria that breaks off right before the repeat of the "A" section: "The composition has been given to us as a fragment. However, it is certainly in and of itself satisfactory, regardless of its beginning in F major and ending in A minor."[31] We can only assume that Mendelssohn, too, thought highly of this movement (highly enough to perform it, anyway). Did he also agree with Marx that it had not survived in its original, complete state? If so, Mendelssohn may have played the first nine bars as a reprise, followed immediately or shortly thereafter by a cadence in F major, which is a practice that has become especially customary when performing just the first movement.[32]

What *is* certain is that the Pastorale impressed Schumann, to quote from his review, as something "mined from the deepest depths in which such a composition may be found." Considering that Schumann mentored his wife, Clara, in all things Bach, his high opinion of the work might explain why she championed it throughout her career as a pianist: she played it both in concert and in her teaching studio, and considered it one of Bach's most significant organ compositions.[33] Clara, in turn, probably introduced the Pastorale to her

---

27. On the Andreas Bach Book, see Hill 1991; Schulze 1984, 30–56; and Kilian 1978–79, 122–31.

28. On this print, see Kilian 1988, 178.

29. The once very close relationship between Mendelssohn and Marx had begun to deteriorate already in 1832–33. See Sposato 2004, 256–58.

30. "Kaum wagen wir, etwas über dieses herrliche Pastorale zu sagen; denn so ganz ist es von der innigsten, wahrhaft ländlichen Empfindung durchdrungen, so ausdrucksvoll und reich und reizend vom ersten bis zum letzten Takte jede Stimme geführt…dass man nur empfinden und staunen und schweigen kann." See Glöckner et al. 2007, 520–21.

31. "Die Komposition ist uns als Fragment übergeben, doch gewiss für sich allein befriedigend, ob sie gleich F-dur in A-moll schliesst."

32. On this practice, see Keller 1967, 97.

33. Clara described the Pastorale in this manner in a letter to Theodor Kirchner of November 2, 1862. See R. Hofmann 1996, 108. She is documented to have played the work on a concert in London on March 3, 1877, and at a studio class in Frankfurt on March 27, 1895. See, respectively, the collection of Clara's concert programs at the Robert-Schumann-Haus, Zwickau (catalogue no. 10 463, A3), number 1144; and Moser 1990, 79. The London concert was probably the same one attended by E. M. Oakeley in which Clara "began with Bach's (organ) 'Pastorale' and went on to the (organ) E minor Prelude and Fugue," BWV 548. See Oakeley 1904, 57.

dear friend Johannes Brahms, who featured the piece on his piano recitals and listened to Clara render it during his last visit with her shortly before her death.[34] In addition, Clara and Brahms sometimes amused themselves by performing the first movement as a piano duet, just as Marx had recommended in his commentary.[35]

The last Bach work played on the recital was a toccata in D minor, either the "Dorian" toccata (BWV 538/1) or the infamous Toccata (and Fugue) in D Minor, BWV 565. Since Mendelssohn knew the "Dorian" not as a toccata but as a prelude, he must have played BWV 565, a work he once described as "learned and at the same time something for the people."[36] Schumann's response to the opening section of this piece as "typical of Bach's sense of humor" is seriously at odds with the traditional interpretation of gloom and doom (see chap. 7).

It is worth asking why Mendelssohn selected these six compositions in particular, especially when we know that during the year or so leading up to his concert he had other Bach organ works on his mind or under his fingers. Obviously, he chose repertoire that he had played for a long time, save the Passacaglia, but popular appeal was surely a consideration as well. Thus the Fugue in C Major, BWV 545/2, which Mendelssohn practiced repeatedly in the summer of 1839 but described as "very simple," probably due to its slow-moving subject, may not have been flashy enough for inclusion.[37] Also during that summer Mendelssohn acquired what he thought was an incomplete autograph manuscript of Bach's *Orgelbüchlein*.[38] As he wrote to his sister Fanny, he especially treasured this source because it began with "Das alte Jahr vergangen ist" (BWV 614), a work that may have factored into Fanny's piano cycle *Das Jahr*. Felix surely prized "Das alte Jahr" for its complex chromaticism, yet it may have been this very quality, along with the aura of melancholy that pervades the music, that discouraged him from playing it for a dilettante audience. The work would already have been familiar to certain members of the audience because of its publication at the end of 1839 in a supplement to the *Neue Zeitschrift*. Schumann also included in this supplement the *Orgelbüchlein* setting of "Ich ruf zu dir, Herr Jesu Christ" (BWV 639). He had advertised the two works as follows:

> With this issue we present to our readers the eighth of our musical supplements, containing: a hitherto unpublished chorale prelude for organ on the text "Ich ruf zu dir, Herr Jesu Christ" by Johann Sebastian Bach . . . and, with best wishes for the

34. On Clara, Brahms, and the Pastorale, see Stinson 2006, 131–33 and 135; R. and K. Hofmann 2006, 97–98; and E. Schumann 1925, 173–74.

35. According to Marx's commentary, the first movement was "written originally for the organ" but was "performable on the piano, in which case the pedal voice is to be executed by a second player."

36. Stinson 2006, 18–19; and Stinson 2002, 121–22. See also Glöckner et al. 2007, 277–78.

37. Mendelssohn Bartholdy 1863, 202; and Stinson 2006, 48–54.

38. Little 2007; and Glöckner et al. 2007, 381.

end of the year, a *strange* chorale prelude, printed according to the original manuscript, on the text "Das alte Jahr vergangen ist" by Johann Sebastian Bach.[39]

One may conclude from this rather odd sales pitch that if Schumann found "Das alte Jahr" to be a "strange" composition, Mendelssohn's audience might have been absolutely bewildered by it.

There is also the Prelude and Fugue in G Major, BWV 541, one of Bach's most accessible as well as exciting free organ works. Early in 1840 Mendelssohn studied the original print of this piece and dispatched an angry letter to the publisher enumerating the many mistakes he had found therein.[40] His primary purpose in this endeavor, though, was to establish an accurate text from which he could prepare his own edition. He may never have played the piece.

Quite separate from all of these issues are the improvisations that began and ended the recital. The "Introduction" to the E-flat fugue was described by Schumann merely as being short. Perhaps it was not much longer than two minutes, like the "Introduction" supplied by Mendelssohn's organ teacher August Wilhelm Bach to the Fugue in G Minor, BWV 542/2.[41] If so, the selections before the concluding "Freie Phantasie" amounted to no more than roughly fifty minutes of music, or just forty minutes, if just the first movement of the Pastorale were played. It is hard to reconcile these statistics with Schumann's report to Clara that "Mendelssohn's concert lasted somewhat long" unless this improvised "Phantasie" was one of the longest items on the program, if not the longest.[42] In Schumann's words:

Mendelssohn ended with a fantasy of his own in which, then, he showed himself in the full glory of his artistry; it was based on a chorale (if I am not mistaken, with the text "O Haupt voll Blut und Wunden") into which he later wove the name BACH and a fugal passage—the entire fantasy was rounded into such a clear and masterly whole that, if printed, it would appear a finished work of art.

---

39. Wir übergeben unsern Lesern mit dieser Nummer die VIII. unserer mus. Beilagen, enthalten: ein bisher ungedrucktes Choralvorspiel für Orgel zum Text "Ich ruf zu dir Herr Jesu Christ" von Joh. Sebastian Bach ... und als guten Jahresbeschluss ein nach dem Originalmanuscript abgedrucktes, merkwürdiges Choralvorspiel zum Text: "Das alte Jahr vergangen ist," von Joh. Seb. Bach." *Neue Zeitschrift für Musik* 11, no. 47 (December 10, 1839): 188. Similar to how Schumann described "Das alte Jahr," his colleague Oswald Lorenz characterized the equally chromatic *Orgelbüchlein* setting of "Durch Adams Fall ist ganz verderbt" (BWV 637) as "ein merkwürdig schönes Vorspiel." See the *Neue Zeitschrift für Musik* 13, no. 52 (December 26, 1840): 206.

40. Stinson 2006, 54.

41. For a facsimile reproduction of A. W. Bach's "Introduction," see Sieling 1999, 308.

42. In this regard, it should be mentioned that Rudolf Lutz's reconstruction of this improvisation lasts over fifteen minutes. See Lutz 2011, which also includes a recording of the reconstruction. The same recording is available on the CD, featuring Lutz and Martin Schmeding, *Leipziger Orgeln um Felix Mendelssohn Bartholdy* (GEN 89152). The score of Lutz's reconstruction is to be published by Carus-Verlag.

Mendelssohn therefore apparently extemporized on one of his favorite chorales, "O Haupt voll Blut und Wunden," probably in the guise of theme and variations with a concluding fugue, and toward the end combined the chorale with the musical equivalent of Bach's name, B–A–C–H.[43] As to the length of the improvisation, just consider that Mendelssohn once extemporized at the piano no fewer than twenty variations on "The Blue Bells of Scotland."[44] There, too, he demonstrated his keen contrapuntal sense, setting the tune twice as a canon and once as a four-voice fugue with the melody inverted.

Mendelssohn's recital was a tremendous success, both artistically and financially: the critics raved, and the proceeds totaled three hundred thalers, a sum equal to one-third of the artist's annual salary as conductor of the Gewandhaus orchestra. Given these factors, not to mention Mendelssohn's overall celebrity, his performance must have influenced other organists. Take, for example, Carl Ferdinand Becker. As a resident of Leipzig, Becker surely attended Mendelssohn's concert, and, as the only organist in town who regularly played public recitals, he would have taken a special interest in the event.[45] It was during his long tenure as organist at St. Peter's that Becker seems to have begun the tradition of an annual organ recital for the local citizens. As shown in table 3.1, he played one recital per year there in 1834 and 1835, in March and April, respectively.[46] For whatever reasons, his recital in 1836 took place at St. Thomas's, in May, and he continued with recitals in May 1837 and May 1838 at St. Nicholas's, having been appointed organist there in early 1837. There is no record of a recital by Becker in 1839, and the same goes for 1840, when he may have deferred to Mendelssohn. From 1841 to 1844, however, Becker played four more recitals at St. Nicholas's, all of which, like Mendelssohn's concert, took place in August. These data suggest that due to the success of Mendelssohn's concert, Becker switched the scheduling of his annual recital from May to August.[47] Maybe he realized, among other things, how much Mendelssohn's audience had enjoyed the ambience of a lazy summer evening. Again, it is worth quoting from Schumann's review: "A fine summer

---

43. For particulars, see Todd 1995; Lutz 2011; and Wollny 2011, 144–45.

44. Todd 2003, 546.

45. Becker, however, did not sign Mendelssohn's handwritten appeal for subscribers to his concert (Schumann did). See Little 2010, 415–28.

46. The information presented in table 3.1 is derived from the following sources: Stadtgeschichtliches Museum, Leipzig, Sammlung Leipziger Konzertprogramme, Mappe 28; reviews in the *Allgemeine musikalische Zeitung* and *Neue Zeitschrift für Musik*; Rosenmüller 2000, 192–97; and P. Krause 1982, 88–90. See also Glöckner et al. 2007, 668–69. For a facsimile reproduction of the program of the 1837 recital, in which Becker was assisted by his pupil J. G. Bastiaans, see Bokum 1971 (facing p. 12). The "Number of Bach Works Played" includes works of doubtful authenticity that at the time were attributed to Bach, such as the Prelude and Fugue on BACH, BWV 898, as well as works played by Becker and his pupils as organ duets, such as the six-voice ricercar from the Musical Offering. The total number of works cited does not include improvisations, works for orchestral instruments and organ, or organ works played solely by Becker's pupils.

47. All of Becker's recitals from 1834 to 1838 occurred on Wednesdays, whereas all of those from 1841 to 1844 took place on Sundays. His reasons for making this change are by no means clear.

evening shone through the church windows; even outside, in the open air, many may have reflected on the wonderful sounds."

Much more significantly, the proportion of Bach works on Becker's recitals from 1841 to 1844 rose to about 50 percent, implying Mendelssohn's enduring influence. Of particular interest is the 1844 recital, for, according to an anonymous review, it featured an unpublished setting by Bach of "Schmücke dich, o liebe Seele."[48] Once again, the work in question seems to have been the Great Eighteen chorale. Surely the reviewer was not

TABLE 3.1.

Carl Ferdinand Becker's Leipzig Organ Recitals, 1834–47

Date	Location	Number of Bach Works Played
March 12, 1834	St. Peter's	1, out of 10 works altogether
April 8, 1835	St. Peter's	unknown
May 18, 1836	St. Thomas's	2 (total number of works unknown)
May 10, 1837	St. Nicholas's	2, out of 6 works altogether
May 30, 1838	St. Nicholas's	2, out of 7 works altogether
August 1, 1841	St. Nicholas's	4, out of 9 works altogether
August 14, 1842	St. Nicholas's	3, out of 7 works altogether
August 13, 1843	St. Nicholas's	3, out of 5 works altogether
August 18, 1844	St. Nicholas's	4, out of 10 works altogether, including a setting of "Schmücke dich, o liebe Seele" (presumably the Great Eighteen chorale BWV 654)
October 24, 1847	New Church	all nine works by Bach, including the Fugue in E-flat Major, BWV 552/2; the Pastorale in F Major, BWV 590; and a setting of "Schmücke dich, o liebe Seele" (presumably the Great Eighteen chorale BWV 654)

48. *Neue Zeitschrift für Musik* 21, no. 15 (August 19, 1844): 60.

referring to BWV 759, which had been in print for forty years; the only other organ arrangement of this hymn ever attributed to Bach, the unquestionably inauthentic BWV Anh. 74, was essentially unknown at the time (and remains so today).[49]

Becker was by this time the organ instructor of the newly opened Leipzig Conservatory, having been appointed to the post by Mendelssohn, the school's founder and director.[50] Any mutual respect that already existed between the two can only have grown during their four years together there. They no doubt discussed early music in general and Bach's organ works in particular, and they undoubtedly played Bach for each other at the organ. It only stands to reason that these sessions sometimes involved Mendelssohn's favorite Bach organ works, including those he had performed on his all-Bach concert. On one or more of these occasions, Mendelssohn presented Becker with copies of his recently published editions of Bach's organ chorales.[51] (Did Mendelssohn also supply the manuscript from which Becker played "Schmücke dich" in 1844?) All four sources are inscribed "zu freundlicher Erinnerung," but Mendelssohn's inscription on his edition of the Great Eighteen chorales also indicates, in addition to the exact date, the place of the exchange: "Herrn C. F. Becker zu freundlicher / Erinnerung an den 29sten October 1846 / in der Nicolaikirche zu Leipzig / FMB." Either man could have opened the volume to "Schmücke dich, o liebe Seele" in order to play the work on the church's organ.

Perhaps Bach's E-flat fugue and Pastorale were taken up at these meetings, too. At any rate, Becker played both pieces on his only all-Bach recital, which occurred in 1847 in conjunction with an organ dedication at the New Church (see table 3.1).[52] Also on the program was an unspecified setting of "Schmücke dich." The mere fact that Becker mounted an all-Bach recital, of course, suggests that he was emulating Mendelssohn. Moreover, Becker in his printed program indicated Bach's authorship of the music more or less exactly as Mendelssohn had done, with a caption at the bottom of the page that reads "Sämmtliche Tonwerke von J. S. Bach" (Mendelssohn's caption reads "Sämmtliche Compositionen sind von Sebastian Bach"). But the inclusion of two and probably three of the same works featured on Mendelssohn's concert makes it a virtual certainty that Becker was following his lead, considering that well over a hundred Bach organ works were readily available in print by this date. Becker's recital may also have constituted a very personal homage to Mendelssohn as a Bach interpreter, taking place as it did on

---

49. The Göttinger Bach-Katalog lists only three manuscript sources for BWV Anh. 74 (a work that remains unpublished) as opposed to twenty-six for the Great Eighteen chorale. The latter piece had in fact been in print for several years, but only in Johann Nepomuk Schelble's exceedingly obscure arrangement for four-hand piano (Frankfurt, n.d.). On this publication, see Kobayashi 1973, 272; and Schneider 1906, 105.

50. For a recent discussion of Becker's organ studio at the conservatory, see Rosenmüller 2011.

51. For information on these sources, see Rosenmüller 2000, 188–90; and P. Krause 1970, 78–80.

52. These are the only two Bach works on any of Becker's recitals that are unquestionably the same as those played by Mendelssohn on his all-Bach concert. The "Fünfstimmige Fuge von J. S. Bach" on Becker's 1841 recital may have been the same E-flat fugue played by Mendelssohn, but this is not Bach's only five-voice organ fugue.

October 24, just a couple of weeks after the great man had suffered the first in a series of strokes that would lead to his death on November 4. Becker may not even have settled on the radical idea of an all-Bach program until hearing the news of Mendelssohn's failing health.

As director of the Leipzig Conservatory, as well as an instructor in performance and composition, Mendelssohn must also have interacted regularly with Becker's organ pupils, even though he was not their official organ teacher. Indeed, it is documented that he once took a group of conservatory students to St. Thomas's expressly to play Bach for them.[53] One can easily believe, therefore, that Mendelssohn's enthusiasm for particular Bach organ works affected Becker's pupils, just as it did Becker himself. One of these pupils was Jan Albertus van Eijken, who studied with Becker at the conservatory from 1845 to 1846. He studied composition with Mendelssohn, but Mendelssohn also admired the young man's organ playing, especially his "very clean pedal playing."[54] Upon returning to his native Holland in the fall of 1846, van Eijken began to concertize extensively, with an emphasis on Bach. From 1846 to 1848 his recitals featured roughly a dozen different Bach works, including four played by Mendelssohn on his Leipzig concert: the E-flat fugue, the Great Eighteen setting of "Schmücke dich," the A-minor prelude and fugue, and the Toccata and Fugue in D Minor.[55] Counting multiple performances of the same work, roughly half of van Eijken's Bach performances during this period were of these four pieces. He also played the Toccata in F Major, BWV 540/1, another of Mendelssohn's favorite Bach works.

Mendelssohn obviously inspired legions of organists to play Bach's music in general and certain works in particular. But to whom did he look for inspiration? One answer is suggested by the following anecdote:

> One story of Mendelssohn was this: Schneider played to him and another—a Professor of music, I think—the B flat minor fugue from Vol. 2 of "the 48." (He was fond of playing the more "organic" of the "48" on the organ.)...At the end of it, Schneider, seeing the Professor looking around unmoved, feared the piece had failed to "find" its audience. But where was Mendelssohn? He was in tears in a remote gallery![56]

At the console was the redoubtable Johann Gottlob Schneider, organist at the Court Church in Dresden (today the Kathedrale Dresden) from 1825 until his death in 1864. Hailed as an improviser as well as a Bach interpreter and widely sought after as a

---

53. Stinson 2006, 62–64.

54. Bokum 2000, 71 n. 30.

55. Bokum 1971, 85–86 and 94. According to Buitenen 1998, 23, van Eijken may also have appropriated the Great Eighteen setting of "Schmücke dich" as a compositional model.

56. Oakeley 1904, 76.

pedagogue, Schneider was one of the most respected organists in all of Europe. He also specialized in organ arrangements of preludes and fugues from Bach's Well-Tempered Clavier, as evinced by the anecdote just quoted, which is taken from the biography of Herbert Oakeley, one of Schneider's last pupils.[57] As a young man, Mendelssohn had expressed outright amazement when he heard that Schneider could pedal the bass line of the D-major fugue from Book 1 of this collection, and as a resident of nearby Leipzig for more than ten years, he may have been one of Schneider's regular listeners. As another Schneider pupil once stated, "Yes, it is said that Mendelssohn sometimes made the trip from Leipzig to Dresden exclusively to hear Johann Schneider improvise."[58] Furthermore, Mendelssohn is quoted as having told organ students at the Leipzig Conservatory: "Go on to Schneider in Dresden, because you can learn good things [from him]."[59] One student who seems to have heeded this advice was, again, van Eijken, who, upon completing his studies with Becker, spent several months in Dresden as one of Schneider's pupils. Following Schneider's example, van Eijken would later publish his own organ transcriptions of twenty-five movements from the Well-Tempered Clavier.[60] Not incidentally, one of these arrangements is of the same fugue that Schneider played for Mendelssohn.

A final bit of documentation linking Mendelssohn and Schneider comes, perhaps unexpectedly, from Schumann's *Erinnerungen an F. Mendelssohn*. In a section of the manuscript devoted to Mendelssohn's "pronouncements and judgements," Schumann wrote "Ueber Johann Schneider u. sein Orgelspiel," indicating, no doubt, Mendelssohn's positive assessment of Schneider's abilities.[61] Schumann might have taken special pleasure in making this entry, for he had become one of Schneider's devotees himself since moving from Leipzig to Dresden at the end of 1844. It is clear from Schumann's household records that he whiled away many an hour at the Court Church listening to the virtuoso play the church's magnificent Silbermann organ.[62] Schneider unquestionably played for his two famous admirers not only movements from the Well-Tempered Clavier but also legitimate organ works by Bach.[63] In fact, Mendelssohn remarked to William Sterndale Bennett in 1842 that Schneider played Bach's organ fugues "better than anybody in the world."[64] Perhaps Schneider regularly treated both Mendelssohn and Schumann to the

---

57. According to Oakeley's entry on Schneider in the Grove Dictionary, second edition, Mendelssohn was one of Schneider's "greatest admirers." For another account of Schneider's performances of movements from the Well-Tempered Clavier, see Holmes 1828, 208–9.

58. "Ja, man behauptet, dass Mendelssohn manchmal die Reise von Leipzig nach Dresden ausschliesslich gemacht habe, um Johann Schneider improvisieren zu hören." See Sieling 1999, 324. The pupil in question was Willem Frederic Gerard Nicolai.

59. "Gehen Sie noch zu Schneider in Dresden, da können Sie was Tüchtiges lernen." See Sieling 1999, 323.

60. Busch 2002.

61. This entry appears in Eismann 1948, 75.

62. Stinson 2006, 90 and 97–98.

63. By the same token, Mendelssohn must have played for Schneider.

64. Bennett 1907, 126.

"Sechs grosse Praeludien und Fugen," playing from the same "shabby old book" he had used when Mendelssohn's friend Henry Chorley visited him in 1840.[65] If so, Schumann might often have requested the Prelude in C Minor, BWV 546/1, a movement that he once singled out as "wonderful" in a review of the collection.[66]

Two further entries from Schumann's *Erinnerungen* concern Mendelssohn and the organ, either directly or indirectly.[67] One reads "[Ausgaben] der Choralvorspiele v. Bach," a reference to Mendelssohn's four editions of Bach's organ chorales. Like Becker, Schumann had received from the editor inscribed copies of all four of these publications, and the many analytical markings that he made in them betray his close study of the music.[68] The other entry simply reads "Sein Orgelspiel." In writing these words, Schumann was probably thinking of his comrade's brilliance both as an improvisor and a Bach interpreter. As an organist, Mendelssohn rarely did anything else.

---

65. Chorley 1854, vol. 1, 326–27. Schneider played for Chorley the Preludes and Fugues in B Minor and E Minor, BWV 544 and 548.

66. Stinson 2006, 82.

67. These entries appear in Eismann 1948, 34 and 36.

68. Stinson 2006, 93–97.

4

Bach's Organ Works and Schumann's *Neue Zeitschrift*

JUST AS ROBERT Schumann acknowledged J. S. Bach as his most profound musical influence, so he repeatedly proclaimed Bach's organ works to be the master's greatest creations. To give just one example of Schumann's particular affinity for Bach's organ music, he once wrote apropos of the so-called Six Great Preludes and Fugues, BWV 543–48, that it was "only at his organ that [Bach] appears to be at his most sublime, most audacious, in his own element."[1]

This heartfelt tribute would have been read by hundreds of music lovers across Europe, for it appeared in the periodical founded by Schumann under the title *Neue Zeitschrift für Musik* ("New Journal for Music"). As editor of this publication from 1834 to 1844, Schumann promoted Bach's organ works in various ways. He personally reviewed organ recitals and editions of organ music, and he printed his own editions of certain pieces as well.[2] Likewise, he published reviews and full-length articles by organist-colleagues of his in which Bach's organ music was prominently mentioned, whether in the context of music history, musical style, or performance practice. Although several of Schumann's own contributions in this regard have been discussed in the scholarly literature, much remains to be said about how the *Neue Zeitschrift* in general served as a kind of forum on Bach's organ works during this time, a time, it bears mentioning, when Bach's organ music

---

1. *Neue Zeitschrift für Musik* 10, no. 39 (May 14, 1839), 154; reprinted in R. Schumann 1854, vol. 3, 95. See also Glöckner et al. 2007, 420–22.

2. On Schumann's editions of Bach's organ works, see Synofzik 2011.

56

was still relatively unknown to the musical public.[3] This material also constitutes an important chapter in the musical history of the city of Leipzig, where the journal was edited and published, and where the great Bach himself lived.

We already find in the inaugural issue of the *Neue Zeitschrift* a capsule review, presumably written by Schumann, of an organ recital featuring the music of Bach: "In the last concert of the splendid organist Mr. Becker, we heard works by Bach, Handel, Krebs, [and] Pachelbel, among others. For a church concert, there was a very large audience, although it was not [quite] the largest we have seen. With gratitude we recognize the inspired efforts in this regard of this esteemed artist."[4]

Admittedly, this report says precious little, but it does introduce us to Carl Ferdinand Becker, who was then a leading figure within the Leipzig organ community. Becker held organ posts in the city for almost thirty years, starting in 1825 at St. Peter's (where this concert took place), and by all accounts he was an accomplished performer, not to mention the only organist in town who regularly offered public organ recitals. Indeed, no less a musician than Felix Mendelssohn thought highly enough of Becker's abilities to appoint him in 1843 as the organ teacher of the newly opened Leipzig Conservatory. Becker was also an indefatigable collector of music manuscripts, particularly of Baroque keyboard works, and he regularly contributed to the *Neue Zeitschrift* articles about and reviews of early music.

Schumann apparently continued to write favorable reviews of Becker's organ concerts. However, he would later grumble privately that Becker was "not a great musician" and that, as a judge of compositional talent, he could not tell the difference between "Bach, Pachelbel, and himself."[5] One can infer from the latter remark that Schumann and Becker held rather different opinions about Bach vis-à-vis other Baroque composers. Schumann, for example, saw Bach not as the culmination of the Baroque era but as an isolated genius whose compositions were the first in music history to manifest the same spiritual and poetic qualities found in the best works of the early romantic period.[6] Becker, for his part, was an early-music fanatic who collected, researched, and performed the music not only of Bach but, to an equal extent, the music of Bach's predecessors and contemporaries. As a critic for the *Neue Zeitschrift*, Becker happily conceded that Bach was the greatest organist of his day.[7] Yet, in reviewing an edition of seventeenth- and eighteenth-century keyboard works, he also had the temerity to write that "true organ-art does not take place only within the school of Johann Sebastian Bach."[8]

---

3. See especially Stinson 2006, which contains an entire chapter on Schumann's reception of Bach's organ works.

4. *Neue Zeitschrift für Musik* 1, no. 1 (April 3, 1834), 4. See also Rosenmüller 2000, 194.

5. Letter to Eduard Krüger of June 19, 1843. See Kinsky 1953, 250; and Jansen 1904, 192.

6. See Schumann's letter to G. A. Keferstein of January 31, 1840, published in Jansen 1904, 177–78. See also Glöckner et al. 2007, 210.

7. *Neue Zeitschrift für Musik* 9, no. 49 (December 18, 1838), 196.

8. *Neue Zeitschrift für Musik* 1, no. 65 (November 13, 1834), 260.

Schumann may have had second thoughts about publishing this statement, since he was prone to denigrate the very composers being defended by Becker. To cite one instance, Schumann asserted that Johann Kuhnau, even if he had composed both books of the Well-Tempered Clavier, was only one-hundredth of the composer that Bach was.[9] Similarly, C. P. E. Bach was dismissed by Schumann as "nothing more than a rather insipid Prussian chamber musician."[10] Schumann even took this derisive tone once in reviewing an anthology of Baroque keyboard works edited by Becker himself. This critique begins, rather in the spirit of a disclaimer, with the following salvo: "With regard to composition for organ and piano, obviously no one of Bach's century can measure up to him. Indeed, to me, everything else appears in comparison to the development of this giant figure as something conceived in childhood."[11]

In March 1837 Becker was appointed organist at the church of St. Nicholas, where for the next seventeen years he would preside over an instrument by the firm of Trampeli. There was fierce competition for this, the best-paying organ job in Leipzig, with Becker beating out nine other candidates, including August Pohlenz, organist at St. Thomas's, the other principal church in town.[12] Two months later, Becker played his first concert as *Nikolaiorganist*. An anonymous review appeared in the *Neue Zeitschrift*:

> At the organ concert given the day before yesterday by Mr. C. F. Becker as the newly installed organist at the church of St. Nicholas, we heard valuable older works, including one of the most profound chorales of Sebastian Bach, "Wenn wir in höchsten Nöten sein," and the six-voice ricercar from the Musical Offering, one of the most wonderfully entwined fantasies of Bach [and] as a masterpiece of harmony perhaps without equal. Mr. Becker splendidly played the latter work with his pupil, Mr. [J. G.] Bastiaans from Deventer. The chamber musician Mr. C. G. Belcke accompanied with the flute some organ compositions of the concert-giver. The concert was for the benefit of the Institute for the Deaf and Mute, a most noble purpose, like artistic enjoyment itself.[13]

There can be little doubt as to Schumann's authorship of this précis. Its overall tone accords with Schumann's prose style,[14] and the two Bach works are hyperbolized basically to the exclusion of all the other repertory played. (The writer does not even mention that Mozart's F-minor fantasy, K. 608, was also rendered as an organ duet on the concert.)

9. Letter to G. A. Keferstein of January 31, 1840.

10. Letter to Eduard Krüger of June 19, 1843.

11. *Neue Zeitschrift für Musik* 6, no. 10 (February 3, 1837), 40; reprinted in Robert Schumann 1854, vol. 2, 197.

12. Rosenmüller 2000, 23–25.

13. *Neue Zeitschrift für Musik* 6, no. 40 (May 19, 1837), 162. See also Rosenmüller 2000, 195; and Glöckner et al. 2007, 668–69.

14. Fuchs 1982, 221.

Moreover, "profound" was the adjective most often used by Schumann to describe Bach as a composer. The word appears here in reference to one of Bach's two organ arrangements of "Wenn wir in höchsten Nöten sein," either the ornamental setting from the *Orgelbüchlein* or the more expansive work catalogued as BWV 668a. By the nineteenth century, the latter had achieved legendary status as a piece dictated by Bach in his blindness at the very end of his life.[15] Considering that Becker's printed program lists the piece in question as Bach's "last work," he must have played this setting.[16]

As Schumann implies, the dense texture of the ricercar from the Musical Offering allows for some of the most sumptuous harmonies and intricate polyphony Bach ever wrote. There is no proof that the movement was composed for the organ, but organ arrangements may already have begun to circulate around 1750, perhaps with the composer's approval.[17] In Becker's arrangement, which in 1855 was published in F. W. Schütze's *Praktische Orgelschule*,[18] one player takes the top three voices while the other takes the bottom three, first pedaling the lowest voice but then, to accommodate the fast, scalar figuration that begins in m. 116, playing it with the left hand. Schütze recommends a basic registration of full organ, for the sake of a "majestic effect," with a reduction in volume for the middle section (mm. 79–103).

We know from Schumann's diary that in 1843 he again heard Becker's transcription at St. Nicholas's, played this time by Becker and his student Louise Avé-Lallemant.[19] According to an anonymous review in the *Neue Zeitschrift*, presumably of Schumann's authoring, the presence of a female organist gave the recital a "special interest."[20] It is worth mentioning as well that in August 1844 Becker and his student Hermann Schellenberger played the same transcription on a concert at St. Nicholas's.[21] Schellenberger would eventually succeed his teacher as the church's organist and was responsible for the parish's acquisition of the magnificent Ladegast organ that still adorns the rear gallery.[22] As a performer, Schellenberger may also have been something of a showman: his trademark was to thrust both hands high into the air when executing a pedal solo to show his audience that he really was playing with his feet.[23]

---

15. For a comprehensive discussion of this myth, see Wolff 1991.

16. See the facsimile of Becker's program in Bokum 1971 (facing p. 12). The program of Becker's organ recital at St. Nicholas's on August 14, 1842 (Stadtgeschichtliches Museum, Leipzig, Sammlung Leipziger Konzertprogramme, Mappe 28a) documents a second performance by him of this chorale setting, again designated as Bach's "last work."

17. Williams 1980–84, vol. 1, 333.

18. Rosenmüller 2000, 135–36. Schütze's treatise also contains a four-hands arrangement of the Mozart fantasy performed by Becker and Bastiaans, presumably the same arrangement they played on this recital.

19. Eismann and Nauhaus 1971–82, vol. 3, 349.

20. *Neue Zeitschrift für Musik* 19, no. 13 (August 14, 1843), 52. See also Rosenmüller 2000, 196.

21. The concert was reviewed in the *Neue Zeitschrift für Musik* 21, no. 15 (August 19, 1844), 60. See also Rosenmüller 2000, 196.

22. Busch 2004, 33.

23. Frotscher 1935, 19, 1176 n. 2.

In 1841 Becker played another solo recital at St. Nicholas's, reviewed in the *Neue Zeitschrift* as follows:

> On August 1 the organist C. F. Becker gave an organ concert at the church of St. Nicholas and proved himself, as always, a highly esteemed artist on his instrument. The compositions played were by Bach, Handel, and Krebs, and the concert-giver, and they included a fugue on the name BACH. This reviewer has always harbored doubts about the authenticity of this fugue; should not many others agree with him? Bach's hand appears in no way to be recognized in this piece; perhaps this is entirely the work of one of Bach's pupils. Where Bach does interpolate his name in a most profound manner is in the last movement of "The Art of Fugue," his last, but uncompleted work; it gives the same impression as in a painting when the name of the artist is somewhat hidden from view. Incidentally, this reviewer would be happy to hear other opinions about the authenticity [of the fugue on BACH].[24]

Once more, it was probably Schumann himself who penned these lines. For one thing, he is known to have attended Becker's concert.[25] For another, the reviewer again discusses Bach to the exclusion of all the other composers represented. The fugue on BACH played by Becker—actually a prelude and fugue, catalogued as BWV 898—was by this time standard fare for organists and pianists alike.[26] In the realm of composition, it obviously inspired Franz Liszt to write his famous Prelude and Fugue on Bach's name and appears also to have influenced Schumann in the first of his Six Fugues on BACH.[27] Today, though, the work has no place in the Bach canon. Both its harmonic style and pianistic idiom point to a composer from the late eighteenth century.[28] It is worth pointing out that the first dozen notes of the fugue subject of BWV 898 are melodically and rhythmically identical

---

24. *Neue Zeitschrift für Musik* 15, no. 11 (August 6, 1841), 44. See also Rosenmüller 2000, 195. Schumann's personal copy of the Art of Fugue (Robert-Schumann-Haus, Zwickau, catalogue no. 10 552, D1/A4, vol. 3) betrays his close study of this movement: he bracketed every statement of the BACH subject and marked the first four notes of the first soprano statement with the letters B-A-C-H. This volume, which Schumann reviewed in the May 14, 1839 issue of the *Neue Zeitschrift für Musik*, also contains the six-voice ricercar from the Musical Offering.

25. Eismann and Nauhaus 1971–82, vol. 3, 189.

26. Heinemann 1995, 153. According to Glöckner et al. 2007, 668, the work had also been performed a few years earlier at Königsberg in an arrangement for organ and brass. The printed program of Becker's organ recital at St. Nicholas's on May 30, 1838 (Stadtgeschichtliches Museum, Leipzig, Sammlung Leipziger Konzertprogramme, Mappe 28a) documents a second performance by him of BWV 898. See also Rosenmüller 2000, 195. Schumann's personal copy of the piece (Robert-Schumann-Haus, Zwickau, catalogue no. 10 552, D1/A4, vol. 4) contains various corrections in his hand but no comment on authorship.

27. Heinemann 1995, 152–53; and Föller 2004, 32–35.

28. Schmieder 1990, 661; and Schulenberg 1992, 378. Two years later, Schumann heard this same work at the church of St. Thomas, performed by the Dresden organist Carl Kloss. In reviewing Kloss's concert, Schumann again voiced his opinion that the composition was "inauthentic." See, respectively, Eismann and Nauhaus 1971–82, vol. 2, 262; and *Neue Zeitschrift für Musik* 18, no. 34 (April 27, 1843), 138.

to Liszt's, except that Liszt starts his subject a beat earlier and inserts an eighth rest before beginning the second segment of his subject (see exx. 4.1, 4.2, and 4.3). Schumann uses the

EXAMPLE 4.1. Prelude and Fugue on BACH, BWV 898, fugue subject

EXAMPLE 4.2. Franz Liszt, Prelude and Fugue on BACH, fugue subject

EXAMPLE 4.3. Robert Schumann, subject of Fugue No. 1 on BACH, from *Six Fugues on BACH*, op. 60

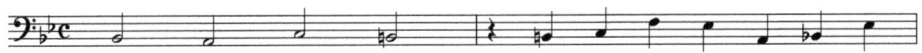

same basic rhythms, but the second segment of his subject amounts to an inversion of the tritone figure used in the other two subjects. Schumann, too, begins his second segment on the "and" of the beat. Since his fugue predates Liszt's by five years, it stands to reason that Liszt imitated Schumann in this regard.

Another figure worthy of our consideration is Eduard Krüger. This learned critic studied aesthetics, history, and philology at the universities of Berlin and Göttingen, graduating from the latter with a dissertation on music in ancient Greece. From 1833 to 1851 he taught at the *Gymnasium* in the East Frisian town of Emden, where under his baton the local choral society mounted works by Haydn and, especially, Handel. But his true passion as a scholar as well as a performer was the music of Bach. Here was an unabashed Bach enthusiast—a true Bach freak—who praised the composer as an "artistic demigod" and the "source of all music."[29] Krüger's specific predilection for Bach's organ works is obvious from his correspondence with Schumann (most of which remains unpublished) as well as from his writings in the *Neue Zeitschrift*. He even resolved, at the advanced age of thirty-one or thirty-two, to teach himself the organ so that he could play Bach's compositions for the instrument.[30]

In accomplishing this feat, Krüger practiced the organ four or five times a week, or as often as the local clergy would allow. Evidently his normal routine was to concentrate on just a few measures of a Bach work for about half an hour at a time, a method that seems to have greatly facilitated Krüger's memorization of the music.[31] As he put it to Schumann,

---

29. "Weniger werden Sie vielleicht der Versicherung trauen, dass ich…dem Urquell aller Musik, dem künstlerischen Halbgott Bach nicht viel weniger ergeben bin, als Sie." Letter to Schumann of June 25, 1839. Like the vast majority of Krüger's letters to Schumann (all housed at the Biblioteka Jagiellońska, Cracow, *Korespondencja Schumanna* collection), this missive is still unpublished. I am indebted to the Robert-Schumann-Forschungsstelle, Düsseldorf, for providing me with facsimiles as well as transcriptions of these materials.

30. Letter to Schumann of December 9, 1842, published in Boetticher 1979, 101.

31. See Krüger's remarks on organ playing in the *Neue Zeitschrift für Musik* 18, no. 50 (June 22, 1843), 199.

"old Sebastian" had him "between his claws."[32] Two and a half years later, in late summer or early fall 1842, he was ready for his first public organ recital, which took place in the nearby village of Aurich. A decidedly positive review, contributed by Krüger's friend and fellow schoolmaster D. R. Stürenburg, appeared shortly thereafter in the *Neue Zeitschrift*:

The famous enemy of the virtuoso, Herr Dr. Eduard Krüger of Emden, is currently well on his way to becoming a virtuoso himself, and, indeed, on the organ. Recently he surprised and delighted the small congregation of our church with a series of almost perfectly rendered classical compositions. Among the gleaming constellations that were illuminated for us, we would have to name above all the lofty, majestic "Symphony in E-flat Major" that opens the Peters collection of J. S. Bach's figured chorales, then the highly poetic Chromatic Fantasy of this same divine master. We acknowledge that this work is rightfully regarded as a keyboard fantasy, but the full power, the true character of the poem, is revealed only on the organ.... Besides these two works was... Bach's "Wachet auf, ruft uns die Stimme," whose introduction... portrays humankind slumbering and daydreaming, when, suddenly, the chorale melody is intoned as a cantus firmus, "high upon the battlement." In addition was the sweet, charming Bach prelude on the chorale "Allein Gott in der Höh sei Ehr," for two manuals and pedal. Next, the Bach "Jubilee" Fugue in G Major, in 4/4 time, with an inventive prelude in 3/4 time, full of heart and strength. Then, a gigantic fugue by Bach in E minor, which appears to represent, in a gripping, restless manner, the pains of a crushed, sinful soul. And then a soaring fantasy by Bach in C minor, shot through with a deeply religious sense and rapturous devotion. And, as the finale, Felix Mendelssohn's Fugue in G Major, a work distinguished equally by its clarity, masculine strength, and originality. (The compatibility of the feminine, modernistic prelude that precedes the fugue to the fugue itself was not clear to us.)

Thanks are due to this enthusiastic disciple of the great Sebastian, this relentless enemy of all unpoetic music, for the enjoyment that he has achieved for us, now, in a practical sense, through his splendid playing. May he also preach the gospel of this noble master in larger cities and on mightier organs than ours.[33]

In effect, then, Krüger played an all-Bach recital, a concept that was still a great novelty at this time. Almost certainly his model was the legendary all-Bach organ concert that

---

32. "Ich habe mich viel zu sehr zersplittert, um ganzer Gelehrter od[er] ganzer Künstler zu werden. Jetzt ists der alte Sebastian, der mich wieder einmal ganz zwischen den Klauen hält - Tag u Nacht orgle ich seine Orgelfantasien..." Letter of October 17, 1841.

33. *Neue Zeitschrift für Musik* 17, no. 32 (October 18, 1842), 130. On the identification of the author of this review, see Tielke 1992, 192–93 n. 75. See also Glöckner et al. 2007, 674–75.

Felix Mendelssohn had performed in Leipzig two years earlier and that Schumann had famously reviewed in the *Neue Zeitschrift* (see chap. 3). The *Neue Zeitschrift* also provides a context for Stürenburg's ironic mention of Krüger as a "virtuoso," for Krüger had published there two lengthy diatribes on virtuosic display.[34] In this endeavor, he surely had his editor's full support.[35] To judge from other articles and reviews published by Krüger in the *Neue Zeitschrift*, his Bach performances were the very antithesis of ostentation. He frowned on registration changes of any kind and pleaded for strict tempo and rhythm even in such a rhapsodic work as the G-minor fantasy.[36] In short, he was a purist whose ideal was to play the music exactly as Bach had notated it.

Stürenburg's fanciful and simplistic descriptions of the works performed by Krüger should be taken with a grain of salt. Still, his review provides enough basic information for most of the pieces to be identified, as long as the publication history of Bach's organ music is also taken into account. The recital began of course with the magnificent prelude in E-flat major that opens Part 3 of the *Clavierübung* and continued with the Chromatic Fantasy, BWV 903/1. Next came Bach's only organ arrangement of "Wachet auf, ruft uns die Stimme," BWV 645. The trio on "Allein Gott" that followed was either that in G major from Part 3 of the *Clavierübung* or that in A major from the Great Eighteen chorales, as these were the only trio-settings by Bach of this chorale that were in print at the time.[37] As for the prelude and fugue cited (curiously) by Stürenburg as the "Jubilee," the only organ work by Bach corresponding to the key and time signatures mentioned by Stürenburg is the brilliant Prelude and Fugue in G Major, BWV 541. Krüger then played a "gigantic" fugue in E minor, which can only mean the very sizable and virtuosic "Wedge" fugue, BWV 548/2, a movement whose chromatic subject suggested to Stürenburg sin and devastation; Bach's other organ fugue in E minor (BWV 533/2) is a mere trifle by comparison. The "deeply religious" fantasy that ensued was obviously Bach's only organ fantasy in C minor to have appeared in print, BWV 562/1. Because this movement had been published by none other than Robert Schumann in a supplement to the *Neue Zeitschrift*, Krüger's choice of repertory here may be seen as a nod both to Schumann and his journal. The concert concluded with Mendelssohn's Prelude and Fugue in G Major, op. 37, no. 2.

Knowing what Krüger's repertoire was, one can only admire his ability to have negotiated this demanding program after only two and a half years of self-tutelage. His own thoughts on three of these pieces are found in his contributions to the *Neue Zeitschrift*,

---

34. *Neue Zeitschrift für Musik* 13, nos. 17–22 (August 26–September 12, 1840); and *Neue Zeitschrift für Musik* 14, nos. 40–43 (May 17–28, 1841).

35. Boetticher 1941, 380.

36. See, respectively, *Neue Zeitschrift für Musik* 18, no. 49 (June 19, 1843), 196–97; and *Neue Zeitschrift für Musik* 19, no. 17 (August 28, 1843), 66. See also Glöckner et al. 2007, 740.

37. Both works are contained in J. G. Schicht's edition *J. S. Bach's Choral-Vorspiele für die Orgel mit einem und zwey Klavieren und Pedal*, published in 1803–6.

where he wrote that the E-flat prelude was a "colossal organ fantasy" evocative of a glorious, old cathedral—and a work deserving of a more grandiose title than "Prelude for Full Organ."[38] Like his friend Stürenburg, he sensed that the "depth and splendor" of the Chromatic Fantasy were revealed only at the organ, with all the stops pulled out and with a pedalpoint on low D added to the last five measures.[39] Krüger also particularly admired Mendelssohn's G-major fugue, at least compared to other fugues by Mendelssohn, citing it as one of only three by him that was more a polyphonic than harmonic entity.[40]

While Krüger learned the organ, he dreamed of proselytizing for Bach's music "in larger cities and on mightier organs" than existed in East Friesland. Specifically, his goal was a pilgrimage to Leipzig, where he would play Bach's organ works on the same instruments performed on by Bach himself, in the presence of his hero and fellow Bach fanatic Robert Schumann. Krüger's many letters to Schumann during this period bear witness to his persistence in this endeavor. Consider, for example, what he wrote in July 1842:

> I had hoped to visit you this summer as part of a Bach organ trip through Frankfurt, Cologne, etc., but extenuating circumstances forced me to change my plans. I'm not giving up, however, and hope next year to oblige you with fantasies and fugues to the best of my ability, God willing. Unfortunately, none of these [works] will be new to you, but, by the same token, is not the old Sebastian eternally new?[41]

After several more months of intense work, Krüger was eager to update Schumann about his progress at the organ: "I am practicing like a fiend and will soon have mastered all of Bach's fantasies and fugues. Those are hours full of eternal bliss, alone in the church, living with, striving with, and enjoying the greatest spirit in music!"[42] Still, according to a letter written in February 1843, Krüger was not quite ready to offer a public recital in a city where organ virtuosos were a standard commodity: "Mendelssohn and Becker are great organists, so I will not risk making an official appearance. But I hope that I can hold

38. *Neue Zeitschrift für Musik* 15, no. 21 (September 10, 1841), 81.

39. *Neue Zeitschrift für Musik* 24, no. 10 (February 1, 1846), 39.

40. *Neue Zeitschrift für Musik* 24, no. 3 (January 8, 1846), 10. The other two Mendelssohn fugues cited by Krüger are the Fugue in B-flat Major for piano, op. 35, no. 6, and the fugue in the last movement of the Sonata in B-flat Major for organ, op. 65, no. 4. One wonders if Krüger was attracted to Mendelssohn's G-major organ fugue because of its thematic resemblance to the aforementioned Fugue on BACH, BWV 898/2.

41. "Als ich vorhatte, Sie diesen Sommer zu besuchen, war es auf eine Bach-Orgelreise über Frankfurt, Köln usw. abgesehen. Durch besondere Umstände ist der Plan für dies Jahr gehindert, doch gehe ich ihn nicht auf, und gedenke nächstes Jahr Ihnen Fantasien und Fugen zum Besten zu geben, so Gott will. Leider wird Ihnen dergleichen nicht Neues sein. Doch ist der alte Sebastian nicht ewig neu?" Letter of July 22, 1842.

42. "Ich orgle ganz entsetzlich und habe bald alle Bachschen Fantasien und Fugen bezwungen. Das sind Stunden voll ewiger Wonne, in der einsamen Kirche, mit dem grössten Geist der Tön allein zusammen zu leben, streben und geniessen!" Letter of October 7, 1842.

my own against second-rate talents."[43] By June 1843, the itinerary was set: Krüger would depart Emden in early July, accompanying his mother-in-law to Göttingen and Gotha, and then journeying alone to Leipzig, even if that meant traveling the almost eighty miles on foot.[44] He explained in the same letter that he would be prepared to play, in addition to preludes and fugues by Mendelssohn and himself, approximately two dozen works by Bach, including, no doubt, the double-pedal arrangement (BWV 686) of "Aus tiefer Not schrei ich zu dir," which Krüger had learned in late 1842.[45] Furthermore, even though he dreaded the prospect of performing in front of Mendelssohn and Becker, Krüger was now open to the possibility of a public concert, asking Schumann to decide whether that would be an appropriate activity.[46] Schumann responded a week later, encouraging Krüger to follow through with his plans and criticizing his old colleague Becker:

> I am delighted at the prospect of seeing you here. Mind you carry out your plan. I plan to be here till July 20th, at all events.... You will probably also find Mendelssohn. Don't be too much afraid of Becker. Between ourselves, I do not consider him a great musician. Bach, Pachelbel, and himself are pretty much the same to him. But he has some good qualities.[47]

The few days that Krüger spent in the "Sebastianstadt" were packed with activities. Most importantly, Schumann arranged for him to play for a small group of connoisseurs at both of the principal churches in town. Perhaps Krüger breathed a sigh of relief that Mendelssohn was in Berlin at the time, but Becker would definitely have attended his performance at St. Nicholas's.[48] In conjunction with his visit to St. Thomas's, Krüger would have seen the newly erected Bach monument by Eduard Bendemann that stands in the church's courtyard today. Even though it was Mendelssohn who had raised most of the funds for this memorial, Schumann had also donated a large sum of his own money toward its completion.[49]

---

43. "Ist Mendelssohn oder Becker gross auf der Orgel, so wage ich in Leipzig keinen öffentlichen Auftritt; gegen die Geister zweiten Ranges hoffe ich die Wage zu halten." Letter of February 28, 1843.

44. "Ich soll im Anfang Juli meine Schwiegermutter auf einer Reise nach Göttingen und Gotha begleiten. Von Gotha aus, wo ich die Weibsen verlasse, wende ich mich fussweise oder p. diligence nach Leipzig, und hoffe bei Ihnen 10–15 Juli einzutreffen. Da spiele ich Ihnen diess u das - ich habe nur ein kleines, doch sehr grosses Repertoir: Bach, Mendelssohn u Ego...Gottlob habe ich eine Auswahl von 20–24 Bachiani." Letter of June 8, 1843.

45. Krüger had informed Schumann about learning this chorale setting in his letter of October 7, 1842: "Einige dieser unendlichen Poesien möchte ich Ihnen zu kosten geben, z.B. das 6 stimmige (dopp. Pedal) 'aus tiefer not'..."

46. "Sie entscheiden, ob ich ein Concert wagen darf, nur um Selbstvertrauen zu gewinnen...nicht ohne Zagen denk ich an Mend: u. Beckers Gegenwart." Letter of June 8, 1843.

47. Letter of June 19, 1843.

48. Todd 2003, 456–57.

49. Eismann and Nauhaus 1971–82, vol. 3, 158.

At Schumann's home, where he was a frequent guest, Krüger played Bach at the piano, and Clara Schumann returned the favor with an "astonishing" performance of Bach's A-minor organ fugue, BWV 543/2, which she evidently took at the breakneck tempo of ♩. = 75.[50] These visits would also have exposed Krüger to Robert Schumann's Bach library, which appears to have included unpublished works from the *Orgelbüchlein* and Great Eighteen chorales.[51] Krüger was overjoyed a few months later when he received from Schumann a manuscript containing a selection of these pieces.[52] Another manuscript that Krüger carried back with him to Emden was one in Schumann's own hand of Bach's Art of Fugue–a not insignificant farewell gift.[53] Imagine, too, Krüger's delight when he saw in the *Neue Zeitschrift* what Schumann had written about his organ playing:

> We have recently gotten to know and appreciate another side of Dr. E. Krüger, to whom the *Zeitschrift* is already indebted for his many outstanding essays. He played for a few music lovers on the organs of the churches of St. Thomas and St. Nicholas, and showed himself to be a splendid performer, especially in Sebastian Bach's most difficult pieces.[54]

Krüger's trip to Leipzig that summer was the musical highlight of his long life. This was definitely not the case with Joseph Maria Homeyer, an organist who had concertized in Leipzig the previous year. Witness the following review, presumably of Schumann's authoring, which appeared in the November 15, 1842 issue of the *Neue Zeitschrift*:

> Mr. L. J. M. Homeyer, a native of Hannover, gave on the 8th [of this month] an organ concert at St. Thomas's Church. The young man appears to possess much talent. Yet, as a virtuoso he still has much to master (not at all to mention his attempts at composition, which to us are not without merit but are still immature and not even appropriate as pieces for the organ). One may attribute his not always clean playing to an unfamiliarity with the instrument. Or did the thought of sitting

---

50. See Krüger's letter to Robert Schumann of September 18 (?), 1844 and Krüger's essay on metronome markings in the *Neue Zeitschrift für Musik* 20, no. 31 (April 15, 1844), 121. See also Glöckner et al. 2007, 740–41.

51. Stinson 2006, 79–82.

52. See Krüger's letter to Schumann of November 1, 1843, in which he thanks Schumann for sending this source ("Herzlichen Dank für die ersehnte Sendung des Bachschen Heftes, das ihn in aller Herrlichkeit zeigt."), compliments the copyist enlisted by Schumann for the project ("Dem Notenschreiber ist auch lobend nachzusagen…"), and describes in highly romanticized language several of the pieces contained therein (for a partial translation, see Stinson 2006, 88). After having gotten better acquainted with the music, Krüger also felt compelled eleven days later to continue with a list of erroneous readings from the manuscript, along with his proposed corrections. Altogether, he cites thirteen different works.

53. For a discussion of this manuscript, see Martin 1959.

54. *Neue Zeitschrift für Musik* 19, no. 6 (July 20, 1843), 24. Krüger thanked Schumann for his kind words in a letter of August 5, 1843 ("Ihr freundliches Gedenken in der Mus. Zeitg. hat mich beschämt…").

in the same place as the greatest organ master of all times intimidate him? In the Bach fugue, we could comprehend exceedingly little: the pedal entrance was barely recognizable and none of the middle voices were clearly distinguishable. We would recommend to this youthful virtuoso the most diligent study of this master. Then he would see that this instrument does not lend itself to frivolity or fashionable tricks. But artists often appear to the public completely different than they are, so Mr. Homeyer perhaps knows all the above himself. We hope this to be the case, and in the future we will expect a master.[55]

Nothing is known about which Bach fugue was mangled so spectacularly by Homeyer, but the remark about "sitting in the same place" as Bach foreshadows a line from a short story that Schumann would publish in his journal in June 1843.[56] Written by C. A. Wildenhahn, an old classmate of Schumann's who had also officiated at his wedding,[57] the tale concerns a young Bach enthusiast who journeys from Hamburg to Leipzig expressly to hear Bach play the organ. Upon his arrival, the traveler is asked whether he would not like to play the organ at St. Thomas's himself. Stunned, he explains that even if he were an organist, he "would never have the courage to sit on the same organ bench where the master of organ playing, the great Sebastian Bach," practiced his art. As Schumann read this story, he may well have remembered his review of Homeyer's recital. Perhaps he recalled that years earlier he had written to another of his colleagues on the *Neue Zeitschrift* that to have heard Bach improvise at the organ would have been the ultimate musical experience.[58] The implication behind this statement, to repeat a point made earlier, is that Schumann regarded Bach's compositions for the organ as his ultimate masterpieces.

---

55. *Neue Zeitschrift für Musik* 17, no. 40, 166.
56. *Neue Zeitschrift für Musik* 18, no. 45 (June 5, 1843), 180.
57. Eismann and Nauhaus 1971–82, vol. 3, 160–61; and Daverio 1997, 195–96.
58. Letter to G. A. Keferstein of February 8, 1840, published in Jansen 1904, 181.

5

César Franck as a Receptor of Bach's Organ Works

CÉSAR FRANCK ENCOUNTERED Bach's organ music as a performer, pedagogue, and composer. He played it in concert, taught it to his legions of pupils, and appropriated it as a model for his own compositions Nonetheless, Franck's reception of Bach's organ works is a largely unexplored area of investigation.

FRANCK'S PERFORMANCES OF BACH'S ORGAN WORKS

Considering that no fewer than fifty-four of Franck's organ students at the Paris Conservatory played on their semester exams and annual competitions a total of forty-three compositions by Bach, and considering also that Franck prepared an edition of Bach's organ music for the National Institute of Blind Youths in Paris that preserve his fingerings and pedalings for thirty-one pieces, he must have played, to some degree of proficiency, a goodly number of Bach's organ works. And one can only assume that in this endeavor he was inspired by other Parisian organists who regularly played Bach, most notably Alexandre Guilmant, Camille Saint-Saëns, and Charles-Marie Widor. In fact, Franck is known to have attended a recital by Guilmant at Saint-Sulpice in 1862 that featured the Toccata and Fugue in D Minor, BWV 565, and in 1879 he heard his colleague tackle Bach's F-major toccata when the two of them helped to inaugurate the Joseph Merklin organ at Saint-Eustache.[1] Still, the Parisian who most persuasively steered Franck

---

1. Smith 1983, 26; and Ochse 1994, 230.

in the direction of Bach's organ music was probably his good friend Charles-Valentin Alkan. Performing not on the organ but on the pédalier or pedal piano, Alkan was a celebrated interpreter of Bach's organ works, and he covered everything from the trio sonatas to the chorale preludes. He no doubt premiered more Bach organ works in the French capital than did any organist.[2]

Alas, Franck's own Bach performances are poorly documented. It is not known if he ever played a piece by Bach in a worship service during his roughly fifty years as a church organist. Perhaps he agreed with Saint-Saëns that Bach's organ music simply did not belong in the Catholic liturgy because of the overt Protestantism of the chorale settings and the virtuosity of the free works.[3] If so, however, why did Franck's conservatory students—most if not all of whom were training for careers in the Catholic church—wind up playing Bach on their exams and competitions more than three-quarters of the time, when there was so much music by other composers that presumably would have sufficed for both church services and concerts?

As one of the leading organists of his day, Franck was in demand as a concert organist in and around Paris. From 1854 to 1889 over thirty such performances may be verified, including solo recitals and ones shared with other organists.[4] On these programs Franck tended either to improvise—a skill for which he was greatly renowned—or to play his own (notated) compositions. Only four performances of organ works by Bach can be documented, and three of them may have been of the same piece. It is high time for a detailed look at these performances, if only to sort out all the information in the secondary literature.

The first time Franck is reported to have played a Bach organ work on one of his concerts was in 1859 for the inauguration of the famous Cavaillé-Coll organ at his own church of Sainte-Clotilde. Sharing the bill with Louis Lefébure-Wély, he improvised, played his own *Final*, and served up a prelude and fugue in E Minor by Bach.[5] As to which of Bach's two organ preludes and fugues in E minor was rendered, there has been disagreement. Was it the modest "Cathedral" (BWV 533) or the grandiose and virtuosic "Wedge" (BWV 548)?

Evidently the first writer to address this question was the late Fenner Douglass in his pioneering study *Cavaillé-Coll and the Musicians*, published in 1980. Douglass identified the work played by Franck as the Wedge , primarily for reasons involving the inauguration of the Ducroquet organ at Saint-Eustache in 1854.[6] Franck also performed at this

---

2. For a recent discussion of Alkan's Bach performances, see Eddie 2007, 17–24, 143, and 181.

3. Smith 1992, 59 and 223.

4. See the list in Ochse 1994, 229–30.

5. The program is reproduced in Smith 1997, 21.

6. Douglass 1980, vol. 1, 102-3 and 111. In making this identification, Douglass provided neither a BWV number nor a nickname, but it is clear from his descriptions of the work as Bach's "great" and "magnificent" Prelude and Fugue in E Minor that he meant the Wedge.

event, as did Jacques-Nicolas Lemmens, who offered a prelude and fugue in E minor by Bach. Assuming that a virtuoso like Lemmens would have chosen the Wedge, Douglass reasoned that Franck so admired Lemmens's rendition of this piece that he chose to play it himself when the time came to inaugurate the Sainte-Clotilde organ. In the first of his two invaluable monographs on Franck's organ music, published three years after Douglass's book, Rollin Smith likewise assumed that Franck played the Wedge, but on the basis of a review that mentioned the artist's "long study and perseverance" in learning the Bach work on the program.[7] Smith argued that Bach's Cathedral prelude and fugue would scarcely have provoked this remark.

Writing eight years after Smith, Jean Ferrard criticized both Smith and Douglass for so hastily identifying the work in question as the Wedge, and proposed that Franck's under-developed pedal technique at this point in his career would have precluded him from playing the piece.[8] Contending that none of Franck's own organ compositions approach this level of difficulty, especially on the pedals, Ferrard suggested that Franck performed the Cathedral prelude and fugue. By the publication of his second Franck study in 1997, Smith was in agreement, although there is no indication that he had read Ferrard's article. Rather, Smith had encountered a second review of Franck's performance that denounced the Bach work played as "detached musical phrases that sounded nothing like a fugue."[9] Smith reasoned that this criticism could apply only to the Cathedral prelude, whose disjointed form suggests a written-out improvisation.

Most recently, the Franck scholar Joël-Marie Fauquet has weighed in on the matter, in his magisterial biography of the composer and in a book authored with Antoine Hennion on nineteenth-century Bach reception in France. Fauquet agrees with Ferrard's rationale, but he has also greatly strengthened the case in favor of the Cathedral prelude and fugue by pointing out that the work appeared in 1858—and in a version heavily edited for performance—in the Parisian journal *La Maîtrise* ("the church choir school").[10] The following year, Franck contributed three of his own compositions to this publication, whose mission it was to uphold the ideals of "true" church music.

A consideration of the organs regularly played by Franck as a church organist prior to his 1859 recital only supports the notion that he could not have managed the Wedge prelude and fugue at that time, because the pedal compasses of these instruments were decidedly inadequate for the realization of Bach's pedal parts. Whereas Bach wrote for pedals beginning on C and extending at least two octaves, those at the Parisian churches of

---

7. Smith 1983, 31 n. 58.

8. Ferrard 1991, 163–64.

9. Smith 1997, 23. As to the reviewer's use of the word "fugue," it was customary in the nineteenth century to refer to any Bach organ work as a "fugue." Regarding Felix Mendelssohn's objection to this terminology, see Stinson 2006, 68–69.

10. Fauquet 1999a, 286, 341, and 831 n. 11; and Fauquet and Hennion 2000, 121. For excerpts from the edition of the "Cathedral" prelude and fugue published in *La Maîtrise*, see Peterson 1995, 81; and Smith 1999, 510.

Notre-Dame-de-Lorette and Saint-Jean-Saint-François extended, respectively, from FF to f and C to g.[11] Playing even the easiest of Bach's organ works on such instruments would have been problematic, if not prohibitive.

It is interesting to note that both of these organs were by Cavaillé-Coll, for, starting in the mid-1840s, this prolific builder would manufacture nothing but "German" pedals, thereby paving the way for a veritable renaissance of Bach's organ music in France. As an organist, Franck could not really have participated in this revival without regularly playing on such an instrument. He was surely looking forward to this opportunity in January 1858, upon his appointment as organist at the newly erected church of Sainte-Clotilde, but the organ promised by Cavaillé-Coll would prove not to be ready until the following year. In anticipation of the unveiling of this instrument, and only a month after his appointment, Franck decided to hone his pedal skills by purchasing a pédalier. His confrere Alkan must have heartily approved.

To return to the issue at hand, the bulk of the evidence suggests that the Bach work played by Franck for the dedication of the Sainte-Clotilde organ was the Cathedral prelude and fugue, BWV 533. Franck's second documented public performance of a Bach organ work, in January 1873 at the third program of the Société des Concerts du Conservatoire, was also of a prelude and fugue in E minor. According to the only review, this Bach work was "severely beautiful,"[12] which is obviously too vague a description to identify which of the two E-minor preludes and fugues was played. As organist at Sainte-Clotilde, Franck had now for more than a dozen years presided over a full (C–d ') pedalboard, and his acclaimed performances throughout the 1860s of his *Six Pièces* evince his mastery of various pedal techniques. Thus there is really no reason to doubt that by 1873 he could have taken on a work as demanding as the Wedge, despite Jean Ferrard's argument to the contrary. Still, the matter remains unresolved.

The third time Franck is known to have played a Bach organ work on one of his concerts was in December 1888, in the city of Angers. According to Fauquet, Franck journeyed there at the invitation of the local concert association, having agreed to conduct a concert of his own compositions and to perform an organ recital.[13] The organ, by Louis Debierre, had just been installed in the main hall of the city's Circus, in imitation of Cavaillé-Coll's massive instrument at the Paris Trocadéro. Quite by coincidence, the great violinist Eugène Ysaÿe and the pianist Théophile Ysaÿe (Eugène's brother) had performed in Angers a few days earlier, and they decided to lengthen their stay to participate free of charge in this "Franck festival." Franck was doubtless honored and delighted, as Eugène had worked closely with him in Paris and Théophile had been one of his piano students there. The brothers played works by Franck on both concerts, while Franck held forth at the organ with two improvisations, two of his own compositions (the *Pièce*

11. Douglass 1980, vol. 1, 99.

12. Smith 1983, 18 and 150; and Smith 1997, 33.

13. Fauquet 1999a, 653–55.

héroïque and *Cantabile*), two works by the recently deceased Alkan, and a prelude and fugue in C minor by Bach. But in spite of everything, the proceeds were a paltry thirty-four francs (about a hundred dollars in today's currency), prompting the president of the concert association to scold the local citizenry for its "apathy" toward the fine arts.

As to which of Bach's two C-minor preludes and fugues for organ was featured on this program, all signs point to the longer and more mature composition, BWV 546. Not only did Franck teach this work throughout his tenure at the conservatory, but in 1888, the year of his recital in Angers, he taught it to two of his students (see app. 1). In addition, he had just annotated the piece for his Braille edition of Bach's organ works, published in 1887.[14] Bach's other C-minor prelude and fugue for organ, a youthful work catalogued as BWV 549, was not unknown to Franck, but only one student performance is documented, as opposed to ten of BWV 546. Furthermore, Franck chose not to include this piece in his Braille edition.

Fauquet mentions that in 1889 Franck again played a Bach work on one of his organ recitals.[15] He did so while inaugurating the reconstructed Joseph Merklin organ at the Parisian church of Saint-Jacques-du-Haut-Pas, the parish where Franck lived. On this instrument, which Merklin had fitted with electro-pneumatic action, Franck improvised on themes by Beethoven and Berlioz, played a few of his own works (including the Fantasy in A Major), and accompanied vocal and instrumental solos.[16] One enthusiastic listener was the young Romain Rolland, who wrote in his diary that Franck was "an admirable artist" and that the Bach work on the program was "sober, simple, all-powerful." Perhaps Franck again played the "Cathedral" prelude and fugue: the description of "sober" and "simple" fits both movements, and the registration suggested by Franck in his Braille edition (*Grand-choeur*) corresponds to the ideal of "all-powerful."

MATTERS OF PEDAGOGY

When, in February 1872, César Franck assumed his duties as organ professor at the Conservatoire National de Musique et de Déclamation, the requirements for organ students at that august institution had changed somewhat since his own student days there thirty years earlier.[17] Under the tutelage of François Benoist, Franck had been trained exclusively to extemporize four-part fugues and four-part accompaniments to Gregorian chants. Starting in 1852, though, the memorized performance of a notated fugue with pedal was added to the requirements, and in 1867 the rules specified that the memorized fugue had to be by Bach. During Franck's first year as professor, this condition was again

---

14. For a comprehensive discussion of this edition, see Hastings 1990.

15. Fauquet 1999a, 738–39.

16. The full contents of this very long program are given in Fauquet 1999b, 180 n. 490.

17. Ochse 1994, 149–60.

modified, presumably by Franck himself, to the memorized performance of a *pièce classique*. Franck's students, therefore, while they still concentrated on improvisation, had the option of playing various types of Bach works (including preludes, fugues, toccatas, concerto transcriptions, and chorale settings), usually one movement at a time, as well as works by other composers. According to one of these students, Vincent D'Indy, Franck "was as enthusiastic as any youth over the absolute beauty of Bach's works, which he taught us to interpret on the organ."[18] A complete listing of this repertory, along with the names of the students involved and the dates of performance, is found in appendix 1.

Franck taught his organ pupils not individually but as a group on Tuesday, Thursday, and Saturday mornings from eight to ten o'clock—and on an instrument described by his pupil Louis Vierne as "a poor cuckoo of an organ."[19] Such was the emphasis on improvisation that of the six hours spent in class each week, not more than one hour was devoted to organ literature. The students were expected to bring in the scores of the works they wished to play and to submit them to Franck for his approval, but he no doubt simply assigned repertoire, too. Indeed, one must believe that the vast majority of the compositions played by Franck's students reflect the teacher's own musical tastes, regardless of the extent of "mutual agreement" between teacher and pupil. To judge from Vierne's memoirs, Franck may have been overly helpful to his young charges when they performed these works in class: "There was no need to worry about console management. Franck drew the stops and worked the *pédales de combinaison* and the expression pedal. Everything was simplified, reduced merely to playing on the keyboards and to the observance of style."[20] Whether this coddling in the end discouraged true virtuosity, especially with regard to pedaling, is a matter of opinion, but surely Vierne was exaggerating about the total neglect of the pedalboard. According to Louis de Serres, another of Franck's conservatory pupils, the maître also "assisted" his students when they played Bach fugues "by adding new entrances [of the subject] to those of the composer's."[21] These gatherings, therefore, must have been not only lively but downright fun.

All the conservatory students were expected to perform a final examination for their professors at the end of each semester of the academic year (in January and June), and in conjunction with these exams the professors wrote brief reports about each student's progress. For this purpose the professors were issued forms containing each student's name, age, and year of study, along with any prizes previously won at the school's annual competitions. Within a blank column headed *Rapport du Professeur*, and in rectangular

18. D'Indy 1910, 248.

19. Smith 1999, 39–49; and Smith 1983, 37–43. Vierne does not appear in appendix 1 of the present book because Franck died early during Vierne's first semester at the conservatory.

20. Smith 1999, 45. The *pédales de combinaison* mentioned by Vierne were a series of iron-ratchet pedals that controlled mechanical devices (mostly couplers) designed to facilitate registration changes. See Smith 1983, 49–51.

21. Smith 2002, 182. See also Vallas 1951, 256.

spaces no larger than 1.5 x 4.5 inches, the professor inscribed his reports and then signed his name at the bottom. From June 1872 to June 1890, Franck evaluated around sixty different students this way.

Naturally, the makeup of Franck's organ class varied from semester to semester. He began with only five pupils, three of whom were inherited from Benoist (who retired in 1872), and for the next thirteen years that number fluctuated between two and eight. But starting in the fall of 1885, Franck regularly had about ten pupils in his studio. That semester, the number of students rose dramatically from four to twelve. Of the ten new students in that group, five played preludes and fugues from Bach's Well-Tempered Clavier, a sure indication that these pupils were incapable of playing legitimate pedal parts, even if pedal was used ad libitum.[22] Franck taught this collection to his beginning students throughout his tenure at the conservatory, just as Benoist had done.[23]

The other new students that semester played various *pedaliter* works either written by or ascribed to Bach. Louis de Serres and Dynam-Victor Fumet performed the "Little" Fugue in G Minor and the "Cathedral" fugue, respectively, while Cesarino Galeotti rendered one of the so-called Eight Little Preludes and Fugues, BWV 553–60.[24] All of these pieces are relatively easy to play, and they proved to be popular choices for Franck's first-semester students throughout his years at the conservatory, just as they are favorite works of novice organists today. In fact, the popularity of the "Eight Little" in this respect was surpassed only by the Well-Tempered Clavier, which suggests that Franck established the tradition in modern times of teaching these pieces to beginning organists. A favorite work of more advanced first-semester pupils was the Fugue in C Minor, BWV 537/2, which was performed by Henri Letocart. Obviously the most talented new student that semester was Adolphe Marty, who played the virtuosic Fugue in A Minor, BWV 543/2. It was in his capacity as judge of the annual organ examinations at the National Institute for Blind Youths that Franck first heard Marty perform, and he was so impressed that he admitted the twenty-year-old into his organ class at the conservatory, making Marty the first-ever blind student there.[25] Franck would go on to instruct other blind organists at the conservatory, including Joséphine Boulay, Albert Mahaut, and, of course, Louis Vierne.

Franck's progress reports on his students have survived complete and are easily accessible today at the Archives Nationales, Paris. Surprisingly, however, only about one-fifth

---

22. According to the *Reminiscences* of Franck by his private student John Hinton, Franck inscribed into Hinton's copy of the Well-Tempered Clavier numerous "optional" pedalings for the first twelve preludes and fugues in the collection. See Hinton, 6. Hinton's report is obviously the basis for Herbert Haag's somewhat misleading claim that Franck prepared organ transcriptions of these works "for his students." See Haag 1936, 20.

23. On Benoist and the Well-Tempered Clavier, see Ochse 1994, 150.

24. The authenticity of these eight works, which are not contained in the Neue Bach-Ausgabe, is today very much in doubt.

25. Miramon Fitz-James 1947, 95.

of them have been transcribed. This project was initiated by Marcelle Benoit, who in the late 1950s published all of Franck's reports on exactly a dozen of his pupils.[26] Whatever Benoit's reasons for selecting these particular individuals, his transcriptions (presented in English translation in app. 2) offer a fascinating glimpse inside Franck's studio. Franck normally began by rating the student with a single adjective, ranging from "good" for the weaker pupils to "perfect" in the case of Albert Mahaut, and then continued with remarks on particular strengths and weaknesses. Both talent and effort were taken into account. The reports typically conclude with the title of the "classical piece" played by the student that semester. In designating the multitude of Bach works performed, Franck usually saw no need to write the composer's name but instead the corresponding volume, number, and sometimes even page number from the Peters edition of Bach's complete organ works. In his report on Louis de Serres of January 1887 (see app. 1), Franck cited the Prelude in A Minor, BWV 543/1, as the "Prelude of the Fugue in A Minor," implying that he understood this movement merely as a preamble to the much longer fugue that is its partner. In his reports on Pierre Sourilas of June 1881 and on Louis Landry of June 1884, Franck cited the Fugue in D Minor, BWV 539/2, as a work in five voices (*fugue en re min á 5* and *fugue en re min á 5 parte*). He would have found no such designation in the Peters edition but would have arrived at it through his own study of the movement, which in fact thickens to five parts only in certain passages. Franck was surely motivated here by the rarity of Bach fugues in more than four voices.

Only Franck's more advanced pupils were allowed to participate in the annual competitions sponsored by the conservatory. These contests took place at the end of the school year (each July) and were judged by a panel of experts, which did not include the professor in the performance area being judged. In other words, Franck was ineligible to judge his own organ students. For the organ competitions, the adjudicators included various conservatory faculty as well as such local organists as Guilmant and Widor. The requirements were the same as for the semester exams, but if the ten extant competition reports are any indication, the Bach works played were generally more virtuosic (see app. 1). Whoever prepared these documents also cited these pieces according to their position in the Peters edition, although not as meticulously as Franck did in preparing his progress reports. In 1890, for example, no book or number was given for either Bach work played.

One way of more precisely understanding the issue of Bach reception within Franck's circle is to focus on those students listed in appendix 2, comparing Franck's evaluations of them with the Bach works they were playing at the time. Take, for instance, Auguste Chapuis, who appears to have played nothing but Bach throughout his three years at the conservatory, including six semester exams and three competitions.[27] Chapuis began with

---

26. Benoit 1957.

27. The *pièce classique* played by Chapuis at the 1880 competition is unknown. Otherwise, he performed seven different works by Bach.

a piece (Bach's Pastorale) whose use of pedal is limited mainly to pedal points, but two years later he was negotiating the virtuosic pedal runs of the E-flat prelude. Had he been more diligent during his first two years, he might have reached this level of proficiency sooner. At the 1881 competition, which was the last of the three that he entered, he captured the coveted first prize.[28] Consider, too, Albert Mahaut, who began his only year at the conservatory with one of Bach's flashiest pedal showpieces, the Fugue in D Major, BWV 532/2. Franck's glowing evaluations of this blind prodigy were validated by Mahaut's first prize at the 1889 competition, at which time he rendered Bach's G-minor fantasy. Only four other Franck pupils took first prize after just a year of study: Joséphine Boulay, Henri Dallier, Adolphe Marty, and Henri Pinot. Boulay won with what is probably Bach's most difficult organ fugue altogether, the Wedge (BWV 548).

Two other pupils cited in appendix 2 are notable for their lack of success. In the case of Alfred Bachelet, who, at least nominally, was one of Franck's pupils for three years, it seems that laziness was mostly to blame. Granted, Bachelet was often sick during his first semester, but in all of Franck's subsequent reports—and in rather harsh language for someone dubbed by his pupils as their Pater Seraphicus—he mentions only the student's indolence, inattention to detail, and absence from class. Indeed, Bachelet was not even allowed to take the semester exam in June 1886, let alone enter the competition the following month. Despite being "gifted," he may have been a rank beginner when he matriculated, since he started with a fugue from the Well-Tempered Clavier. By his second year, he had progressed to nothing more taxing than one of the Eight Little Preludes and Fugues. Henri Letocart's problem, conversely, was lack of talent, his exemplary work ethic and "passion" for the organ notwithstanding. Even though he played major works by Bach (and Mendelssohn) throughout his four years of study, Letocart placed no higher than second runner-up in the three competitions that he entered.[29] Perhaps his "difficulty" in extemporizing fugues explains why.

The first pupil listed in appendix 2, Vincent D'Indy, never enjoyed much recognition as a conservatory student either, although Franck rated him higher ("excellent" rather than "good") than either Letocart or Bachelet. D'Indy worked remarkably hard, but, as his teacher observed at the end of their first semester together, he also struggled with improvisation. In this same report, Franck praised D'Indy's "execution," suggesting that the word in this instance refers to how that semester's *pièce classique* (Bach's "Little" Fugue in G Minor) had been handled. Similar to Letocart, then, D'Indy may never have advanced beyond first runner-up in the two competitions that he entered due to his weak improvisational skills.[30] His repertory selections (the Bach-Vivaldi A-minor concerto and the Bach Passacaglia) would certainly have passed muster.

---

28. On the prizes won by Franck's students at the annual competitions, see Fauquet 1999a, 959–64; and Ochse 1994, 231–32.

29. Letocart won this prize in the 1887 competition. He did not place in either 1889 or 1890.

30. D'Indy's prize at his first competition, in 1874, was second runner-up.

In what may be a unique case within the *bande à Franck*, D'Indy's encounter with the Bach works he studied in Franck's organ class is also documented by sources other than the school's records. One of these is a letter from 1876 in which D'Indy described the third and final stanza of his *Madrigal de Bonnières* as "counterpoint (sixteenth notes) in four parts like the last variation of Bach's *Passacaille* (without comparison!)."[31] The Bach work so excitedly referenced here is the same one played by D'Indy at the 1875 competition, the Passacaglia in C Minor, BWV 582, whose final variation (mm. 160–68) does contain the same type of motivic figuration in perpetual-motion sixteenth notes as the piano accompaniment to stanza three of the *Madrigal*. D'Indy completed this charming piece in 1872, around the age of twenty, which means that he knew the Passacaglia years before he studied it with Franck.[32] The Passacaglia was doubtless already a sentimental favorite of his as well, for in 1873 the young aristocrat had delighted in playing it nowhere else than in Leipzig, on the organ at St. Thomas's.

Decades later, by which time D'Indy had become one of the most respected musicians in all of France, he appropriated Bach's Passacaglia as a compositional exemplar of a different type, that is, in his treatise *Cours de composition musicale*. Hailing Bach's work as "the most perfect example" of the passacaglia genre, D'Indy argued that Bach had avoided any hint of monotony in these twenty variations thanks to their "contrapuntal interest" and "melodic-rhythmic exuberance."[33] Curiously, he also wrote that the work's theme had "Gregorian origins," although on what basis he did not say.

Among the many other Bach organ works covered in this study is another piece that its author learned under Franck's supervision, the Fugue in C Minor on a Theme by Legrenzi, BWV 574, which D'Indy used to illustrate both the technique of tonal answer and the genre of double fugue.[34] Given Franck's well-known penchant for combining themes in his own compositions, one can easily imagine how he was drawn to this fugue, and it should be pointed out that he taught the work to roughly a half-dozen of his students. Other multi-subject Bach fugues used by Franck as teaching repertory are the Fugues in E-flat Major, F Major, and C Minor, BWV 552/2, 540/2, and 546/2, respectively, and especially the Fugue in C Minor, BWV 537/2, which Franck taught to more of his pupils (twelve) than any other movement by any composer. The fact that this movement's partner, the Fantasy in C Minor, BWV 537/1, was played by only seven students underscores Franck's tendency to teach *fugues* by Bach rather than the movements (preludes, fantasies, and toccatas) with which they are paired. Thus, despite his role in broadening the repertoire played by the organ students at the Paris Conservatory, Franck maintained Benoist's emphasis on fugue.

As for other patterns within Franck's teaching repertory (see app. 1), we have already mentioned that the Well-Tempered Clavier and the Eight Little Preludes and Fugues

---

31. Fauquet and Hennion 2000, 84–85.
32. Thomson and Orledge 2001, 374.
33. D'Indy 1903–50, vol. 1, 458.
34. Ibid., vol. 1, 80, and vol. 2, 41–42.

dominated the first semester of the 1885–86 academic year. Both collections served to accommodate the many new students who enrolled at that time, all of whom continued playing from either collection for at least a semester. Meanwhile, Franck's more advanced pupils were plowing through the Mendelssohn sonatas, a trend that distinguishes the 1883–84 and 1887–88 academic years as well. During Franck's last full year at the conservatory (1888–89), he taught four different Bach works for the first time: the Prelude in G Major, BWV 568; the Fantasy in C Minor, BWV 562/1; the Concerto in C Major after Prince Johann Ernst, BWV 595; and the Aria in F Major, BWV 587. In so doing, he seems to have been exploring new (and relatively obscure) repertoire to sustain his interest in teaching organ literature, after more than fifteen years on the job. For the same reason, presumably, he also taught for the first time that year the opening movement of Bach's Toccata, Adagio, and Fugue in C Major.[35]

Another pattern presents itself during the 1875–76 academic year, when Franck's pupils essayed chorale settings by Bach for the first time. Two such works were played, the *Orgelbüchlein* setting of "O Mensch, bewein dein Sünde gross" and the arrangement from the Great Eighteen chorales of "O Lamm Gottes, unschuldig," each of which received two additional student performances from 1884 to 1889.[36] For reasons undocumented—but chief among which was surely an incompatibility with Catholic practice rather than any musical bias—these are the only Bach organ chorales that Franck ever taught. In speculating about what could have attracted Franck to these two works in particular, one need look no farther than his comrade Charles-Valentin Alkan, for Alkan during the 1870s introduced Parisian audiences to various organ chorales by Bach, and the *Orgelbüchlein* setting of "O Mensch" was definitely part of his repertoire.[37] As a concert pianist, Alkan might well have gotten acquainted with this sublimely poignant piece through the collection *Choralvorspiele für die Orgel von Johann Sebastian Bach für das Clavier übertragen von Carl Tausig*, published in 1873.[38] Tausig transcribed six Bach organ chorales to comprise this set, which happens to include not only "O Mensch" but also the Great Eighteen setting of "O Lamm Gottes." Given this circumstance, Alkan may have learned both chorales through Tausig's transcriptions, performed both of them in recital, and, at some point before the fall of 1875, alerted Franck to their existence.

35. As a rare example of a prelude and fugue "interrupted" by a slow movement, this work may well be the structural model for Franck's *Prélude, Choral et Fugue*, a piano work from 1884. See also Vallas 1951, 184. At any rate, Franck's composition is obviously a tribute to Bach, and it may have been conceived with the Bach bicentennial of 1885 in mind. On these points, see Fauquet 1999a, 605–7.

36. See also Ochse 1994, 189. The misinformation on this subject found in Busch 2003, 126, should be emended accordingly.

37. Eddie 2007, 19–23 and 181. Eddie refers to Alkan's performance in 1880 of the Bach chorale prelude "Pleure ô morte," which, in the context of Lutheran hymnody, is an obvious misprint for "Pleure ô monde" or "O mankind, bewail [your great sin]." The *Orgelbüchlein* setting is Bach's only keyboard arrangement of the chorale "O Mensch, bewein dein Sünde gross."

38. On this publication, see Stinson 2006, 120–21.

Franck made sure to include both of these chorales in his Braille edition of Bach's organ works, published in 1887 under the title *Choix de pièces pour orgue*. Aided by an anonymous transcriber, he prepared these five volumes specifically for the organ students at the National Institute for Blind Youths in Paris, where he judged the annual organ examinations and served as superintendent of studies. Obviously, this publication constitutes another important source for understanding Franck's pedagogical practices vis-à-vis Bach, but, with its many performance instructions, it also affords valuable insights into how Franck must have played these pieces himself. (Unfortunately, though, it does not evince the claim of Franck's pupil Henri Libert that his teacher used rubato in playing Bach and "heightened the tempo in episodes of the fugues.")[39] The complete contents are given in table 5.1.[40]

Franck's edition is the subject of an excellent and detailed study by Karen Hastings, who seems to have grasped about every aspect of these mysterious tomes except that they closely follow the order of the nine-volume Peters edition, the same Bach edition used in Franck's organ class at the Paris Conservatory.[41] (Not surprisingly, in view of these circumstances, the readings of Franck's edition follow those of the Peters edition.) Its opening work—none other than the Passacaglia in C Minor—is the only one taken from volume 1 of the Peters edition, while the next ten are taken from volume 2, and mostly in the same order as well. This pattern continues with volume 3 of Franck's edition (based entirely on vol. 3 of Peters), volume 4 (based on vols. 3 and 4 of Peters), and volume 5 (based on vols. 4, 5, 6, 7, and 8 of Peters).

From the approximately 250 compositions contained in the Peters edition, Franck selected only thirty-one, limiting himself with very few exceptions (see BWV 554, 653, 740, and possibly 547) to those works he is documented to have taught at the conservatory. Accordingly, preludes and fugues abound, while the trio sonatas are conspicuously absent.[42] From the roughly 170 chorale settings published by Peters, Franck included only four: the two that he taught at the conservatory ("O Mensch" and "O Lamm Gottes"); the arrangement from the Great Eighteen chorales of "An Wasserflüssen Babylon," BWV 653; and the miscellaneous setting of "Wir glauben all an einen Gott, Vater," BWV 740, a work now commonly attributed to J. L. Krebs. That Franck titled these pieces merely according to genre and key (for example, *Choral en sol* in the case of "An Wasserflüssen") suggests that he placed less value on the chorale texts involved than on purely musical matters.[43] With "O Lamm Gottes," he chose a rare specimen from the

---

39. Dunham 1954.

40. Table 5.1 is based on Hastings 1990, 92. According to Fauquet 1999a, 500-501, the last ten works of Franck's edition are evenly divided between two volumes, making for a six-volume set.

41. Hastings 1990.

42. During Franck's second full year at the conservatory (1873–74), and perhaps as a kind of experiment, he taught the first movement of the first trio sonata. Otherwise, there is no record that his students played any of these works.

43. This is precisely how Franck cited "O Mensch" and "O Lamm Gottes" in his progress reports on his conservatory students.

TABLE 5.1.

The Contents of César Franck's Braille Edition of Bach's Organ Works

Volume	Work
1	Passacaglia in C Minor, BWV 582
	Prelude and Fugue in C Major, BWV 545
	Prelude and Fugue in G Major, BWV 541
	Prelude and Fugue in A Major, BWV 536
	Fantasy and Fugue in G Minor, BWV 542
	Prelude and Fugue in C Major, BWV 547
2	Prelude and Fugue in F Minor, BWV 534
	Prelude and Fugue in C Minor, BWV 546
	Prelude and Fugue in A Minor, BWV 543
	Prelude and Fugue in E Minor ("Wedge"), BWV 548
	Prelude and Fugue in B Minor, BWV 544
3	Prelude and Fugue in E-flat Major, BWV 552
	Toccata and Fugue in F Major, BWV 540
	Prelude and Fugue in D Minor, BWV 539
	Fantasy and Fugue in C Minor, BWV 537
	Prelude and Fugue in E Minor, BWV 533
4	Toccata, Adagio, and Fugue in C Major, BWV 564
	Prelude and Fugue in C Major, BWV 566
	Prelude and Fugue in G Major, BWV 550
	Prelude and Fugue in D Major, BWV 532
	Toccata and Fugue in D Minor, BWV 565
5	Prelude and Fugue in D Minor, BWV 554
	(Eight Little Preludes and Fugues)
	Fugue in C Minor on a Theme by Legrenzi, BWV 574
	Fugue in G Minor ("Little"), BWV 578
	Fugue in B Minor on a Theme by Corelli, BWV 579
	Canzona in D Minor, BWV 588
	"O Mensch, bewein dein Sünde gross," BWV 622
	"O Lamm Gottes, unschuldig," BWV 656
	"An Wasserflüssen Babylon," BWV 653
	"Wir glauben all an einen Gott, Vater," BWV 740
	Concerto in A Minor after Vivaldi, BWV 593

huge repertory of Baroque chorale partitas in which the music flows seamlessly from one variation to the next (and in which the chorale melody migrates between variations from the soprano voice, to the alto, and finally to the bass). In the other three works, the hymn tune is subjected to extravagant ornamentation and played on a separate manual, whether in the soprano voice or, as happens in "An Wasserflüssen," the tenor. "Wir glauben," furthermore, features double-pedal. It is hard not to believe that these pieces, with their diversity of approaches to arranging a cantus firmus, influenced Franck in the realm of Gregorian chant, both as an improviser and a teacher of improvisation.

Franck's edition preserves literally thousands of fingerings and pedalings, and they are entirely consistent with the legato style of Bach playing associated with the modern French organ school. Every conceivable legato technique is represented, including finger, foot, and hand substitution; finger and foot crossing; finger, foot, and thumb glissando; and a liberal use of the heels. Moreover, Franck twice provided the instruction *soutenu*, both times for fugue subjects whose many repeated notes might otherwise lead to a choppy articulation. One of these subjects commences the opening section of the Fugue in C Major, BWV 566/2, an extremely popular movement within the Franck circle.[44] Likewise, Franck tended to add registration indications and tempo markings only to his favorite pieces for teaching or playing. Thus the first movement of the Concerto in A Minor after Vivaldi, BWV 593, contains the instruction *jeux de fond* (foundation stops) and the "Cathedral" prelude and fugue (BWV 533) the directions *Grand-choeur* (foundation and reed stops) and *Très largement* ("Very broadly").

FRANCK'S COMPOSITIONAL RESPONSES TO BACH'S ORGAN WORKS

As someone who cherished Bach's oeuvre, and who played and taught the composer's organ works for most of his career, Franck incorporated elements of Bach's style into his own organ compositions. This fact has been acknowledged ever since the publication more than a hundred years ago of Vincent D'Indy's biography of Franck.[45] Since that time, the issue of Bach's influence on Franck's organ works—arguably the greatest organ music of the nineteenth century—has been touched on by various writers, but their comments rarely go beyond casual observations on particular pieces.

Let us first consider four relatively straightforward examples, most of which involve thematic borrowing of some kind. To begin with, there is the *Offertoire* in F Minor that opens Franck's *Pièces posthumes pour Harmonium ou Orgue à Pédales* (better known as vol. 2 of *L'Organiste*), a collection that was not published until after Franck's death in 1890 but whose contents originated between 1858 and 1863.[46] This little-known work

---

44. The other fugue in question is the Fugue in G Major, BWV 541/2.

45. D'Indy 1910.

46. Verdin 2004, 166–67.

begins with a theme whose first five notes are melodically and rhythmically identical to those of the theme of Bach's C-minor passacaglia (see ex. 5.1).[47] Furthermore, the two

EXAMPLE 5.1. César Franck, *Offertoire* in F Minor, mm. 1–11

themes are about the same length, they are both introduced monophonically in the bass register, and they both serve as the basis for a set of variations. Likewise, Franck seems to have cribbed the fugue subject of his most popular organ work, the *Prélude, Fugue et Variation*, from Bach's Fugue in A Major, BWV 536/2.[48] Both melodies use the same basic rhythms and the same sequentially descending contour, beginning on the fifth degree of the scale, rising to the sixth degree, and then falling to the tonic; both are eight bars long, and both are in sharp keys. In view of these similarities, it may not be coincidental that both themes appear initially in the order tenor-alto-soprano-bass. There is also Franck's *Pastorale*, whose main thematic material, stated initially in the first four measures, closely parallels the first movement of Bach's organ work by this name (BWV 590) in its use of two moderately fast (and at least quasi-imitative) manual voices above a pedal point.[49] Finally, the fugue that concludes the *Grande Pièce symphonique* contains a segment of three bars lifted from the "Little" Fugue in G Minor, BWV 578 (see exx. 5.2 and 5.3). No doubt what Franck found so attractive about Bach's handiwork here is the long (and, according to the Peters edition, optional) trill that runs throughout the passage. Bach's trill is preceded by an anticipatory eighth note, while, according to the original print of the *Grande Pièce*, Franck's begins with this sort of gesture (but might Franck's trill also begin on the second note?). In addition, Franck's trill is accompanied by manual figuration in nonstop eighth notes and pedal figuration in eighths and quarters, which is precisely what Bach writes, except in diminution.[50]

---

47. See Fauquet 1999a, 369, which refers to a "thematic relationship" between these two works.

48. According to Mohr 1942, 151, the two themes share a "family resemblance."

49. Sabatier 1982, 72.

50. The Toccata and Fugue in D Minor, BWV 565, contains in the middle of its fugue a very similar passage, but both voices that accompany the trill there are limited to a single rhythm, whether eighths or sixteenths.

EXAMPLE 5.2. Fugue in G Minor ("Little"), BWV 578, mm. 19–21

EXAMPLE 5.3. César Franck, *Grande Pièce symphonique*, mm. 525–28

More complex is Bach's influence on Franck's *Final*, a work, like the three just dis-cussed, published in 1868 as one of Franck's *Six Pièces*. According to Hermann Busch, this influence may be traced all the way back to 1844, when the German virtuoso Adolph Friedrich Hesse astonished the city of Paris with his rendition of Bach's F-major toc-cata.[51] Hesse had been invited to the French capital to inaugurate the Daublaine-Callinet organ at Saint Eustache (an instrument that only a few months later would go up in flames); he was joined by several French organists, including Franck's teacher Benoist. Assuming that the young César Franck would have attended this event, Busch proposes that the *Final* was Franck's compositional response to Hesse's playing, since the work's opening section contains, strikingly enough, two lengthy and virtuosic pedal solos, just as the opening section of Bach's toccata does. Considering that Franck waited about fif-teen years to actually compose the *Final*,[52] I would argue that his initial impulse may have been nothing more specific than to write a pedal showpiece. Regardless, any decision made by Franck to emulate Bach's toccata would have resulted primarily from his long friendship with the Bach specialist Charles-Valentin Alkan, for Alkan per-formed the F-major more often than any other Bach organ work.[53] The notion that Franck did appropriate Bach's toccata in this manner is supported not only by Busch's observation about the two pieces but also by one additional aspect of the music: in each

---

51. Busch 2003, 123. See also Ochse 1994, 38–41.

52. Smith 1997, 151.

53. Eddie 2007, 18–22, 143, and 149.

work the two pedal solos are in different keys, yet they consist of the same thematic material.

There can be no question that in the coda of the *Final*—the work is in sonata form—Franck borrows from another staple of the organ repertoire, namely, the Toccata and Fugue in D Minor, BWV 565. He actually begins this process two bars earlier, in m. 303, with a massive D-major triad identical in texture (seven voices) and layout (the hands span the interval of a thirteenth, with the fifth of the chord at the bottom) to the B-flat-major chord that sounds immediately before the "coda" of BWV 565 (see exx. 5.4 and 5.5).

EXAMPLE 5.4. Toccata and Fugue in D Minor, BWV 565, m. 127

EXAMPLE 5.5. César Franck, *Final*, mm. 303–6

What is more, each chord is either extended or immediately followed by a fermata, a grand gesture that capitalizes on the organ's capacity to prolong pitches indefinitely. Each work then accelerates, hands alone, to *perpetuum mobile* figuration derived from the same basic motive, a four-note figure that begins off the beat and proceeds mostly in ascending, stepwise motion. And each work then continues for the next several bars by alternating between such chords and figuration, leaving the listener to wonder where things will finally end.

But nowhere in Franck's output is the influence of Bach's organ music more tangible than in the *Trois Chorals*, Franck's last compositions of any kind. Authored in late summer and early fall of 1890, they are also among his greatest works for any medium. Franck's use of the word "choral" here implies a tribute to the undisputed master of that genre, and his indebtedness to Bach is apparent throughout, most obviously, perhaps, in those passages (found in all three pieces) written in the same, homophonic texture as the Baroque master's *371 Four-Part Chorales*. Yet another source of inspiration was Bach's chorale preludes, as Franck in 1889 had confessed to his pupil Pierre de Bréville: "Before I die, I am going to write some organ chorales, just as Bach did, but on quite a different plan."[54] Franck's "different plan," ultimately, was to write loosely constructed sets of variations on one or more themes, including variations in the style of Bach's ornamental organ chorales. In these works Bach profusely embellishes the hymn tune and presents it on its own manual.

Such ornamental passages are found in both the first and third *Chorals*, and it should be mentioned that four-voice texture predominates, just as in most of Bach's ornamental chorales. In mm. 65–80 of *Choral No. 1*, for example, Franck varies the opening theme in this manner, first in the soprano voice and then in the tenor (see ex. 5.6). He would have

EXAMPLE 5.6. César Franck, *Choral No. 1* in E Major, mm. 65–68

found models for either approach in the three ornamental chorales included in his Braille edition of Bach's organ works. Furthermore, in editing "An Wasserflüssen Babylon," the only one of these three Bach works featuring a tenor cantus firmus, Franck called for the same registration as he does here, a reed melody with flute accompaniment. Witness, too, in m. 67, the appoggiatura "sigh" figures in parallel tenths between the soprano and tenor, a procedure that recalls another Bach organ chorale contained in the Braille edition, "O Mensch, bewein dein Sünde gross."[55] The other two such ornamental passages are mm. 126–37 of *Choral No. 1* and mm. 46–64 of *Choral No. 3*, both of which constitute exceedingly free variations on the "chorale" themes of these works. In both cases, moreover, Franck indicates again that the melody is to be played on reed stops, accompanied by flutes.

The primary exemplar for *Choral No. 2*, by way of contrast, is Bach's Passacaglia in C Minor,[56] the same work that thirty years earlier had served as the thematic model for Franck's *Offertoire* in F Minor. While Franck may also have been bowing to the genre of the Baroque passacaglia by composing an ostinato-bass work in triple meter

---

54. "Avant de mourir, j'écrirai des chorals d'orgue, ainsi qu'a fait Bach, mais sur un autre plan." See Bréville 1938, 95; and Fauquet 1999a, 757.

55. See mm. 12 and 21 of "O Mensch," wherein such figures involve parallel fourths and sixths between the soprano and the middle two voices.

56. This is basically the conclusion reached, without further discussion, in Fauquet 1999, 758.

and in the minor mode, he specifically and unmistakably follows Bach's Passacaglia in the ersatz double fugue contained in this piece (see exx. 5.7 and 5.8).[57] At approxi-

EXAMPLE 5.7. Passacaglia in C Minor, BWV 582, mm. 168–74

EXAMPLE 5.8. César Franck, *Choral No. 2* in B Minor, mm. 148–52

mately the midpoint of his work, Bach took the unprecedented step in the history of ostinato-bass composition of jettisoning the second half of his theme in favor of a permutation fugue on its first half—the fugue extends for more than a hundred measures to the very end of the piece—and he begins by stating the truncated theme simultaneously with one based on a series of five eighth notes beginning on the "and" of the first beat. Franck follows Bach's highly unusual procedure to the letter, at least for the first three bars, and he adopts both the positioning and range of Bach's voices as well (observe also the phrase markings, which may have been suggested by Bach's slurs). As to why Franck was drawn to Bach's Passacaglia at this time in his life, surely one reason is that he had just taught the work to two of his pupils (see app. 1), one of

57. On this point, see also Frith 2006, 33.

whom played only the concluding fugue, cited by Franck in his progress report as the *Fugue de la Passacaglia*.

The passage in *Choral No. 2* that immediately precedes this fugue is apparently derived from Bach's Fantasy in G Minor, BWV 542/1, a movement taught by Franck to several of his students. As examples 5.9 and 5.10 illustrate, this passage begins in the same distinctive way as Bach's fantasy, with high-pitched rhapsodic figuration that moves in fits and starts, supported by quarter-note triads in exactly three voices in the alto-tenor register and by reiterated tonic pedal points. Franck's label of "con fantasia" probably represents a further allusion to Bach's work.

EXAMPLE 5.9. Fantasy in G Minor, BWV 542/1, m. 1

EXAMPLE 5.10. César Franck, *Choral No. 2* in B Minor, mm. 127–28

Finally, it is patently obvious that the opening theme of *Choral No. 3* was influenced by that of Bach's Prelude in A Minor, BWV 543/1 (see exx. 5.11 and 5.12). This argument was made about eighty years ago by Franck's pupil Charles Tournemire and was generally accepted until Rollin Smith dismissed it as an untenable theory "suggested by the rhythm and the first four notes [of the two works] being identical."[58] In looking beyond the first four notes, however, one sees that Franck not only imitated the rhythm of Bach's passage-work for several measures but that he also closely followed its contour for more than two bars, starting on A and descending chromatically to D. The likelihood that Franck had

---

58. Tournemire 1931, 33; and Smith 1997, 253 n. 4.

EXAMPLE 5.11. Prelude in A Minor, BWV 543/1, mm. 1–3

EXAMPLE 5.12. César Franck, *Choral No. 3* in A Minor, mm. 1–3

just taught the Prelude to one of his students (see app. 1) could help explain his "compositional" attraction to this movement at this juncture in his career.

As a composer for the organ, therefore, Franck simulated (and actually wrote in) several of the same organ genres mastered by Bach, including, in the order of our discussion, the passacaglia, fugue, pastorale, toccata, ornamental chorale, fantasy, and prelude. As part of this process, specific pieces by Bach guided Franck on such crucial matters as melody, rhythm, harmony, texture, timbre, and tonal structure. Perhaps Franz Liszt was thinking of these similarities when he declared Franck's organ works, in reference to the *Six Pièces*, "poems [that] have their place beside the masterpieces of Sebastian Bach."[59] As a champion of Bach's organ music, Franck also exerted great influence as a teacher. Both as a pedagogue and composer, he played a critical role in the revival of Bach's music in nineteenth-century France.

---

59. Smith 1997, 161.

6

Edward Elgar as a Receptor of Bach's Organ Works

LIKE CÉSAR FRANCK, Edward Elgar played Bach's organ music and used it as an exemplar for his own compositions. He prepared orchestral transcriptions of certain pieces as well. His reception of the music is also evinced by the many markings that he made in his personal copy of the Peters edition and by his heavily annotated copy of Albert Schweitzer's book on Bach. The time is ripe for a detailed investigation of these (and other) archival materials and for an examination in general of Elgar's encounter with this repertory.

ELGAR AS BACH INTERPRETER

Compared to Franck, Edward Elgar enjoyed neither a long nor a particularly distinguished career as an organist. Rather, Elgar's involvement with the king of instruments was confined largely to his youth and early adulthood, during which time he toiled as a church organist in his native Worcester. Elgar was still a teenager when, in 1872, he became the unofficial assistant organist at St. George's Catholic Church; in 1885 he was appointed organist there. As he disclosed the following year, he was not especially happy in his work: "I am a full fledged organist now &—hate it. I expect another three months will end it; the choir is awful & no good to be done with them."[1] Three years later, he

---

1. Letter to Charles Buck of January 1886. See Anderson and Kent 1987, v; and Kent 1994, 98.

resigned this post to seek his fortune in London as a freelance composer and musician. He would never again play the organ professionally.

Despite Elgar's misgivings about being a church organist, there is ample evidence that he admired Bach's organ music. It follows, therefore, that he regularly programmed compositions by Bach as voluntaries for worship services at St. George's. Whatever the case, Elgar's personal copy of the Peters edition of the complete Bach organ works has survived, and the numerous markings that he made in this source (catalogued as no. 1365 in the archives of the Elgar Birthplace Museum, Lower Broadheath) shed light on how he performed various pieces. These markings, many of which illuminate aspects of the music that might otherwise go unnoticed, have yet to be thoroughly investigated.[2]

Elgar worked from a revised version of the Peters edition in which volumes 1–4 and 5–8, respectively, are bound together as massive single volumes. That he owned only the tome containing volumes 1–4 implies an aversion to Protestant chorales on the part of a Catholic musician, for these volumes are completely free of chorale settings, whereas volumes 5–8 contain hundreds.[3] In a moment of youthful exuberance, Elgar saw fit to rubber-stamp with the appropriate volume number every single right-hand page of both the main musical text and the appendix, which contains variant versions from all four volumes. On the pages containing four of these variants (those of BWV 532/2, 536, 542/2, and 566), and obviously for the sake of comparison, he also indicated which pages of the main text contain the standard version. Elgar's pride in this publication is attested to by a four-page inventory that he made of it (Elgar Birthplace Museum, no. 92) containing thematic incipits of the individual movements of all forty-two pieces.

Not all of Elgar's markings relate exclusively to performance practice. For example, in m. 17 of the B-minor prelude, BWV 544/1, which resembles a concerto movement for the organ, he inscribed an X exactly where the first episode begins. His perusal of the D-major fugue, BWV 532/2, led to the inscription *app* over the last beat of m. 5, to signify that the variant version found in the appendix offers a different reading. And in four other movements, he made queries about possible misprints, wondering whether m. 129 of the Wedge fugue should not begin with B instead of A; whether m. 44 of the fugue from the Toccata, Adagio, and Fugue should not conclude like m. 58, with F-sharps rather than a mixture of F-sharp and F-natural;[4] whether the second, third, and fourth notes of the left-hand voice in m. 15 of the Prelude in C Major, BWV 531/1, should not be a third lower, thus creating the same "horn fifths" as on the third beat of measure 10; and whether Bach really intended all those chromatic dissonances in the youthful Prelude in A Minor, BWV 569 (see mm. 33, 34, 71, 115, 127, and 131). Only one of these queries, however, is corroborated by philological evidence. That instance involves m. 131 of BWV 569, where

---

2. For a helpful general discussion, see Kent 1996, 182–85.

3. According to Kent 1996, 180, Elgar owned both sets of volumes.

4. Elgar's copy of the Peters edition lacks in m. 44 the soprano F-sharp found in other printings.

Elgar questioned why the soprano voice should move to F-natural rather than to F-sharp, when F-sharp is the pitch being sustained by the tenor. He would have been pleased to find in one of the manuscript sources for this work a reading of F-sharp for both voices.[5]

The performance markings made by Elgar throughout this edition, most of which were entered in very faint pencil, encompass virtually everything but fingerings. There is but one brief set of pedalings, for mm. 21–24 of the Prelude in E Minor, BWV 548/1, where the use of both toe and heel is indicated. Tempo markings, however, appear in no fewer than eighteen movements, with *Andante* as the favorite tempo for preludes and *Allegro* the favorite for fugues, even in the case of the relatively somber "Dorian" fugue. The fact that these instructions are all double-underlined in red ink suggests they were entered at the same sitting. Only two metronome markings are given, and both for the Fugue in C Minor, BWV 546/2: a sprightly $\quarternote = 76$ and a more conventional $\quarternote = 56$.

Phrasings and articulation markings occur in only four works, and always in tandem. They are used for the subject and countersubject of the "Little" Fugue in G Minor; for the first two subjects of the permutation fugue that concludes the C-minor passacaglia; for both subjects of the Legrenzi fugue (BWV 574); and for the first four bars of the Prelude in E Minor. The specificity—even fussiness—of these markings would seem to reflect Elgar's training as a violinist. For example, in the Little fugue, starting with the pickup to m. 7 and continuing in mm. 9–10, one hand often plays staccato while the other plays legato (see fig. 6.1, which also illustrates Elgar's tempo marking for this work). In all three of these fugues, Elgar inscribed decidedly un-Baroque phrasings that begin on a weak beat or off the beat entirely, such as that between the first two bars of the subject of the Little fugue.

The issue of ornamentation arises in only three works, and in two very different contexts. In the case of the B-minor prelude, Elgar notated six different times how the appoggiatura motives in the main theme should be played, whether with two sixteenths (mm. 1, 27, and 28) or two eighths (mm. 8, 9, and 10). In annotating the Prelude in C Major, BWV 545/1, he added in red ink a series of trills to the sequential sixteenth-note pedal passage in measures 24–26, with the trills occurring on the third note of each eight-note grouping. Since this is exactly how the prelude is printed in volume 15 of the Bachgesellschaft edition of Bach's complete works, published in 1867, Elgar must have used that edition as his guide.

As his crescendo-decrescendo markings in three works show, Elgar had no compunctions about using the swell pedal in Bach, even though the practice has no historical basis. In employing this device, he was no doubt aiming for a certain Romantic expressivity. His tack in the first movement of the Pastorale was simply to open and close the swell box according to the rise and fall of the melodic line, initially (thinking four beats to the bar) from the fourth beat of m. 3 to the first beat of m. 6, and then in mm. 9–10. This, at any

5. On this reading, see Kilian 1978–79, 550.

FIGURE 6.1. Fugue in G Minor ("Little"), BWV 578, mm. 1–17. Edward Elgar's personal copy (Elgar Birthplace Museum, Lower Broadheath, catalogue no. 1365)

rate, is where the markings appear, but surely he treated the remainder of the movement likewise. He would have done so with relative ease, for this pedal line consists of little more than low pedal points, which he would have played with his left foot, leaving his right foot free to work the swell pedal to his heart's content.

Not so in the Prelude in E Minor, where the only such indication is a crescendo hairpin on the very first beat. Although it would have been tricky business, with regular octave leaps for the left foot, we may surmise that for the first four measures the swell box was opened on each downbeat chord and closed by the end of each measure, and that this process was repeated whenever this segment of the ritornello returns. Elgar also added on the first beat a bracket for the three manual quarter notes, which means they are all to be taken by the left hand while the right hand plays only the top voice. To enhance this melody-with-accompaniment layout, he specified the use of two manuals, writing "Gt. Gamba" above the right-hand staff and "Swell Reed" beneath the left hand, along with a pedal registration of 16'.

That leaves the Prelude in E-flat, BWV 552/1, another concerto-like movement, where crescendo-decrescendo hairpins were entered in mm. 98–99 and 174–75.[6] Each of these

---

6. Elgar made two other additions in mm. 101–3, a brief countermelody (m. 101) and a line indicating hand distribution (mm. 102–3). For a transcription, see Kent 1996, 185.

passages, too, commences a statement of the ritornello, and they are the only statements that begin in a minor key (they both modulate to the major after two bars). Elgar may not have precisely positioned his markings, but it seems that in both instances he meant for the crescendo to begin with the lone dominant note on the third beat and to end, approximately five beats later, on the tonic triad that establishes the minor key. However inauthentic, the technique effectively highlights the thickening in texture between the third and fourth beats as well as the dissonant harmony (a dominant-seventh chord sounding above the tonic pitch) that immediately precedes the tonic triad. Elgar was also concerned here about maintaining a legato touch, for in both instances he drew a slur from the lone dominant note to one (B-flat and F, respectively) in the thick chord that follows. A break in the musical flow would have undermined the whole idea of a lengthy crescendo.

The E-minor prelude is hardly the only work in which Elgar reveals his preference for a variegated organ sonority, especially where reed stops are concerned. Consider, for example, his indication of oboe for the ornamental right-hand melody at the beginning of the G-minor fantasy, BWV 542/1, which undoubtedly means that the left-hand chords are to be played on a separate manual. The concept is compelling—and not so different from the second movement of the first Brandenburg Concerto, where a florid solo oboe line sounds against soft repeated chords in the string section. He furnished a similar but more detailed registration for the Fantasy in C Minor, BWV 537/1, with the left hand taking the tenor line on a loud reed (marked "Choir," even though the organ at St. George's lacked this division) and the right hand playing the soprano and alto on the Great, along with a soft 16′ stop in the pedals. Here—and in contrast to both the G-minor fantasy and E-minor prelude—the figuration and texture stay basically the same, which would have allowed for the two-manual layout to be maintained for the duration, despite some large reaches for the right hand. What is gained, though, by singling out the tenor voice in the many passages where one of the main themes sounds in another voice? In two other works, Elgar instructed that a reed be used to underscore new melodic material: in m. 5 of the E-flat prelude, where the inscription "P[iano]. Reed" appears for the second phrase of the ritornello; and in m. 23 of the B-minor prelude, to introduce the barrage of thirty-second notes for the right hand.

Most of Elgar's registrations, not surprisingly, are consistent with the specifications of the organ at St. George's.[7] Except, that is, in the case of the Legrenzi fugue. For this piece, he called for a 32′ pedal stop, which would have been available in Worcester only on the Hill organ that had been installed in 1874 at the city's cathedral.[8] Elgar's enthusiasm for this instrument is well known. Inspired by this great machine, and presumably seated at its console, he inscribed in m. 1 the registration of "16 & 8 Ft" for the hands and 32 & 16 Ft" for the feet; in m. 37, where the second subject is introduced, "REEDS"; and in m. 70,

---

7. Kent 1996, 182 and 184. The specifications of this instrument are given in Kent 1994, 94.

8. For the specifications, see Anderson and Kent 1987, vi; and Clark 2002, 29–30.

where the two subjects are combined for the first time, "MIXTURES &C." Thus, in registering this textbook double fugue, Elgar added stops at the two main formal junctures, creating a steady buildup of sound. He presumably began just with diapasons but by the end of the piece had augmented this registration with reeds and mixtures, and most likely some mutation stops to boot.

The page from Elgar's edition containing his inscription of "REEDS" is reproduced in figure 6.2. Observe here also the large rubber stamp of the number "4" in the upper right corner, denoting the volume number, and what appears to be, in Elgar's hand, the number "6," which is the number of this work within volume 4. His phrasings and articulation markings for the two fugue subjects are present as well (note the staccato dots), in the first three systems. Additionally, Elgar chose in mm. 43–44 to restore the first pedal statement of the second subject to its original, unsimplified state by inserting sixteenth notes and altering the rhythm of the following notes accordingly. Barely visible due to an erasure is a sixteenth note on g that was originally notated between the last two pedal notes of m. 43—and that created parallel fifths with the soprano voice. The added notes in m. 44 pose no such problem.

Arguably the most interesting (and certainly the boldest) of Elgar's performance instructions in this source is a note found near the end of the E-minor prelude. Penned above mm. 115–18, the note reads: "six bars on p 67 in G—then open theme & coda."

FIGURE 6.2. Fugue in C Minor on a Theme by Legrenzi, BWV 574, mm. 26–45. Edward Elgar's personal copy (Elgar Birthplace Museum, Lower Broadheath, catalogue no. 1365)

Preceding this inscription, and placed directly above the bar line that begins m. 115, is a large *X*. This is the same symbol used twice by Elgar two pages earlier in this edition, on page 67, to mark the beginning and end of the six bars of music at mm. 69–74. He therefore means to skip directly from the end of m. 114 to the beginning of m. 69 and, literally, to transpose the music found there to G major. Elgar, though, could more accurately have referred to this transposition in terms of an interval—either up a fourth or down a fifth—because the music of mm. 69–74 constantly modulates; the key of G major obtains only for the first beat or so. With m. 64 transposed in this way, the same V–I progression in that key occurs between mm. 114 and 69 as between mm. 114 and 115.

This transposed passage leads directly to the "open theme" and then to the "coda." There can be little doubt that "open theme," which is obviously short for "opening theme," refers to the lengthy ritornello stated at the very beginning of the prelude and that "coda" refers to the material that concludes it. But the precise amount of material being referred to in each instance is, on the face of it, unclear. To help clarify this matter, let us consider three aspects of the music: (1) the last statement of the ritornello, found in mm. 125–37, and presented by Bach in the key of E minor, lacks the first six bars of the theme; (2) the only time these six bars are stated by Bach in the key of E minor is in mm. 1–6; and (3) if transposed up a fourth or down a fifth, m. 74 ends on the leading-tone chord in the key of E minor and therefore leads naturally to the tonic triad in that key, which, of course, is also the harmony at the beginning of m. 1. It would seem, therefore, that "open theme" refers only to the first six measures of the ritornello, that "coda" refers to all thirteen bars of the concluding fragmentary ritornello statement, and that the main objective behind Elgar's cut-and-paste job was to combine these two fragments for the sake of a complete statement of the ritornello in E minor to end the prelude, even if that meant discarding the long episode at mm. 115–24.[9]

Elgar performed this surgery, evidently, because he perceived an imbalance in how the prelude ends. As composed by Bach, the movement is not evenly framed by complete ritornello statements; it does not begin and end with the same amount of material. But rather than attempting to symmetrize this masterpiece—which forces it into a procrustean bed—it seems that Elgar would have been better off appreciating that Bach does not always do the obvious.

ELGAR AS BACH DEVOTEE AND BACH CRITIC

Elgar did not approach Bach's oeuvre with a blindly undiscriminating eye. According to his friend Billy Reed, he "loved some of Bach's music, but by no means all,"[10] and on one

---

9. In accordance with these changes, the highest note at the end of m. 74 would presumably be removed to avoid an unresolved seventh.

10. Reed 1936, 86.

occasion he even pronounced certain Bach cantatas "infernally dull."[11] But those Bach works that Elgar did love affected him to the point of veneration. For example, he admitted in 1896 to playing "three or four preludes and fugues from the Well-Tempered Clavier every day."[12]

There can be no question that certain compositions by Elgar, especially those involving fugue, are heavily indebted to his study of Bach's music. Furthermore, the very fact that he composed organ fugues betrays the influence of Bach's organ works.[13] Scholars have acknowledged this influence for decades, and some have argued that Elgar modeled certain compositions after particular organ works by Bach, most famously in variation 11 of the *Enigma Variations*, which allegedly depicts the fast organ-pedaling of George Robertson Sinclair, a good friend of Elgar's and the organist of Hereford Cathedral.[14] Still, not one of these arguments is especially convincing, and further speculation along these lines should probably be avoided. Thus, instead of considering Elgar's compositions as evidence of his respect and enthusiasm for Bach's organ works, we will focus here on biographical data. We will also observe Elgar as an opinionated critic of this music.

One of Elgar's fondest memories of his youth was hearing Samuel Sebastian Wesley hold forth at the newly constructed Hill organ at Worcester Cathedral. The year was 1875, and the occasion was the annual Three Choirs Festival, an event involving the choirs of Gloucester, Hereford, and Worcester Cathedrals that is still thriving today. Wesley had been engaged as the organist at the festival that year, and Elgar remembered the great man's penchant for playing Bach. Wesley, of course, inherited this predilection from his father Samuel, who, as the most ardent Bachian in all of England at the time, had even chosen to name his son after Bach.

Two posthumous reports on Elgar's reaction to Wesley's playing have survived, and they mention two different organ compositions by Bach (although most commentators cite only one or the other). The first comes from Elgar's friend Emmie Leaver, who in her reminiscences of the composer wrote: "Elgar had visited Worcester Cathedral since the age of four. On someone mentioning the acoustics of the building, he told of the impression he had once received from the improvising of S. S. Wesley, who had built up a wonderful climax of sound before, in Elgar's words, crashing into the subject of the 'Wedge' Fugue."[15] As we have seen, Elgar's study of this fugue is documented by a query that he made in his Peters edition. There, he also inscribed the tempo indication of *Allegro* at the beginning of the movement; Elgar was so taken with the Wedge that he even considered transcribing it for orchestra.

---

11. Letter to Ivor Atkins of February 2, 1926. See Atkins 1984, 386.

12. Moore 1984, 192; and Kent 1996, 179–80.

13. These fugues are published in Anderson and Kent 1987.

14. Parrott 1971, 48–49; and Clark 2002, 17–20.

15. Leaver 1934, 869.

The second such report stems from Elgar's friend and colleague Ivor Atkins, organist of Worcester Cathedral, who, in addressing the Royal College of Organists in 1935, offered these remarks:

> Elgar heard him [S. S. Wesley] at Worcester in 1875, and often spoke to me of the thrilling effect Wesley's playing had upon him. The occasion was the outgoing voluntary at a Three Choirs Festival evensong. Wesley began with a long extemporisation, designed to lead up to Bach's Choral Prelude "Wir glauben all an einen Gott" [the so-called Giant Fugue, BWV 680, from Part 3 of the *Clavierübung*], breaking off the extemporisation in an arresting way before entering upon the Prelude. The effect upon Elgar was so great that in after years when he returned to live in Worcester and would constantly slip into the old cathedral, which had so many memories for him and which he greatly loved, he almost invariably asked me to play him something, and we always had to end with the *Giant*. But I do not know that I was ever able to recapture the impression left upon him by Wesley.[16]

Decades after hearing Wesley play, Elgar made some jottings in his copy of Albert Schweitzer's monograph on the music of Bach that reveal his curiosity about—of all things—the nickname of this piece. To understand these annotations, a brief discussion of the history of that nickname is in order. It appears to have originated around 1845, when the organist George Cooper published the work as *John Sebastian Bach's Fugue on a Chorale in D minor: The Giant Fugue*.[17] Cooper did not explain his subtitle, but there seems to have been a general understanding that the sobriquet somehow involved the "striding" pedal theme. Approximately seventy years later, the organist Herbert Hodge proffered an explanation, namely, that the moniker "Giant Fugue" was due to "the constantly recurring figure in the pedal part, which is supposed to represent a giant ascending the stairs, and who, having arrived at the top, tumbles and bumps his way down to the bottom again every time." Hodge's commentary originated merely as a program note to one of his recitals, but it was given wide exposure when reprinted (as an "Occasional Note") in the April 1, 1916, issue of the *Musical Times*, the leading music journal in Britain at this time.[18] Not that all English organists of the day were happy about the nickname or Hodge's interpretation of it. Witness, for example, these words of Harvey Grace: "It may

---

16. Atkins 1984, 475. Wesley essayed this same Bach work on a recital in 1855. The piece was also a favorite of his father Samuel, who found it an "electrifying" work. See, respectively, Horton 2004, 222; and Olleson 2001, 105–6.

17. Cooper's edition is cited in Thistlethwaite 1990, 169.

18. There followed in the June 1 issue a letter to the editor from "W. W. S." claiming that the nickname had Handelian roots: "The independent pedal motive, 'the constantly recurring figure' which is an obbligato part to the fugue proper, suggested to [Cooper] the song of the giant Polyphemus, 'O Ruddier than the Cherry,' in Handel's *Acis and Galatea*." At issue, undoubtedly, is the jagged ascending melody sung to the text "O nymph more bright than moonshine night."

be well to point out that the ground bass is obviously intended to typify faith, and that the less we think of a giant walking upstairs and tumbling down again (*vide* some programme notes) the better."[19] Rather, the point is that English organists at around the time of World War I were well acquainted with both the locution "Giant Fugue" and Hodge's particular explanation of it, whether or not they appreciated or accepted either.

As the relevant page (vol. 2, 60) of his copy of Schweitzer's study shows, Elgar was no exception to this rule. There, he first questioned (with good reason) Schweitzer's description of "Wir glauben" as "gentle" and "almost dreamy" by underlining the text and drawing a question mark in the margin. Elgar then moved on to the illustration of the pedal theme, marking off with two *X*'s its concluding stepwise descent (see ex. 6.1). These

EXAMPLE 6.1. "Wir glauben all an einen Gott," BWV 680, mm. 4–9, pedal part

letters correspond to another *X* inscribed by Elgar at the bottom of the page, after which he charmingly wrote: "Then this may be tumbling down stairs, I conclude." Obviously, Elgar alludes here to the mythology behind the "Giant Fugue" nickname, and his use of the word "tumbling," as opposed to, say, "falling," suggests a knowledge of Hodge's explanatory note. More significantly, Elgar's use of the modal auxiliary "may" implies that he had never seen the score of this piece, even though it was a favorite work of his. This would accord with the total absence of Bach's organ chorales from Elgar's library. All things considered, the note smacks of whimsy as well as naiveté. It also represents Elgar's only annotation in this source made in reference to one of Bach's organ chorales—further evidence that he neglected these works.

The source in question is Elgar's heavily annotated personal copy (Elgar Birthplace Museum, no reference number) of Ernest Newman's two-volume English translation of the German version of Schweitzer's book, which, in turn, is Schweitzer's own translation (1908) from the French (1905).[20] Newman's translation was brought out in 1911 by Breitkopf & Härtel under the title *J. S. Bach*. According to an inscription in Newman's hand at the front of volume 1 (*To Edward Elgar / from En. / 8 Nov 1911*), Elgar received the book from the translator himself, hot off the press.[21]

Save the inscriptions just discussed, all of Elgar's markings pertaining to Bach's organ music are found in volume 1. They touch on various issues, and often in ways that denigrate Schweitzer's commentary. To begin with, Schweitzer loathed the piano transcriptions of Bach's organ works that were flooding the market at the time, and he asked why

---

19. Grace 1922b, 214–15.

20. I would like to thank Chris Bennett of the Elgar Birthplace Museum for alerting me to this source.

21. Elgar provided a similar inscription at the front of vol. 2: *Edward Elgar / Nov 1911 / (from E. N.)*.

so many pianists were producing these arrangements instead of original piano compositions (p. 262). Elgar answered by slamming the organ community: "Simply because the
organists sound ineffective." Five pages later, Schweitzer discusses the relationship between the Fugue in D Minor for organ, BWV 539/2, and the Fugue in G Minor for unaccompanied violin, BWV 1001/2, writing that "The theme of the D minor fugue is
identical with that on which the fugue in the first sonata for violin solo (G minor) is
constructed, the priority belonging to the violin fugue." In response, Elgar underlined
"the priority" and wrote: "I doubt this." Another five pages later, Schweitzer states cate-
gorically that the subject of the Fugue in G Minor, BWV 542/2, is borrowed from the
North German master J. A. Reinken, and he refers the reader back to a musical example
illustrating the alleged model. Elgar's retort is a single word: "nonsense." As to the validity
of Elgar's pronouncements here, it is hard to know what to make of the first one, but there
is absolutely no reason to question the "priority" of the violin fugue. Regarding
Schweitzer's third point, Elgar had every reason to object, as the resemblance between
these two themes is superficial at best.

Schweitzer then turns his attention to various early organ works by Bach, and without
exception he extols their virtues (pp. 269–70). Elgar, for his part, was singularly unim-
pressed, not only with the works themselves but also with Schweitzer's comments on
them. Apropos of Schweitzer's contention that the Little Fugue in G Minor and the
Toccata and Fugue in D Minor, BWV 565, "affect the hearer almost more powerfully
than any other of Bach's organ works," Elgar underlined "more powerfully than" and
drew a question mark in the margin. With regard to the Little Fugue, which might be
characterized as charming but certainly not "powerful," the question mark is entirely jus-
tified. Schweitzer then writes about "the wonderful pathos of the prelude and fugue in
D major…and the toccata and fugue in C major," in the latter case referencing the work
better known as the Toccata, Adagio, and Fugue in C Major, BWV 564. Elgar responded
by circling both instances of the word "fugue" and scribbling in the margin: "rubbish."
Schweitzer begins his next paragraph by describing these movements as "brilliant and
dashing fugues," which prompted Elgar to circle "dashing fugues" and to inscribe the
same insulting marginalium. And Schweitzer begins his next paragraph by describing
these two works, as well as the Prelude and Fugue in C Major, BWV 531, as "masterpieces
of [Bach's] youth," a phrase derisively underlined by Elgar. He evidently preferred to dis-
miss all of these pieces as flawed juvenilia. Likewise, in his copy of the Peters edition Elgar
expressed his disdain for the youthful Prelude and Fugue in C Major, BWV 566—a work
that was a perennial favorite within the organ studio of César Franck—by writing on its
score "early" and "rubbish."

Elgar felt differently about the Fugue in C Minor, BWV 537/2, as his orchestral transcription of this movement attests. Thankfully, he also reacted to one of Schweitzer's
remarks about this fugue in slightly less elliptic terms than we have just seen. Schweitzer
here speaks of the fugue's "chromatic counter-theme" (p. 274), obviously referring to the
slow, chromatically ascending idea introduced in mm. 57–60. Bach actually pairs this

theme with another, much faster one in the manner of a double fugue, although neither melody is ever paired with the main subject of the fugue, that featured in mm.
1–53 and 104–28. Elgar's response was to underline the text in question and pen the following gloss: "this is a separate theme; i.e., not a countertheme but subject." In modern
parlance, Elgar's inscription means that the chromatic theme is not a countersubject to
the main subject of the fugue, as Schweitzer's terminology suggests, but a subject in and
of itself.

ELGAR'S BACH TRANSCRIPTIONS

Over the course of his long career, Elgar produced only two arrangements of Bach's music,
and they both happen to be of organ works. His orchestration of the Fantasy and Fugue
in C Minor, BWV 537, is one of the most famous (and successful) Bach transcriptions
ever committed to paper. Consequently, the arrangement has figured in the Elgar literature since it was premiered in the early 1920s. Despite all that has been written, however,
scholars have tended to discuss either Elgar's techniques of orchestration or certain letters
written by or to him about the transcription. By considering both the music and all the
source material, which includes a good deal of correspondence, a more balanced and
complete picture emerges.

Elgar's other Bach arrangement, that of the conclusion of the Toccata in F Major,
BWV 540/1, is virtually unknown. It owes its existence to a request made by Ivor Atkins
in connection with the Three Choirs Festival held at Worcester Cathedral in September
1908. Atkins had selected for the opening service Heinrich Esser's orchestration of the
toccata (published in 1859), but he so disliked the arranger's rather banal coda, which
replaces the last two measures composed by Bach, that he asked Elgar to re-orchestrate

EXAMPLE 6.2. Heinrich Esser's coda for the Toccata in F Major, BWV 540/1 (piano reduction)

the ending (see ex. 6.2). Elgar chose to dispense with Esser's coda altogether and back-
track to m. 417, from which point he orchestrated the final twenty-two bars composed by
Bach without altering the movement's length in any way. In this hybrid form, the transcription was unveiled on Sunday, September 8.

Elgar's fragment is still unpublished (although it will be included in a forthcoming
volume of the *Elgar Complete Edition*), but the recent acquisition of his autograph man-

uscript by the Elgar Birthplace Museum (reference no. 138) has now made it generally accessible.[22] Signed *Edward Elgar / July* 1908, this score augments Esser's orchestration by a total of nine instruments: a third flute, an English horn, a bass clarinet, a contrabassoon, a third trumpet, a tuba, a third timpani, a bass drum, and—most importantly—an organ. As is often the case with Elgar's orchestral manuscripts, his wife, Alice, lovingly inscribed all the part names.[23] A modern source worth consulting is a recently re-released recording from 1932 of the entire joint arrangement, conducted by Albert Coates.[24] This remains the only recording in existence.

In sampling this disc, there is no mistaking when Esser leaves off and Elgar takes over, as Elgar's orchestration is both larger and more imaginative. For example, as if to herald Elgar's arrival,, the two sustained C's in mm. 417–22 are played by the trumpet section, and the second one is set to a dramatic crescendo (simultaneously, the organ crescendos on a C pedal point). Tremolo string writing takes over at m. 430 and continues until the middle of m. 434, where the sixteenth-note figuration is now assigned to the low brass as well as the low strings. What is missing from this recording, though, is Elgar's organ part, which must have added exponentially to any sense of grandeur felt at the premiere performance. In a gesture no doubt meant to exploit the 32′ pedal diapason of the cathedral organ—and one that recalls the optional organ part in the final movement of the *Enigma Variations*—the part begins by sustaining a pedal C for seven bars, then switches to chords for the next eleven measures, and ends by duplicating the last four bars of the original.

Two days after completing the fragment, Elgar dispatched it to Atkins with the following note: "I send the climax of the Bach which will sound fine. I fear it will snuff out the earlier part somewhat, but anyhow it will be climactick & *final*. Do play it: it fires me to 'do' the E minor one: I *will* in time."[25] Thus he was concerned—and rightly so—that his contribution might overwhelm rather than complement Esser's score (cited by Elgar as "the earlier part"). Yet on the whole he was satisfied with his handiwork, to the extent that he planned now on orchestrating an entire Bach work . Elgar refers to this work as being in the key of E minor, and it only makes sense from the context of his letter (one written to an organist about an organ work) that he means an organ composition. Excluding the E-minor prelude and fugue from the "Eight Little" (which Elgar did not own) and the E-minor trio sonata (which evidently did not interest him in the least), there are only two other free organ works composed by or attributed to Bach that are in

22. For particulars, see Kent 1993, 241–42.

23. My thanks to Chris Bennett for this identification.

24. *Johann Sebastian Bach: Great Orchestral Transcriptions* (Biddulph Recordings: BID 83069/70). Esser's original version has evidently never been recorded in its entirety.

25. Letter of July 19, 1908. See Atkins 1984, 179. Completion date of Elgar's fragment according to Kent 1993, 242.

this key: the Prelude and Fugue in E Minor, BWV 533 (the "Cathedral") and the Prelude and Fugue in E Minor, BWV 548 (the "Wedge"). All indications point to the latter piece as the one Elgar had in mind. It was this fugue, after all, as played by S. S. Wesley, that had so thrilled Elgar as a young man. Moreover, Elgar's interest in both the prelude and fugue is documented by various markings that he made in his Peters edition, as opposed to only one marking in the score of BWV 533 (the tempo indication of *Andante* for the prelude). Finally, with his strong bias against Bach's early organ works, Elgar would have chosen a mature masterpiece over a relatively inferior product of Bach's youth.

Atkins wrote back to Elgar the very next day, full of compliments and encouragement:

> The Bach additions look grand and ought to sound magnificent. You will now do the E minor, I am quite sure, and by Jove! won't it be a worthy tribute from Maestro to Maestro! There's a glow about those final pages that you have done for me that would please John [i.e., Johann Sebastian] highly. Let us hope he'll be there. I don't know how I shall snare you in—what form of decoy I may have to resort to—but come you must on the Sunday for the E minor depends on it. Your addition shall be copied, if with my own hands. You *are* a craftsman.[26]

Atkins, then, was more than satisfied with his friend's efforts, to the degree of effusive praise. Since Elgar was in town to conduct his own music at the festival, he probably did hear his Bach "addition(s)" on the day in question.[27] That he never followed through on his plans to "do the E minor" was undoubtedly to Atkins's chagrin.

Three points about Elgar's toccata transcription remain to be made. First of all, certain inscriptions in Elgar's Peters edition show that he worked from this source as he prepared the arrangement: exactly where the transcription begins (m. 417) he inscribed an *X*; seven bars later, where in the transcription the organ part changes from a pedal point to chords, he drew a diagonal line; and two bars from the end he inscribed *rit*, which corresponds to the marking of *rit molto* found in the transcription. Second, in 1929 Elgar was asked by his publisher Novello whether the Esser-Elgar arrangement might be added to that vast archive known today as the Edwin A. Fleisher Collection of Orchestral Music.[28] He responded in the affirmative and suggested that Mr. Fleisher be notified as to the "reinstatement of Bach's ending." Third, in 1932, two years before his death, Elgar once again had the opportunity of hearing this transcription at Worcester Cathedral at the opening service of the Three Choirs Festival.[29] The experience must have been rife with nostalgia.

---

26. Atkins 1984, 180. Atkins's organ repertory included both BWV 533 and 548. See Clark 2002, 31–32.

27. Moore 1984, 541–42.

28. Moore 1987, 861–62. This otherwise authoritative study gives the wrong date for the premiere performance of the transcription. The correct date is 1908, not 1929.

29. Young 1955, 239.

Turning to Elgar's transcription of the Fantasy and Fugue in C Minor, BWV 537, it is important to realize that the fugue was completed first. According to the diary of his daughter Carice, by April 19, 1921, Elgar had begun to orchestrate the movement.[30] He worked initially from his Peters edition, numbering every measure of that source in addition to notating rehearsal numbers, but probably due to the bulkiness of this tome his primary working score proved to be several pages conveniently removed from a copy of the Novello edition (Elgar Birthplace Museum, no. 1479).[31] A first draft was completed on April 24, and the final manuscript was mailed to Novello on May 25.

Certain critics denounced Elgar as a "vandal" for his flamboyant style of orchestration and especially for the ubiquitous material of his own composition, but the transcription was a smash hit with the public.[32] Three performances took place in London that fall, and at the two conducted by Eugene Goossens the audience demanded an encore. The premiere on October 27, led by Goossens, was chronicled by Carice in her diary: "great enthusiasm—had to be repeated & Father called down to platform to bow—Thrilling evening—sounded quite wonderful."[33] Elgar also attended both of Goossens's dress rehearsals, after which he wrote glowingly about the young maestro ("I heard G. do the fugue yesterday, & he makes it really go") as well as his hand-picked orchestra.[34] At this time, Elgar famously explained his arrangement to Goossens in terms of a confession: "Now that my poor wife has gone I can't be original, and so I depend on people like John Sebastian for a source of inspiration."[35] Lady Elgar had succumbed to cancer in April 1920, and her husband had written no music since.

Somewhat more detailed explanations may be found in two letters from Elgar to his friends. Read, for instance, what he wrote to Ivor Atkins roughly a fortnight after completing the transcription:

> I have orchestrated a Bach fugue *in modern way*—largish orchestra—you may not approve. I did want you to see it before printing but I had to send it to the engraver—however, many arrgts [i.e., arrangements] have been made of Bach on the "pretty" scale & I wanted to shew how gorgeous & great & brilliant he would have made himself sound if he had had our means.... This is the one [at this point, Elgar inscribes the first two bars of the fugue subject, making sure to include the added slur found throughout his score between the first two notes] & the climax is pretty brilliant—take my word for it.[36]

---

30. Anderson 1990, 156–61.

31. Kent 1993, 321–23.

32. Grace 1922a.

33. Anderson 1990, 158.

34. Moore 1990, 357; and Moore 1989, 266.

35. Goossens 1951, 298.

36. Letter of June 5, 1921. See Atkins 1984, 330. In a subsequent letter to Atkins, Elgar referred to his transcription as a "wild wark." See Atkins 1984, 331. It should also be mentioned that Atkins accompanied Elgar to Goossens's first dress rehearsal of the transcription. See Atkins 1984, 334.

Thus, in an attempt to "modernize" Bach—and to distance himself from the "prettiness" of such transcriptions as Esser's of the F-major toccata—Elgar deployed virtually every orchestral instrument in use at the time, including two harps and a full percussion battery (timpani, bass drum, snare drum, triangle, tambourine, cymbals, and glockenspiel). Nowhere does he use these instruments more compellingly than from rehearsal no. 27 to the end, which must also be the passage referred to by him as the "climax" of the arrangement. Marked *allargando* by Elgar, these eight measures suggest a final statement of the fugue subject in augmentation (as do the repeated brass notes at rehearsal no. 22 and between rehearsal nos. 18 and 19). Furthermore, this is the only passage in the original version where the subject is either lengthened or decorated with rhythms faster than an eighth note: the second, third, and fourth notes of the third bar of the subject are restated at the upper octave, while simultaneously the fourth note is embellished with two sixteenths and one eighth note. Elgar chose to underscore these extraordinary gestures not only by slowing down the tempo even further (he writes *rit. al fine*) but by hammering out the rhythm of the restated segment with all the percussion instruments except the glockenspiel. (He achieves the same effect shortly after rehearsal no. 23, but in conjunction with his own rhythmic sharpening of the subject.) In the very last measure, while the rest of the orchestra is crescendoing on a sustained dominant-seventh chord, the harps are frantically arpeggiating the same harmony in accordance with Elgar's instruction to "repeat the arpeggio rapidly as many times as may be required by the *ritenuto* in the other orch. parts." This chord is held for a full eight beats, as opposed to only two beats in the original version, constituting the only instance in either the fantasy or the fugue where Elgar lengthened his model.

The other missive in question was penned by Elgar on October 26, after attending Goossens's first dress rehearsal that same day. It was sent, along with an advance copy of the printed score, to Ernest Newman, one of the leading music critics of the day (and whom we have already encountered as the translator of Albert Schweitzer). Here, Elgar describes his manner of orchestration in explicitly organistic terms, as if he began with principals only and then gradually built up to full organ:

> Here is the score; I only got it today, &, as [it] is not to be published until the 31st, I must ask you to keep it *quite private* & not, as you will understand, use it for journalistic purposes: I had a childish wish that you shd see it.... Goossens rehearsed it today with his gorgeous orchestra & it comes off well.... P.S. You will see that I have kept it quite solid (diapasony) at first;—later you hear the sesquialteras & other trimming stops reverberating & the resultant vibrating shimmering sort of organ sound—I think[37]

---

37. Letter of October 26, 1921. See Moore 1990, 357–58.

Elgar's treatment of the orchestra also increases in virtuosity as the transcription unfolds, and it enhances the ABA design of the fugue as well. Shortly after rehearsal no. 8, for example, the harps glissando onto the scene, followed by a flurry of sixteenth-note scales in the woodwinds and strings. To mark the end of the first A section (rehearsal no. 13), the tambourine makes its first appearance, while in the aforementioned *allargando* passage there is a cascade of thirty-second notes for the trumpets.

The history of the transcription continues in December 1921, when Elgar conducted the first recording ever made of it.[38] Performed by members of the Royal Albert Hall Orchestra, the disc was praised by the recently knighted Landon Ronald at a press conference in his honor on January 10, 1922. Also during that month, Richard Strauss was making his first postwar visit to London. He and Elgar were old friends (and mutual admirers), and Elgar arranged a sumptuous luncheon on Strauss's behalf that was attended by several of the city's leading musicians, Goossens included. One timely topic of conversation was the orchestration of Bach's organ works, which apparently was a subject the two composers had discussed some years earlier. Strauss preferred a more restrained approach than Elgar had shown with the C-minor fugue, whereupon Elgar challenged the German to transcribe the fantasy. Strauss demurred, however, and Elgar undertook the task himself, working initially from the same fragmentary organ score (published by Novello) he had used for the fugue.[39] Exactly when is unclear, but the orchestration of the fantasy was definitely completed by June 1922, when Elgar began to correspond with Novello about publishing it. He conducted its first performance (along with the fugue) at the Three Choirs Festival held at Gloucester Cathedral in September of that year.

Compared to how he had transcribed the fugue, Elgar hewed closely to his model here, as if he were following Strauss's advice (he also used fewer percussion instruments). Still, his genius as an orchestrator is fully evident. Consider, for example, the opening pedal point, which lasts for more than thirteen bars.[40] It begins, very quietly, with sustained notes for the double basses (and, initially, for the bassoons and first violas as well), tremolo effects for the cellos and second violas (*con sordino*), and a measure-long timpani roll. Starting in the second bar, however, the timpani and bass drum begin to trade quarter notes in what will become a lengthy hemiola, and by m. 9 muted horns have been added to the mix. Meanwhile, the principal theme sounds first in the woodwinds and then in the strings. Elgar marks the latter *legato*, an indication realized in his 1926 recording with portamento technique.[41]

---

38. Moore 1974, 41–45.

39. Kent 1993, 322.

40. As opposed to the six and a half measures in Bach's original version. The reason for this discrepancy is that Elgar changed Bach's time signature from 6/4 to 3/4 for the sake of, as he states in the score, "convenience in performance." In a letter to his publisher Novello of June 23, 1922, Elgar estimated that this alteration would "save ½ the time & trouble in rehearsing." See Moore 1987, 824.

41. For a re-release of this disc, which also includes the fugue, see *Johann Sebastian Bach: Great Orchestral Transcriptions* (Biddulph Recordings: BID 83069/70). Elgar made a separate recording of the fantasy in 1923. See Moore 1974, 49 and 59.

As the music continues, the volume steadily increases until the deceptive cadence two bars before rehearsal no. 8, which is preceded by the first harp glissando in the arrangement. These are also the instruments used to enhance the inverted statement of the "sigh" figure between rehearsals nos. 12 and 13, but this time in the form of loud, blocked chords. The true point of climax occurs at the second big deceptive cadence at rehearsal no. 19, where the low brass shines through à la Wagner. By the authentic cadence two measures later, the sound has died down to *piano*, and for the most unusual link between fantasy and fugue that follows, a solo oboe (which plays an inverted mordent of Elgar's devising) is delicately accompanied by harp harmonics. The concluding *pianissimo* marking serves as the perfect foil to the *fortissimo* start of the fugue.

The exquisite transition composed by Bach between these movements (mm. 47–48 of the original version of the fantasy) proved to be something of a sticking point—and an amusing one at that—between Elgar and his publisher Novello. Elgar had suggested that he be paid the same one hundred guineas as for his orchestration of the fugue, yet the firm initially agreed only on the condition that the half cadence provided by Bach at the very end of the fantasy be replaced with an authentic cadence. Elgar replied on June 16, 1922, in no uncertain terms: "I cannot add anything to the Bach Fantasia—I have orchestrated it as it stands & an *ending* wd. be out of place. I really think I ought to receive the same fee as for the fugue."[42] This was all the convincing that Novello needed from its most popular composer, as Elgar's check was delivered to him the very next day. An accompanying note explained the firm's previous position: "Our idea was that the fantasy cannot possibly be as successful *commercially* as the Fugue, because it cannot be performed by itself, as it has no ending other than the Fugue which follows it."[43] Feeling guilty, or at least conscientious, Elgar returned the check three days later, along with some most revealing comments:

> I began the fantasia before I "did" the fugue—but dropped it. Your Mr. West (?) & some one else (Harold Brooke *I think*) said "Why not 'do' the fantasia?" I am not trying in the least to shift the responsibility (if there's any) on to anyone else. I cannot ask you for a fee which you cannot see your way to recover from the public. As I said before, the actual work was more arduous than that required by the fugue.... Here is my proposition: let sufficient M.S. copies be made, entirely at my expense, for Dr. [Herbert] Brewer's Gloucester festival performance (which is announced) & after that I will "scrap" the whole thing & we will say no more about it. How will that do?[44]

The check made its way back to Elgar for good on the following day, causing him to write, somewhat tongue in cheek: "All right: many thanks. Here's the formal receipt & the

---

42. Moore 1987, 821.
43. Ibid., 822.
44. Ibid.

agreement shall follow. I am, of course, hard up (more or less) but I didn't want my memory to be cursed by generations of impoverished shareholders."[45] Later that year, Novello would publish Elgar's orchestration of the fantasy, along with that of the fugue, as the composer's op. 86.

We learn from this exchange two important facts about what is arguably the greatest Bach transcription of the twentieth century. First and most important, Elgar had already attempted an arrangement of the fantasy before he took on the fugue, but for whatever reasons decided to abandon the project. Second, his decision to return to the fantasy had been prompted, at least in part, by a suggestion made by the Novello staff, who surely were hoping for a repeat of the "commercial success" they had enjoyed with Elgar's fugue transcription. Why this information has gone virtually unnoticed in the musicological literature is a bit of a mystery.

---

45. Ibid., 823.

7

Aspects of Reception from Bach's Day to the Present

GIVEN THE LARGE quantity and high quality of Bach's organ works, it is hardly surprising that for centuries they have garnered the attention—and usually the admiration—of performers, composers, scholars, critics, and music lovers in general. The thirteen analyses offered here represent especially interesting examples of this phenomenon, whether in the domain of classical music or, in certain instances, popular culture. I have gathered and synthesized as much new information as possible, in addition to providing my own thoughts, and I have drawn from a wide variety of musical and cultural contexts, including film, literature, politics, and rock music. Unlike the previous four chapters of this book, these case studies are organized according to works rather than individuals, although the individuals cited include many of the greatest luminaries in music history. The order is that of the Bach-Werke-Verzeichnis (BWV).

THE SIX TRIO SONATAS, BWV 525–30

"In addition to the chorale settings and variations that Bach wrote for the organ...various trios have become known, particularly six for two manuals and pedal that are written in such *galant* style that they still sound very good, and never grow old, but on the contrary will outlive all revolutions of fashion in music."[1] Writing in 1788, this anonymous prognosticator (probably Bach's son Carl Philipp Emanuel) rather missed his mark as far

---

1. David and Mendel 1998, 406.

as organ playing is concerned, because organists basically ignored Bach's trio sonatas until the early twentieth century. This neglect may be attributed to the notion (going back to Forkel) that the pieces were intended merely as exercises; they also constitute some of the most technically demanding works ever written for the organ. They remain the ultimate test of coordinating hands and feet, due to the composer's tendency toward fast figuration in all three parts, with the hands crossed. As Hubert Parry opined roughly a hundred years ago, "these Sonatas gain quite a special character from the manner in which Bach makes use of the device of crossing the hands and interlacing the parts which are given to them. It seems, indeed, to be his cue in these works, and the effect is to make the works extraordinarily serviceable to develop independence of hand and feet."[2]

The remarkable Elizabeth Stirling, who was still a teenager at the time, is documented to have played the second, fifth, and sixth sonatas in London in 1838.[3] But the first two organists who exerted any influence in championing the collection were both continentals. One, Carl August Haupt (1810–91), was based in Berlin, and his students there included John Knowles Paine and Wilhelm Middelschulte, both of whom would go on to enrich musical life in America with their performances of these works—even if Middelschulte specialized in the slow movements.[4] Middelschulte's prize pupil was Virgil Fox, who regularly featured the fast movements of the sonatas, at breakneck speed, on his legendary "Heavy Organ" programs.

The other organist in question was the Belgian virtuoso Jacques-Nicolas Lemmens (1823–81). Lemmens could play all the trio sonatas from memory, and he must have instilled in his pupils a special passion for this music as well.[5] His most important pupil, Charles-Marie Widor, was renowned for his meticulously phrased renditions of the set, and Widor expected nothing less from his multitudinous students.[6] One of the most prominent of these, Albert Schweitzer, proclaimed in his monograph on Bach, published originally in 1905, that

> To this very day [the trio sonatas] are the *Gradus ad Parnassum* for every organist. Whoever has studied them thoroughly will find scarcely a single difficulty in the old or even in modern organ music that he has not met with there and learned to overcome; and before all he will have attained that absolute precision that is the chief essential for good organ playing, since in this complicated trio-playing the slightest unevenness in touch is heard with appalling clearness.[7]

---

2. Parry 1909, 501.

3. Barger 2007, 82.

4. On Middelschulte, see the repertoire list in Meyer 2007, 383–433. On Paine, see Owen 2003, 8.

5. Douglass 1980, vol. 1, 76.

6. Hiemke 1994, 111.

7. Schweitzer 1911, vol. 1, 279.

Essentially this same encomium would reappear eight years later in the edition of the trio sonatas prepared jointly by Schweitzer and Widor (vol. 5 of their edition of Bach's complete organ works). Seven years later, in 1920, another Widor pupil performed all six pieces on a series of recitals at the Paris Conservatory in which he played all of Bach's organ works from memory.[8] The performer was Marcel Dupré, whose use of the sonatas as pedagogical material may be demonstrated by how he (sadistically) taught them to the young Virgil Fox in the early 1930s: Fox had to learn all six works, one movement per week, and would occasionally be asked by his maître on the spot to transpose them into another key, often without the music![9]

Organists may have been slow in warming to the trio sonatas, but no other Bach organ works have been transcribed so often or for so many different combinations of instruments. Considering that movements from nos. 1, 2, and 4 appear to have originated as chamber music, it is only natural that most of these arrangements have been for some type of chamber ensemble.[10] This tradition, which has lived on in recent times with such groups as the Palladian Ensemble, can be traced back to around 1750, when an anonymous transcriber adapted the outer movements of the first sonata, transposed to C major, for violin, cello, and double bass.[11] To form a three-movement "concerto," he also included the slow movement of the A-major flute sonata, BWV 1032. Another relatively early arrangement is one of the entire collection for two harpsichords. This adaptation is probably the work of Carl Philipp Emanuel or Wilhelm Friedemann Bach, and it may reflect how the composer and his progeny enjoyed these pieces as *Hausmusik*.[12] The first harpsichord plays the top and bottom voices, while the second plays the middle and bottom voices. During the 1770s and 1780s, this arrangement was heard in the salons of Fanny von Arnstein in Berlin and of Gottfried van Swieten in Vienna. It was also presumably for van Swieten's salon that three movements (the second and third of no. 2 and the second of no. 3) were transcribed for violin, viola, and double bass. These arrangements have traditionally been ascribed to Mozart—they are catalogued as part of the K. 404[a] set—but there is no hard evidence that he had anything to do with them.

The first complete edition of the trio sonatas, published in London in 1809–10, constitutes a further transcription, courtesy of Samuel Wesley and C. F. Horn.[13] Printed like Bach's original organ score, but in a country where the art of organ pedaling was largely unknown at the time, it was intended for "three hands upon the pianoforte," with the top

8. Murray 1985, 61–66.

9. Curley 1998, 59 n. 6.

10. Williams 2003, 10, 14, and 23–24.

11. Kilian 1988, 70–71. Between 1995 and 2006 the Palladian Ensemble recorded all six of the trio sonatas (Linn Records CKD 036 and 275).

12. Kilian 1988, 98–100.

13. Ibid., 61–62. For facsimile reproductions of the first two pages of this print, see Kassler 2004, between 234 and 235.

voice simply played an octave higher than notated. As for later arrangements, the trio sonatas experienced a brief vogue as orchestral repertory at the turn of the twentieth century. H. H. Wetzler's orchestration of the first sonata was heard in New York, while in the early days of the Proms, Henry Wood's arrangements of the Andante of no. 4 and the Vivace of no. 6 delighted Queen's Hall audiences.[14] Another devotee of the sixth sonata was Béla Bartók, who shortly before 1930 transcribed all three movements for piano, two hands.[15] With its frequent octave doublings and occasional added harmonies, this arrangement makes enormous demands on the performer, which may explain why Bartók himself never played it in public. The many added accents and articulation markings impart to the transcription the same "percussive" quality found in Bartók's own compositions.

THE PRELUDE AND FUGUE IN D MAJOR, BWV 532

The Göttinger Bach-Katalog lists seventeen manuscript sources for this work, eleven of which contain only the fugue. This is an indication that the prelude and fugue originated at different times and that the fugue was by far the better known of the two movements during the eighteenth and early nineteenth centuries. By 1900 the fugue had achieved such popularity that Vincent D'Indy could call it "a battle horse for modern organists."[16] He might also have remarked that the fugue is Bach's ultimate pedal showpiece. As such, it was featured on organ (and pedal-piano) concerts given in Paris by Alkan, Guilmant, Hesse, Saint-Saëns, and Widor.[17] Widor, who, like Alkan, Hesse, and Saint-Saëns, rendered the fugue without the prelude, maintained that it was one of only four Bach organ fugues that could be played "briskly" without obscuring the polyphony.[18] In England, meanwhile, the movement had become known as Bach's "Concert Fugue in D," probably because of Griepenkerl's peculiar idea that the word "Concertato" found in one of the sources implied use outside church.[19] Harvey Grace felt compelled to set the words "That's THAT!" to the final pedal leap of the fugue, while, several decades later, the German recitalist Karl Richter was known to push himself off the bench with the last pedal note and simultaneously spin around, landing on the floor behind the console and then taking a bow—all in one rapid motion.[20]

---

14. Greer 2003, 61 and 98–99; Hull 1929, 157–58; and Grace 1922b, 179.

15. Somfai 1995, 692–96. For a recent recording, see *Petronel Malan: Transfigured Bach* (hänssler CLASSIC CD 98.424). This disc also includes Dinu Lipatti's piano transcription of the Pastorale in F Major, BWV 590.

16. D'Indy 1903–50, vol. 1, 80.

17. See, respectively, Eddie 2007, 21–22; Ellis 2005, 86; Busch 2003, 125; Smith 1992, 30 and 35; and Smith 1995, 289.

18. Smith 1999, 74–75. The other three fugues in question are the Fugue in G Major, BWV 541/2; the Fugue in C Major, BWV 564/3, and the Fugue in D Minor, BWV 565/2.

19. Statham 1909, 66; and Grace 1922b, 52–53.

20. Grace 1922b, 59; and Setchell 2008, 10.

Such showmanship would have been anathema to Albert Schweitzer, who was also the first to suggest (and rightly so) that the fugue is the weaker movement from a compositional perspective.[21] But the prelude was one of his very favorite recital offerings, and he played it to the near exclusion of its partner: more than forty performances are documented, only one of which includes the fugue. What especially attracted him to the prelude was its "wonderful pathos," a reference unquestionably to the concluding Adagio section, whose minor tonality, dissonant harmonies, and thick double-pedal texture are diametrically opposed to the movement as a whole.

Little could Schweitzer have foreseen that this same music, because of its "pathetic" nature, would figure in one of the most famous scenes in all of cinema, the climactic five-minute-long baptism sequence toward the end of Francis Ford Coppola's *The Godfather*, released in 1972. Also featuring Bach's Passacaglia in C Minor as well as organ music presumably written by Nino Rota, the composer of the film's score, this scene qualifies as the most effective use of Bach's organ music anywhere in the movie genre. As film scholar Royal Brown has written:

Coppola mixes flamboyant crosscutting with almost imperceptible metamorphoses on the music track to suggest the final transformation of Michael Corleone (Al Pacino) into the new godfather. The sequence begins with a long shot of the interior of a cathedral in which Michael's nephew (also named Michael) is being baptized, with Michael standing as godfather. On the (apparently diegetic) music track, a solo organ modulates athematically through a series of major-mode chords. Some twenty-four seconds later, following a close-up of the baby Michael, the sequence cuts away for the first time to the preparations for what will become a series of five rubouts. But although we see the arms and hands of a killer preparing his weapon, we still hear the voice of the priest reciting the baptismal ceremony. And we still hear the organ music, although the tone has become slightly more ominous through the modulation to a minor-mode chord. This carefully choreographed pattern will continue: throughout the sequence, the crosscutting between the baptism and the executions moves along its ironic course, accelerating as the moments of the actual shootings approach. Never leaving the solo organ, on the other hand, the music seems to emanate solely from the church, although it backs both the baptism and the killings. A careful listening, however, reveals that if the timbres of the music belong to the church, the harmonies, form, and, ultimately, genre belong increasingly to the rubouts. Once the camera returns to the church following the first cutaway (described above), for instance, the music begins to suggest the passacaglia from Johann Sebastian Bach's famous Passacaglia and Fugue in G Minor [*sic*], a morose work decidedly unsuitable for a baptism. During the third cutaway, which begins with Albert Neri (Richard

---

21. Schweitzer 1911, vol. 1, 269; and Schützeichel 1991, 19–68 (esp. 50) and 164.

Bright) taking a gun and a policeman's badge out of a bag, the passacaglia solidly establishes its identity. The music has moved into its second phase.

But the musical metamorphoses do not stop here, even though *The Godfather*'s end titles attribute the music for the "baptism sequence" simply to "J. S. Bach." In the next (fourth) cutaway, which begins with Barzini (Richard Conte) walking toward the screen, the music enters a third phase by actually switching genres into what might be called "silent-film doom-and-gloom," which begins to swell in the lower registers of the organ. In the next baptism shots the diegetic sound of baby Michael's crying adds an additional note of tension as the organ continues to crescendo. Then, preceding the first and second rubouts (the sixth and seventh cutaways), the organ, in classic silent-film fashion, crescendos to a sustained chord that acts as a prelude for each of the murders, which also, for the first time, include diegetic sound (gunshots, screams). By the end of the fifth rubout (Barzini's), the organ music metamorphoses back into its second phase, moving to the end of Bach's passacaglia. A sustained seventh chord accompanies the final cutaway (a series of three corpse shots) and then a shot of Michael with a candle in the foreground. A cut to the exterior of the cathedral, with its bell tolling, signals the end of this virtuoso sequence in which even diegetic sound—the baby's crying (all shots of the infant show an entirely placid, sleeping child), the church bells—tends, as a kind of musique concrète, to slip away from the diegesis.[22]

Trenchant analysis, to be sure, but Brown's remarks on the purely musical elements of this scene deserve to be corrected and qualified, starting with his misidentification of the key of the Passacaglia.[23] What he perceives as a "minor-mode chord" early on in the sequence is actually the first of two excerpts from the Passacaglia (mm. 20–25). And this excerpt does continue to sound, ever so briefly, "once the camera returns to the church following the first cutaway," where Brown senses merely a suggestion of the work. But he is absolutely right that "during the third cutaway…the passacaglia establishes its identity," since for most of this excerpt (mm. 1–6 and 8–11) all that is heard is the work's theme, as opposed to one of the variations. Beyond this point, and contrary to what Brown states ("moving to the end of Bach's passacaglia"), the Passacaglia never returns.

The end titles attribute the music to Bach alone because the scene contains roughly a minute's worth of material not only from the Passacaglia but also from the D-major prelude. Brown identifies the latter as generic "silent-film" music, surely owing to the high-pitched diminished-seventh chord in the middle of m. 97 and probably also the thirty-second-note scale passage that precedes it. In actuality, once Michael says for the first time "I do renounce him," in response to the priest's question "Michael Francis Rizzi,

---

22. R. Brown 1994, 80–81.
23. The same mistake occurs in Cooke 2008, 378.

do you renounce Satan?" the last eleven bars of the prelude are played, and with a louder, brighter organ registration than before. (Between this question and answer, we hear a brief passage inspired by m. 97 of Bach's prelude, one that begins with the same sort of flourish and continues with diminished-seventh chords on F-sharp and E-sharp.) Rather than one continuous segment, two distinct excerpts are heard. The first begins on the second beat of m. 97 and extends to the downbeat of m. 102, while the priest asks "And all his works?" Without any musical accompaniment, Michael answers "I do renounce them." Then the second excerpt commences, starting on beat three of m. 102 and continuing until the end of the prelude, although Bach's concluding D-major triad is barely heard before the music segues into a dissonant chord that lasts until the sequence is over. Brown may be correct in hearing a "sustained seventh chord" here, as this final sonority appears to include a diminished-seventh chord.

THE PRELUDE AND FUGUE IN E MINOR, BWV 533

The "Cathedral" Prelude and Fugue (or the "Little E Minor" or "Nightwatchman") remains to this day one of Bach's most frequently performed organ compositions. One reason, no doubt, is ease of performance. The work circulated throughout Germany in the eighteenth and early nineteenth centuries, becoming a favorite of the young Mendelssohn. Ever since 1858, when Louis Niedermeyer published the piece in his church-music journal *La Maîtrise*, it has also been very popular with French organists. Probably inspired by Niedermeyer's example, César Franck in 1859 seems to have played it for the inauguration of Cavaillé-Coll's organ at Sainte-Clotilde, and in the following decades Franck would teach the work to his organ students at the Paris Conservatory. By 1865 it had been adapted for household use in an arrangement for piano and harmonium by Clément Loret, the organ instructor at the school of church music founded by Niedermeyer.[24] More than a thousand people heard Jules Grison essay the piece in 1878 on the huge Cavaillé-Coll at the Trocadéro, although one critic objected to how the performer "transposed an octave higher the beginning and other parts of the fugue, whose melancholy character hardly calls for a change."[25]

Today, players correctly render the mordents in the fugue subject as starting on the beat and using A-natural, since A-sharp would suggest B minor as the home key. There was scarcely any such norm in earlier times, as may be seen by comparing Niedermeyer's edition with that of J. F. Bridge and James Higgs, issued in the 1880s by Novello: the latter advocates A-sharp, while in the former these same ornaments are realized as inverted mordents (B, C-natural, and B).[26] Such was the influence of Niedermeyer's edition in

24. Ferrard 1991, 164.
25. Smith 1995, 294.
26. On Niedermeyer's edition, see Smith 1999, 509–10.

France that, according to Louis Vierne, most organists around 1920 still performed the ornaments this way. Vierne, in his own edition, recommended the correct practice, but he recorded the fugue with the mordents starting before the beat and using A-sharp, because, amusingly enough, the organ's A-natural refused to speak. Roughly fifty years earlier, the Bach biographer Philipp Spitta had maintained that the fugue's effect would be "grievously impaired" with A-sharps in the subject, implying that the work was commonly played that way in Germany.[27]

THE TOCCATA AND FUGUE IN F MAJOR, BWV 540

This toccata is Bach's longest organ prelude, not to mention one of his most virtuosic. Consequently, it has been played throughout much of music history to the near exclusion of its partner, which might be regarded as one of the finest organ fugues that Bach ever wrote. This trend seems to have begun, shortly after the publication of the work in Leipzig around 1832, with the Breslau organist Adolph Friedrich Hesse.[28]

The information is sketchy, but there is reason to believe that for the first ten years of his career as a concert organist, Hesse played virtually no legitimate organ music by Bach, relying instead on the Well-Tempered Clavier.[29] For his six-week tour of Germany in the spring of 1838, however, his Bach repertoire contained some of the composer's most demanding preludes and fugues for the organ (BWV 541, 543, 546, and 548, and probably also 542) as well as the F-major toccata. As a seasoned concert artist, Hesse undoubtedly chose the latter for the crowd-pleasing potential of its two long pedal solos. Six years later, in what was a watershed in the reception of Bach's oeuvre in France, Hesse's footwork amazed a Parisian audience of seven thousand—which included Berlioz and possibly Chopin as well—when he played the toccata for the inauguration of the Daublaine-Callinet organ at Saint Eustache.[30] Although it has been suggested otherwise,[31] Hesse was not "handicapped" by a pedalboard whose top note was middle C, because he would have played the version of the toccata in which Bach's wide-ranging pedal part was rewritten precisely for a pedalboard of this sort (see chap. 1). The standard, authentic version of the movement would not be published until the following year, in volume 3 of the Peters edition of Bach's complete organ works.

---

27. Spitta 1873–79, vol. 1, 402 n. 18.

28. Kilian 1978–79, 260–61.

29. See the discussion of Hesse's concert repertoire in Seyfried 1965, 12–33. See also Glöckner et al. 2007, 663–67.

30. On the possibility that Chopin attended this performance, see Rottermund 2008. Hesse again rendered the toccata at St. Eustache a couple of weeks later, when he played a farewell concert for a few friends. That program also featured the Prelude and Fugue in A Minor, BWV 543.

31. Douglass 1980, vol. 1, 36.

Hesse's performances of the F-major toccata, whether in Germany or France, presumably inspired other players to learn it. For instance, August Freyer, organist in Warsaw and one of Hesse's closest colleagues, who in the summer of 1849 is known to have played the toccata on his church's organ for the composer Mikhail Glinka—and so "wonderfully" that the Russian was reduced to tears.[32] Three years later, back in Paris, Cavaillé-Coll was raving about a performance of the toccata that Alkan had just given on pedal piano. It is reasonable to assume that Alkan had taken up the movement in response to Hesse's performance in 1844, even if he did not attend, which seems unlikely. At any rate, the toccata became one of Alkan's signature pieces on the Petits Concerts de musique classique that he offered in Paris from 1873 to 1880, and on which he appeared both as a pianist and a pedal pianist.[33] Not by coincidence, another Parisian pedal pianist who was playing the toccata in 1873 was Elie Miriam Delaborde, Alkan's pupil and allegedly his illegitimate son.[34]

This is not to suggest that the toccata was being neglected by the organists of the 1870s. To cite the most prominent example, Anton Bruckner began with this movement when in 1871 he represented his native Austria in a series of demonstration concerts on the new Willis organ at London's Albert Hall.[35] Immediately thereafter, he improvised on the toccata, much to the dismay of the critic who asserted that "nothing can be added to a toccata of Sebastian Bach." At the end of the decade, and once again back in Paris, both Guilmant and Eugène Gigout performed the toccata at the Trocadéro.[36] Guilmant, who made the pedal part even harder by playing m. 348 as a straight scale, used the toccata as the finale to his recitals there, while Gigout began his with the movement, billing it as Bach's Toccata in F "with pedal solos."

Meanwhile, Johannes Brahms had been featuring the "heavenly barrel-organ toccata" (as he called it) on his piano recitals for approximately twenty years.[37] He never bothered to notate this arrangement, which he played everywhere from Budapest to Amsterdam, but he did make some jottings to this effect in Clara Schumann's "Bach book." The piano transcription published in 1884 by Brahms's friend Julius Röntgen provides further clues, such as the use of hemiola phrasing for the pedal solos, as to how Brahms might have performed the toccata. According to eyewitness accounts, he did so at a blistering pace and in a "peculiarly organ-like" manner.

---

32. On Freyer and Hesse, see Rottermund, 83. On Freyer and Glinka, see Zwetzschke 2008, 149.

33. Eddie 2007, 17–24.

34. Delaborde performed a "pedalier-pianoforte" arrangement of the toccata in 1872 at St. James's Hall in London, on a concert sponsored by the local Philharmonic Society. See Foster 1912, 331–34.

35. Howie 2001, 301–8; and Busch 1975, 13. According to Bruckner's heavily annotated personal copy of the toccata, he played it with a liberal use of the heel. For facsimile reproductions of the first two pages of this source, see Horn 1997, 113–14.

36. Ellis 2005, 84–86; and Grace 1922b, 160.

37. Stinson 2006, 126–40; and Stinson 2008, 28–29.

By the turn of the twentieth century, the toccata had fallen victim to modern technology in the form of the *Rollschweller*, a foot-operated device similar to the crescendo pedal that automatically adds or subtracts stops as it is rolled forwards or backwards. Judging from a remark by Albert Schweitzer, organists often used this gadget specifically for the opening two canons: "It is to be hoped that some day the practice will cease of employing the *Rollschweller* at the beginning of the F major toccata, instead of starting with a good *forte* and leaving the *crescendo* to the dramatic unfolding of the canon."[38] The preferred technique, evidently, was to begin each canon quite softly and then gradually build up to full organ by the start of the ensuing pedal solo.

A later proponent of this practice was Virgil Fox, as we learn from Ted Alan Worth's memoir about the artist. Fox happened to be performing the toccata the first time that Worth heard him play, and Worth was more than a little impressed: "With the opening pedal point—thunderingly deep 32-foot stops that shook the building—the canons started as if far in the distance, and began to get louder and more intense with each measure until almost the full organ was on. Suddenly, as every stop was clearly on, the powerful pedal solo began—played completely from memory at a speed I'd never dreamed possible."[39] Some years later, at the dedication of the Aeolian-Skinner organ at Lincoln Center's Philharmonic Hall (now Avery Fisher Hall), Worth again heard Fox essay the movement, but he might have written about that performance that those who live by the crescendo pedal die by the crescendo pedal:

> Virgil must have felt like a racehorse at the starting gate, for when he came out, he tore into the Bach F Major Toccata at a tempo faster than I had ever heard it played. (The word "frantic" comes to mind.) All went well until, during a de-crescendo midway in the work, he closed the crescendo pedal...only to find that no other stops were on. There was dead silence for a second or two, as Virgil's fingers and feet continued to fly over the mute keyboards![40]

The F-major toccata is also a rare example of a Bach organ work other than the Toccata and Fugue in D Minor, BWV 565, that has been appropriated by a rock band.[41] The band, as any baby boomer reading this book probably knows, is Emerson, Lake and Palmer, and the song is "The Only Way (Hymn)," from the group's 1971 album *Tarkus*. For the first

---

38. Schweitzer 1911, vol. I, 305.

39. Torrence and Yeager 2001, 13. Fox rendered the beginning of the Prelude in A Minor, BWV 543/1, essentially the same way, as may be heard on the recording of his "Heavy Organ" concert at San Francisco's Winterland (Decca DL 75323).

40. Ibid., 167.

41. The only other example that comes to mind is the *Orgelbüchlein* setting of "Durch Adams Fall ist ganz verderbt," as arranged by the progressive-rock trio Egg (see the track "Boilk" from the album *the polite force*). This work was chosen, no doubt, because of its extreme chromaticism.

forty seconds of this track, Keith Emerson plays the first of the two introductory canons on a real pipe organ (that at the London parish of St. Mark's, Finchley), thus underscoring the allusion to the Christian church that is already clear from the song's subtitle. But this is no ordinary song of praise. Instead, it is a "hymn to agnostic humanism" loaded with such simplistic rhymes as "Can you believe God makes you breathe? Why did He lose six million Jews?"[42] And the unspoken irony provided by the organ introduction is only heightened by the fact that a "paragon of Protestant piety" like Johann Sebastian Bach is its author (Bach is referenced again in the middle of the track, with a quotation for piano, bass, and drums from the Well-Tempered Clavier). Otherwise, Emerson's "reception" of Bach's organ works, excluding the Toccata and Fugue in D Minor, is linked to his cocaine habit, circa 1977, as he regularly received the drug through the mail in box sets of *The Complete Organ Works of Bach*![43] In tribute, he suggested *The Works of Emerson, Lake and Palmer* as the title for one of the group's promotional tours.

THE FANTASY AND FUGUE IN G MINOR, BWV 542

Of the thirty-five extant manuscripts of this celebrated work, a whopping twenty-seven contain the fugue only, indicating that it was at one time much better known than the fantasy and that the two movements originated as independent pieces.[44] Indeed, they may not have been paired until after Bach's death. In preparing one of his two copies of the fugue—and in a rare instance of a scribe enthusing over the work being copied—the Hamburg organist J. S. Borsch (ca. 1744–1804) dubbed this movement "the very best pedal piece of Mr. Johann Sebastian Bach." He probably had in mind not only the overall quality of the music but also the fugue's brilliant pedal part. By 1812 the fugue had become standard fare as an instrumental transcription at the Berlin Singakademie, and the Prussian capital is also where, in 1829, the movement was first published, in A. W. Bach's anthology *Orgel-Stücke für das Konzert*. Four years later, Felix Mendelssohn and the theorist Adolph Bernhard Marx issued both the fugue and the fantasy, but as separate pieces, in the collection *Johann Sebastian Bach's noch wenig bekannte Orgelcompositionen*. The two movements were not printed as a prelude-fugue pair until 1844, in volume 2 of the Peters edition of Bach's complete organ works.

Both the fantasy and the fugue, of course, went on to become staples of the organ literature, to the extent that the first several measures of the fantasy served for more than

---

42. Macan 2006, 159–61.

43. Emerson 2004, 306. Emerson first appropriated the toccata and fugue as a member of The Nice, playing two quotations from the work on the track "Rondo," from the album *The Thoughts of Emerlist Davjack* (1967). According to Macan 2006, 553, he sometimes played these same excerpts when Emerson, Lake, and Palmer performed live.

44. Bates 2008, 2–3; Stauffer 1980, 110; Kilian 1978–79, 110; Stinson 2006, 22 and 32; and Schünemann 1928, 145–46.

twenty-five years as the opening theme of John Obetz's weekly radio show *The Auditorium Organ*. Unlike Edward Elgar (see chap. 6), but like practically every other organist who has performed the movement, Obetz rendered this material at full volume, thereby invoking the stereotype of sinister-sounding chords played "with all the stops pulled out." Roughly a century earlier, C. A. Haupt was playing the entire movement this way, with nary a manual change. His pupil Arthur Bird found the effect downright monolithic: "the fantasie he played organo pleno from beginning to end without any change...like a massive granite building with a rigid cold façade."[45]

Widor and Schweitzer, conversely, recommended a multitude of registration changes, not to mention the frequent use of the swell pedal, even where such pedipulation seems out of the question. To quote from the preface to their edition, "During the course of measures 31–34 the swell box opens. In order that the right foot may be free to work the swell pedal, the last three and the first two eighths in the bass in these measures should regularly be taken by the left foot."[46] These measures are reproduced in example 7.1, both to help the reader visualize these outrageously difficult foot crossings and to show how Bach writes his own crescendo here by gradually thickening the texture from three to six voices. The latter technique enhances one of the longest circle-of-fifths progression in

EXAMPLE 7.1. Fantasy in G Minor, BWV 542/1, mm. 31–35

Bach's entire output, one that in the span of only four bars modulates from D major all the way to D-flat major. Vincent D'Indy hailed the passage as "a unique example in the history of the organ," whereas its pedal line made Harvey Grace pine for a pedalboard with four octaves, so that "the scale might be carried down in one sweep."[47]

Explaining the popularity of the fugue in the early twentieth century, Grace rightly observed that "in melody and rhythm the subject is one of the most attractive ever devised" and that the treatment of the subject is "marked by a clarity and finish that defy criticism."[48] He acknowledged, too, that the movement was esteemed "even in the most unlikely quarters," probably an allusion to Dan Godfrey's arrangement for military band.

45. Bird 1915, 140.

46. Widor and Schweitzer 1913, xii.

47. D'Indy 1903–50, vol. 2, 81; and Grace 1922b, 166.

48. Grace 1922b, 169–70; Grace 1922a, 22; and Hull 1929, 186.

Perhaps it comes as an even greater surprise that the first twelve notes of the subject are quoted during the second act of Gilbert and Sullivan's *The Mikado*, while the title character patters on about the music-hall singer who for his "crimes" is forced to attend "a series / Of masses and fugues and 'ops' / By Bach, interwoven / With Spohr and Beethoven / At classical Monday Pops." As an organist, Arthur Sullivan must have taken particular pleasure in making this citation.

THE SIX GREAT PRELUDES AND FUGUES, BWV 543–48

Known by this nickname for most of the nineteenth century, these works originated as independent compositions, and there is no evidence that Bach himself ever assembled them into any kind of group.[49] Rather, that distinction seems to belong to Bach's pupil Johann Philipp Kirnberger, since the earliest source in which these pieces are found as a self-contained collection is a manuscript prepared sometime after Bach's death by Kirnberger and one of his scribes. Bearing an ornate title page in Kirnberger's hand that reads *Praeludia und Fugen für die Orgel von Hrn. Joh: Seb: Bach*, the manuscript was copied for the music library of Princess Anna Amalia of Prussia, which Kirnberger supervised from 1758 until his death in 1783. In this source, the works appear in the order BWV 545, 546, 547, 548, 543, and 544. Kirnberger probably devised this rising key sequence (C major–C minor–C major–E minor–A minor–B minor) in imitation of two authentic keyboard collections by Bach, the Well-Tempered Clavier and the Inventions and Sinfonias.

The first edition was brought out in 1812, not in Berlin but in Vienna, with the pieces now presented in the alphabetical key sequence of the BWV and titled *Sechs Praeludien und SECHS FUGEN für Orgel oder Pianoforte mit Pedal von Johann Sebastian Bach*.[50] Observe the capitalization of the words "sechs Fugen," which represents an era that viewed Bach almost exclusively as a composer of fugal polyphony, to the degree that any organ work by him could be called a "fugue." But the title is misleading, at least in the context of musical life in Vienna at the time, in its mention only of organ and pedal piano as performance media, because there were few players in the city who could have negotiated such demanding pedal parts and probably no instruments there, either organs or pedal pianos, with a full two-octave pedalboard.[51] Instead, the average Viennese customer would have used a normal piano, either unassisted, in which case it would often have been impossible to play all the notes written (due to those same demanding pedal parts), or

49. Kilian 1978–79, 15–16, 51, 107–8, 217–19, 256–57, and 271; Kilian 1988, 98–100; Schmieder 1990, 513; Thistlethwaite 1990, 169–71; Palmer 1997, 197; and Stinson 2006, 108.

50. In sequencing the large free organ works for the BWV, published in 1950, Wolfgang Schmieder merely duplicated the order used by Wilhelm Rust for vol. 15 of the Bachgesellschaft edition, published in 1867. In sequencing the Six Great Preludes and Fugues, Rust obviously followed the order of the first edition.

51. Biba 1978, 31–33; and Blanken 2011.

with a second player for the pedal line. Only in the case of Simon Sechter's four-hand arrangements of the first four works from the set, however, have any of these performances been preserved in the form of notated transcriptions.[52]

The music most likely made its way from Berlin to Vienna through the agency of Baron Gottfried van Swieten—the same early-music enthusiast in whose Viennese salon Mozart famously heard "nothing but Handel and Bach." For in his capacity as the Austrian ambassador to Berlin during the 1770s, van Swieten belonged to Anna Amalia's circle, and, like Amalia herself, he was even one of Kirnberger's music students.[53] To judge from these circumstances, the "half dozen fugues by Bach" played by Beethoven at van Swieten's residence as a "good night blessing" may have been none other than the Six Great.[54] Perhaps the anonymous string arrangements of two of the fugues from the collection (those in C minor and E minor) housed today in Vienna at the Österreichische Nationalbibliothek were also fashioned for performance at van Swieten's.[55]

The set was reissued, either as a reprint or a revised edition, nine different times between 1815 and 1852, which means that these were by far the most widely circulated of any of Bach's organ works during this period. Of particular interest, in terms of performance practice, is the reprint published in 1836 by the London house of Coventry & Hollier, as Book 2 of the series *John Sebastian Bach's Grand Studies for the Organ*, since it includes "A Separate Part for the Double Bass or Violoncello, Arranged from the Pedale by SIGNOR DRAGONETTI." The double-bass virtuoso Domenico Dragonetti, that is, who carefully rewrote the pedal parts of all six pieces (indeed, of all nineteen *pedaliter* works in the series) to range only as low as G, thereby allowing for performance on a three-stringed instrument with the bottom string tuned down a step from its normal pitch.[56] Dragonetti is known to have played these arrangements at various concert venues in London and to have rehearsed them on the very premises of the publisher, with the composer John Barnett at the piano.[57]

A slightly later edition, dating from before 1848, and the second of two issued by the Viennese firm of Haslinger, is noteworthy for its added dynamics, phrasings, fingerings, and tempo markings. The rather detailed crescendo and decrescendo indications found throughout—four of the movements end, curiously, with a lengthy *decrescendo*—are undoubtedly intended for pianists and not organists, and this must also be true of the brisk metronome markings, especially where the preludes are concerned.[58] For example,

---

52. On Sechter's arrangements, see Zenck 1986, 105.

53. Marshall 1998, 61–62.

54. On this anecdote, see Leisinger 2006, 5.

55. On these manuscripts, see Leisinger 2006, 6.

56. Palmer 1997, 197–98.

57. Buckley 1905, 1; and Young 1955, 21.

58. On this point, see also Thistlethwaite 1990, 520, where the date given for this print is erroneously that of the *first* edition published by Haslinger.

the B-minor prelude is to be played at ♪ = 100, the C-minor at ♩ = 116, the C-major "9/8" at ♩. = 80, and the E-minor at ♩ = 88.

When, in 1844, these six pieces were published, along with four others, in volume 2 of the Peters edition of Bach's complete organ works, F. C. Griepenkerl advocated significantly slower tempos: for the B-minor prelude, ♪ = 80; for the C-minor, ♩ = 66; for the C-major "9/8," ♪ = 126; and for the E-minor, ♩ = 60. He explained himself first with the general remark that "A large space and a large instrument (church and organ) require a slower tempo for a musical work than a cramped space and an instrument with little volume."[59] Then, after listing his suggested metronome markings, he commented specifically on performing the music at the piano: "On the pianoforte all these pieces must be taken faster, but not at such an exaggerated speed that they lose their sublime character."[60] He did not explain why he began the volume with the Prelude and Fugue in C Major, BWV 545, and ended it, after four intervening pieces, with the other five preludes and fugues in the sequence BWV 546 (C minor), 547 (C major), 543 (A minor), 548 (E minor), and 544 (B minor), but this fragmented and seemingly arbitrary ordering scheme implies a certain skepticism about the validity of the Six Great as a collection.

Meanwhile, during the years 1844 and 1845, and far from the European mainstream, one Iwan Karlowitsch Tscherlizkij (1799–1865), an organist and pianist based in St. Petersburg, was busy issuing his two-hand piano arrangements of all six pieces, thereby beginning a series of transcriptions that would ultimately cover no fewer than eighty-five organ works by Bach.[61] His arrangements of the Six Great, therefore, were the first for the piano ever to be published, predating Franz Liszt's by several years. Russian musicologists have been justifiably proud of this fact, yet they have not considered the very real possibility that Tscherlizkij got the idea for this project only after hearing Liszt perform his transcriptions.[62] And if Tscherlizkij's arrangement of the A-minor prelude and fugue is any indication, he may even have modeled his transcription style after Liszt's: essentially the only added material in either arrangement involves the use of left-hand octaves to play the pedal line, a practice that is at once an idiomatic piano technique and an effective simulation of 16′ organ stops.[63]

---

59. "Ein grosser Raum und ein grosses Instrument (Kirche und Orgel) fordern eine langsamere Bewegung des Tonstücks als ein enger Raum und ein Instrument mit kleinem Ton."

60. "Auf dem Fortepiano muss man die Stücke sämtlich schneller nehmen, doch dürfen sie auch da durch übertriebene Geschwindigkeit den Charakter des Erhabenen nicht verlieren..."

61. Rojsman 2001, 209–13; and Zwetzschke 2008, 42–44 and 185.

62. Liszt concertized in St. Petersburg in 1842 and 1843. See Walker 1988–97, vol. 1, 295. On Liszt's performances of the Six Great in Berlin during the winter of 1841–42, see Stinson 2006, 105–6.

63. Tscherlizkij's transcription of the A-minor prelude and fugue appears in the anthology of his Bach transcriptions published in 1952 by Musgis and edited by Leonid Rojsman. I have not seen his transcriptions of any of the other five works.

Whereas Tscherlizkij's arrangements never really circulated outside his homeland, Liszt's transcriptions of the Six Great were known throughout the world.[64] They quickly entered the repertoire of such leading pianists as Carl Czerny and Hans von Bülow (Liszt's teacher and pupil, respectively), and eventually even Clara Schumann (one of Liszt's strongest detractors for most of his career). In addition, they were performed by Liszt's young students at the master classes he gave for them, toward the end of his life, in Weimar, Rome, and Budapest.

Another nineteenth-century musician who knew the Six Great—and who by the middle of the 1850s had become a staunch advocate for the music of Bach—was Richard Wagner. For one thing, Wagner's personal copy of Liszt's transcriptions of these works has survived.[65] For another, the diaries of Wagner's wife Cosima, who was also Liszt's daughter, document various performances of the Six Great in the couple's presence by the pianist Joseph Rubinstein. (It is unclear whether Rubinstein was playing from Wagner's score, from a score of his own, or from memory.) In terms of compositional influence, scholars have recently suggested that certain ritornello forms found in Wagner's later operas were informed by his study of Bach, and they have pointed to the B-minor prelude from the Six Great as a movement that might have specifically factored in this process.[66] The C-minor and E-minor preludes from this collection would have to qualify, too, as they represent equally grand ritornello structures. In any case, Bach's music proved to be a decisive catalyst in the formation of Wagner's late style, to the extent that, in Wagner's own words, it "predestined" his all-important concept of "endless melody."[67]

In view of Wagner's imposing stature as an artist, it seems appropriate to consider each one of Cosima's diary entries pertaining to the Six Great Preludes and Fugues. Presumably the first was penned early in 1871, at the couple's villa in Tribschen, when the guest of honor was the young conductor Hans Richter, who five years later would conduct the first complete *Ring* cycle at Bayreuth. Richter and Wagner were already well acquainted, and we know that a few years earlier, when Richter was working for Wagner as a copyist, they had played through the preludes and fugues of the Well-Tempered Clavier, four hands, an experience that revealed to Richter the "demonic power" of Bach's art.[68] (Wagner had already "converted" to Bach's music after hearing Liszt play the Prelude and Fugue in C-sharp Minor from Book 1 of that incomparable collection.[69]) But on that

64. Stinson 2006, 113–14 and 121–25.

65. This source is housed today at the Richard-Wagner-Museum, Bayreuth (catalogue no. 1-1-03-4). Unfortunately, it contains no markings in Wagner's hand. For this information, I am indebted to staff member Kristina Unger.

66. Newcomb 1989, 220, esp. n. 29; and Thorau 1999, 186. For general discussions of Wagner's Bach reception, see also Geck 1969; Dahlhaus 1988; and Geck 2000.

67. Gregor-Dellin and Mack 1978–80, vol. 2, 200.

68. Geck 1969, 128; and Geck 2000, 171.

69. Dahlhaus 1988, 440–41; Thorau 1999, 171; and Geck 2000, 171–72.

evening in 1871, Richter had apparently been extolling the virtues of nineteenth-century French and Italian opera, which Wagner found insufferable and which made Cosima "physically sick." Then, somehow, the conversation turned to "Bach's organ fugues." In Cosima's words:

> Richter had to play two of them, and then we found ourselves back on a plane where we could contemplate and wonder to the full. I told R. that, as far as my own feelings were concerned, the difference between Bach and Beethoven lay in the fact that the former called on all my powers, to follow him was a test of intelligence and character, whereas I could give myself over to Beethoven without any effort of will. R. says: "Bach's music is certainly a conception of the world, his figurations, devoid of feeling, are like unfeeling Nature itself—birth and death, winds, storms, sunshine—all these things take place just like such a figuration; the idea of the individual, in Bach always extraordinarily beautiful and full of feeling, is the same which asserts itself in all this to-ing and fro-ing, as steadfast as the Protestant faith itself. Mozart gives us a picture of this juxtaposition of the two things in *Die Zauberflöte*, where the two guides sing to Tamino about eternal wandering and toiling; this is Bachian in feeling. And it belongs to the organ, which is as devoid of feeling as the universal soul, yet at the same time so powerful. In the themes dance motives alternate with the chorale.[70]

The two Bach works (or movements) essayed by Richter on this occasion were in all likelihood taken from the Six Great Preludes and Fugues, as transcribed by Liszt. Cosima may have been somewhat overwhelmed by their complexity, but they elicited from Richard a series of ruminations on the subject of "feeling" (or the lack thereof) in Bach's music, including an implicit analogy between Bach's organ works and the setting of "Ach Gott vom Himmel sieh darein" from Mozart's opera *The Magic Flute*. Wagner recognized the unabashedly Bachian style of this number, which, after all, is an imitatively textured chorale arrangement. But he also sensed something inherently organlike about the music, probably the presentation of the hymn tune by sustained woodwinds simultaneously in four different octaves. At any rate, Wagner's remarks suggest some knowledge of Bach's organ chorales, and it has been proposed that the influence of these works may be heard in the so-called fight scene at the end of the second act of Wagner's opera *Die Meistersinger von Nürnberg*, composed in the 1860s.[71]

Cosima's next diary entry involving Bach's organ music definitely does not concern the Six Great but is nonetheless worth citing. It dates from the couple's stay in Berlin during

---

70. Diary entry for February 12, 1871. See Gregor-Dellin and Mack 1978–80, vol. 1, 335–36. As is typical of her diaries, Cosima writes "R." for "Richard." She tends to abbreviate the names of friends and colleagues in this manner, too.

71. Breig 1992, 470.

the spring of 1871: "In the evening Tausig comes and plays Bach chorales for us."[72] The pianist Carl Tausig, that is, one of Wagner's strongest supporters and also one of Liszt's most prodigious pupils, who by this date had completed piano transcriptions of six of Bach's organ chorales (published posthumously in 1873 and virtually forgotten today, despite having been featured in concert by the likes of Sergei Rachmaninoff).[73] Since Tausig is not known to have transcribed any other "Bach chorales," surely the ones he performed for the Wagners were taken from this collection. The arrangement most likely to have been played was that of the Passiontide hymn "O Mensch, bewein dein Sünde gross," BWV 622, which, in a letter written to Liszt written less than three weeks later, Tausig referred to as his "passion" as well as a "sublimely sad piece."[74] Whether or not he intended a pun on the word "passion," Tausig's personal circumstances at this time were rather dire in their own right, for he was stricken with typhus and, at the shockingly early age of twenty-nine, had only two months to live.

Cosima mentions nothing about Wagner's response to Tausig's chorale transcriptions. Luckily, however, her diaries contain plenty of information about how her husband reacted to Bach's Six Great Preludes and Fugues for organ, as played on seven or eight occasions for them by Joseph Rubinstein. Nowhere does Cosima state explicitly that Rubinstein performed from the "Six Great," but whenever she cites the key of a Bach organ prelude and/or fugue that was played by him, the key corresponds to a work from that collection. Furthermore, in one instance she identifies a Bach organ fugue played by Rubinstein as "No. 6." All these performances took place at the couple's villa in Bayreuth, where, from 1874 to Richard's death in 1883, the two lived like musical royalty. A regular visitor to this kingdom, which Wagner dubbed "Wahnfried," was the aforementioned Joseph Rubinstein. Indeed, Rubinstein was on the grounds so often that he was known as "Wahnfried's supreme court pianist."[75] He played music of all kinds for the Wagners, but especially preludes and fugues by Bach, from the Well-Tempered Clavier as well as from the Six Great Preludes and Fugues for organ. Rubinstein's story is actually more tragic than Tausig's, as he approached Wagner to seek deliverance from his "Jewish deficiencies" and ultimately committed suicide, in his late thirties, the year after Wagner's death.

According to Cosima's diaries, the first time that Rubinstein played for the Wagners from the Six Great was in late 1878: "J. R. first of all plays Bach organ fugues (A minor,

---

72. Diary entry for May 2, 1871. See Gregor-Dellin and Mack 1978–80, vol. 1, 361.

73. Listed in Kehler 1982, 1019–20, are two performances by Rachmaninoff of a Bach-Tausig organ chorale in the key of A major, obviously, from Tausig's collection, the arrangement of "O Lamm Gottes, unschuldig," BWV 656. This arrangement is also by far the most technically demanding of the six, which may explain why it appealed to a virtuoso such as Rachmaninoff.

74. Stinson 2006, 120–21. According to Geck 1969, 133, Wagner owned Bach arrangements by Tausig as well as Liszt, but no such arrangements by Tausig are listed in the online catalogue of Wagner's library (*Katalog der Wahnfried-Bibliothek*) maintained by the Richard-Wagner-Museum (http://www.wagnermuseum.de).

75. Millington 1992, 30–31.

C minor), very well, 'a little overdramatized,' says R., but he enjoys them greatly."[76] Three months later, Rubinstein treated his formidable hosts to the B-minor prelude and fugue: "In the evening Herr R. plays to us the B-minor organ fugue by Bach, the prelude of which delights R."[77] This performance was followed by one three months later of the Prelude and Fugue in C Minor: "R. asks Herr Rubinstein for something by Bach, and he chooses the C-minor organ prelude with its fugue; R. finds it beautiful, though toward the end rather *un*-fugue-like."[78] Five months later, Rubinstein returned to the B-minor, which prompted from Wagner a positively metaphysical outburst: "R. asks Rubinstein to play a fugue by Bach, and he chooses the B-minor (for organ), to our supreme joy. 'These things are elemental forces, like planets, endowed with psychic life.' 'There is the musician *par excellence*,' he also exclaims."[79] Wagner's reaction to the B-minor when Rubinstein played it in early 1881 was similarly ontological but more in the direction of Schopenhauer's notion of will: "Bach's B-minor fugue is played. 'What a world that is,' he exclaims. 'Planets circling around each other, no feeling, yet all of it is passion, will—no intellect at all.'"[80] In responding to Rubinstein's next performance, which took place only three days later, Wagner enigmatically invoked the name of one of his favorite authors: "Rub. plays organ fugues by Bach. R. says to me, 'This is something like Cervantes's stories, but nobody would understand what I mean.'"[81] One can only assume that Rubinstein again played from the Six Great early that spring, when Cosima wrote: "We listen in a cheerful mood to an organ fugue by Bach...R. says there is much conventional stuff in the fugue (not in the prelude)."[82] Cosima's final diary entry concerning Rubinstein and the Six Great reads as follows:

> I ask Herr Rub. to play us something by Bach, which he does (organ fugues by Bach), first the famous A-minor and then the smaller one, I believe No. 6. At the start of the latter, R. says he is pleased by its fantastic anarchy. He describes the theme as a human voice that turns into a bird's voice; it is the bird species speaking. Bach was a true musician, he says....He advises Rub. to be careful with rubato and repeats that it is impossible to indicate where it should occur and that no tempo marking can show it.[83]

---

76. Diary entry for December 15, 1878. See Gregor-Dellin and Mack 1978–80, vol. 2, 229.

77. Ibid., 276 (diary entry for March 11, 1879).

78. Ibid., 328 (diary entry for June 21, 1879).

79. Ibid., 398 (diary entry for November 18, 1879).

80. Ibid., 623 (diary entry for February 15, 1881).

81. Ibid., p.626 (diary entry for February 18, 1881).

82. Ibid., p. 649 (diary entry for April 1, 1881).

83. Ibid., p. 659 (diary entry for April 24, 1881).

A number of conclusions may be drawn from this material. One, regrettably, is that the last of Cosima's entries is erroneous with respect to the "smaller" fugue played by Rubinstein, the one so fancifully described by Wagner. To begin with, it seems that she would have used a comparative such as "smaller" only in reference to one of the two works from the Six Great that are in the same key, which would be the two in C major, BWV 545 and 547. And this makes all the more sense considering that the prelude of BWV 545 is about one-third the length of the prelude of BWV 547; in fact, it is by far the shortest movement in the entire collection. Cosima, however, tentatively identifies the work in question as "No. 6," which in Liszt's set of transcriptions is the Prelude and Fugue in B Minor, BWV 544.

This matter notwithstanding, one can still assert that Rubinstein preferred those works from the Six Great that are in minor keys, just as nineteenth-century composers like Wagner were attracted to dark subject matter. Undoubtedly the most "famous" of these works, as Cosima put it, was the A-minor prelude and fugue, BWV 543, which, thanks to Liszt's transcription, had by this time earned for itself a permanent place in the piano literature. Who knows how many times Cosima had already heard this piece? Her father seems to have played it for most of his adult life, and her first husband, the Liszt pupil Hans von Bülow, included Liszt's transcription of it at least fifty-eight times on his piano recitals.[84] Rubinstein, for his part, seems to have rendered the work like a true Romantic, taking too many liberties with the music for Wagner's taste.

On the whole, it appears that both Richard and Cosima approved of Rubinstein's playing. More importantly, they appreciated his repertoire selections, except perhaps for the fugue criticized by Wagner as "conventional." Regarding the one with the "un-fugue-like" passage near its conclusion, Wagner can only have meant the C-minor fugue, which contains a lengthy and quasi-*galant* episode at mm. 121–39, about three-fourths of the way through the movement. Nowhere in this episode, declared by one modern commentator to be "unlike any other in Bach," is the fugue subject even hinted at.[85] Of all the movements played by Rubinstein, the one that seems to have pleased Wagner the most was the B-minor prelude, but exactly why is impossible to ascertain.

To reiterate, Cosima identified none of the works played by Rubinstein as belonging to the "Sechs grosse Praeludien und Fugen," even though, as letters written by Mendelssohn and Schumann evince,[86] this is how the pieces were known in Germany as early as the 1830s. Although their "greatness" is both quantitative and qualitative, the moniker refers primarily, if not exclusively, to the former. It also reminds us of Bach's tendency in the prelude-fugue genre to write longer movements for the organ than for other keyboard

---

84. Stinson 2006, 105–14 and 200 n. 30; and Hinrichsen and Sackmann 2004, 41.

85. Williams 2003, 110.

86. Stinson 2006, 56–66. See also the discussion of Schumann's letter in chap. 3 of the present book.

instruments, which may be understood as an attempt to match the vast dimensions of the instrument and its vast, churchly surroundings.

The Prelude and Fugue in A Minor, BWV 543

More pianists have played this piece than any other organ work by Bach, and the vast majority of them have chosen Liszt's transcription. Nonetheless, almost thirty different piano arrangements have survived.[87] Contrary to what one source states,[88] this list does not include a four-hand transcription by the American composer and pianist Louis Moreau Gottschalk (the results of which might have been fairly outrageous!) but Liszt's pupil Alexander Wilhelm Gottschalg.

The number of nineteenth-century organists who championed the A-minor was also legion. Let us consider three who played it in London. Mendelssohn's performances of the work there during the 1830s ignited a veritable revolution in organ playing across England, owing to his pedal virtuosity.[89] In 1837 he played it first at St. Paul's—where the organ blower infamously aborted the proceedings—and two days later at Christ Church, Newgate Street, in the presence of Samuel Wesley. One would like to believe that Mendelssohn's audience on at least one of these occasions also included the teenage prodigy Elizabeth Stirling (one of the few local organists who could have managed such a pedal part), who in a recital given the very next month would essay the A-minor herself, and to critical acclaim.[90] Was her interpretation of the work influenced by Mendelssohn's?

The third organist is Camille Saint-Saëns. When, in 1879, he rendered the A-minor at St. James's Hall on a program of the Philharmonic Society—he was also the soloist in his own G-minor piano concerto—one of his listeners was the young George Bernard Shaw, who years later would argue on the basis of that "excellent" performance that the public deserved to hear organ music in concert halls as well as in churches.[91] In addition, Shaw singled out the A-minor prelude as the best specimen altogether of Bach's "poetically ornamental vein." He mentioned nothing about the huge Gray & Davison organ on which Saint-Saëns played, known by organists of the day as "The Beast," but the fact that this instrument had only one manual obviously restricted the number of registration changes he could have made. Saint-Saëns included this same prelude and fugue on his "farewell recital" in 1913, where again he appeared as organist, pianist, and composer, eight years before his death at the age of eighty-six.

---

87. Schanz 2000, 491–92 and 512.

88. Hull 1929, 179.

89. Stinson 2006, 29 and 44–48.

90. Barger 2007, 78–81. This recital also featured, from the Six Great, the C-minor, the E-minor, and the "smaller" C-major.

91. Shaw 1932, vol. 3, 25 and 161; Smith 1992, 120 and 165; Thistlethwaite 1990, 283; and Foster 1912, 369–72.

The Prelude and Fugue in B Minor, BWV 544

Though not nearly as popular with piano transcribers as the previous work, the B-minor prelude and fugue was appropriated by two of the greatest pianists of the nineteenth century, Hans von Bülow and Clara Schumann. Bülow played Liszt's arrangement of both movements more than thirty times in public, while Clara evidently played her own transcription of the prelude.[92] Perhaps she felt, as did Schweitzer, that the "quiet world" of the fugue made that movement more of an acquired taste.[93] Similarly, Spitta perceived in the fugue "a vein of quiet melancholy," but he also maintained that Bach in both movements "strikes a chord of deep elegiac feeling such as is found nowhere else in the organ works."[94] Writing in the 1890s, Widor cited the piece in reference to the renaissance of Bach's organ music in France that had been initiated by the organs of Cavaillé-Coll: "Since Cavaillé-Coll, the study of Bach has begun. Will you believe that sixty years ago one would have searched Paris in vain to find two organists who knew the Fugue in B Minor?"[95] This suggests that the B-minor was not only a known quantity in Parisian organ circles at the turn of the twentieth century but a prized commodity as well.

Despite his apathy toward the fugue, Schweitzer contended that the "flowery arabesque" of the B-minor prelude, that is, the swirling thirty-second-note figuration found throughout, was one of the most striking characteristics of any of Bach's Leipzig organ works. This filigree also constitutes a particularly attractive feature of the autograph manuscript, whose first page has been emblazoned onto everything from coffee mugs to T-shirts to neckties. Bach took great pains in this source to produce what is an eminently legible fair copy, and he notated the upper staff in treble rather than soprano clef—an indication of a relatively late composition date.[96] Therefore, it is by no means impossible for modern organists, whether in the spirit of gimmickry or authenticity, to perform directly from one of the three available facsimile editions of this manuscript.[97] Witness, for example, the late Gustav Leonhardt in Jean-Marie Straub's film *Chronik der Anna Magdalena Bach*.[98] Posing as J. S. Bach and seated at the Silbermann organ in the village of Grosshartmannsdorf, Leonhardt plays from one of these facsimiles the prelude's opening ritornello statement only, but with a Picardy-third ending, as at the conclusion of the

---

92. The collection of Clara's concert programs housed today at the Robert-Schumann-Haus, Zwickau, documents seven performances of the prelude by her from 1865 to 1881; see also Oakeley 1904, 97–98. On Bülow and this work, see Hinrichsen and Sackmann 2004, 41.

93. Schweitzer 1911, vol. 1, 277.

94. Spitta 1873–79, vol. 2, 689.

95. Pirro 1902, xix.

96. On the chronological implications of Bach's clef usage in his keyboard music, see Stinson 1989, 442–53.

97. For a detailed discussion of these editions, as well as the autograph itself, see Kilian 1978–79, 35–40 and 487–88.

98. This outstanding production, released in 1968 and now available on DVD, includes three additional organ works by Bach: the C-minor trio sonata; "Vor deinen Thron tret ich hiermit," BWV 668; and, from Part 3 of the *Clavierübung*, the five-voice setting of "Kyrie, Gott Heiliger Geist."

movement proper. This fragment lasts longer than many of Bach's harpsichord preludes, including several from the Well-Tempered Clavier.

The Prelude and Fugue in C Major, BWV 545

In Germany, whole generations of wedding couples have processed to the strains of this majestic prelude (which is sufficiently short not to need any cuts for this purpose). The fugue, conversely, is sober enough to have been the first musical selection at the funeral in July 2009 of fabled anchorman Walter Cronkite. D'Indy thought so highly of this movement as a fugal specimen that he devoted ten pages to it in his *Cours de composition musicale*, complete with musical examples in open score.[99] According to D'Indy's analysis, the fugal entries fall into seven distinct sections: an opening exposition in the tonic (mm. 1–19), a "Contre-Exposition" in the dominant (mm. 28–48), an exposition in the relative minor (mm. 52–65), a second counterexposition (mm. 73–82), an exposition in the subdominant (mm. 84–87), an exposition in the relative minor of the subdominant (mm. 89–92), and a final exposition that incorporates a "Pédale de Dominante" (mm. 100–109).

Probably not by happenstance, the only known orchestration of this prelude and fugue is that of D'Indy's pupil Arthur Honegger, a composer who claimed Bach as his "great model."[100] The transcription originated in 1928, as the first and last of several movements by Bach arranged by Honegger for the ballet *Les Noces d'Amour et de Psyché*. Published posthumously in 1977, it was first recorded in 2000, with Leonard Slatkin and the BBC Philharmonic.[101] Honegger's use of two saxophones adds a quintessentially French gloss to the music.

The Prelude and Fugue in C Minor, BWV 546

To quote Robert Schumann on the subject of the Six Great Preludes and Fugues, "Number 4 is the wonderful Prelude in C Minor."[102] His contemporary J. N. Schelble (1789–1837) must have agreed with this assessment, for this Frankfurt-based conductor and singer—he was also a good friend of Mendelssohn's—scored the prelude for strings, brass, woodwinds, and timpani, resulting in the earliest extant orchestration of any movement from the collection.[103] Its ritornello alone contains, in Hermann Keller's

---

99. D'Indy 1903–50, vol. 2, *Première Partie*, 45–54.

100. Honegger 1966, 94; and Cantoni 1998, 14–16.

101. *Bach Transcriptions* (Chandos Records 9835).

102. Stinson 2006, 82.

103. Stinson 2006, 24–27; and Bormann 1926, 71–72 and 143. According to the latter source, Schelble is also responsible for a fragmentary orchestral transcription of the E-minor fugue, but this arrangement seems not to have survived.

words, "a wealth of great effects,"[104] including, in the first four bars, a series of chords suggestive of a dialogue between two different choruses. Schelble's choice of trumpets and horns for the upper "chorus" and three trombones for the lower one nicely enhances this impression.

Schumann's colleague J. G. Schneider (see discussion at the end of chap. 3) should also be considered here, since, in what is an exceptional case for that era, we know how this great organist essayed both the prelude and the fugue.[105] He took the prelude at a "moderate" tempo, with the statements of the ritornello played on the Hauptwerk, full organ, and with the six-note pedal motive introduced in m. 5 played staccato. The episodes he rendered on a subsidiary manual and with a softer registration, although in m. 82, for the statement of the "fugue theme" at the bottom of the pedalboard, a 16′ reed was added. He played the fugue proper at the relatively slow tempo of $\rfloor$ = 40, and with 8′ flues, grouping the sixteen notes of the subject into phrases of five, four, and seven notes, respectively. For the lengthy *manualiter* episode starting at m. 59, he changed manuals for the sake of a brighter but softer sound, using 4′ as well as 8′ stops. For the reinstatement of the subject in m. 87, his left hand returned to the main manual, whose registration now included 4′ stops; his right hand quickly followed, probably in m. 99. He switched manuals again in mm. 123 and 125, creating an echo effect for the material restated there. Starting in m. 140, and to fortify the final statements of the subject, he changed to a "stronger and fuller" registration, though probably not as big as that used for the ritornello statements within the prelude. Compared to A. W. Bach and C. A. Haupt, who tended to play Bach full organ from start to finish, and with no registration changes whatsoever, Schneider seems to have been something of a free spirit.

The Prelude and Fugue in C Major, BWV 547

Spitta grouped this work together with the B-minor, E-minor, and the Prelude and Fugue in E-flat Major from Part 3 of the *Clavierübung* as "four stupendous creations in which are embodied the highest qualities that Bach could put into *this branch of art*,"[106] meaning organ composition. Still, it is safe to say that the piece was not regularly played until about fifty years ago.[107] This neglect may be attributed to a perceived scholasticism within the fugue, which by any measure is one of Bach's most complex movements.

Richard Wagner, though, may have been drawn to this fugue precisely because of this contrapuntal artifice. We refer here to the prelude to *Die Meistersinger von Nürnberg*, a movement so Bachian in style that Wagner described it as "applied Bach," just as he

---

104. Keller 1967, 149.

105. Sieling 1999, 323–29. The basis for this discussion is a report by Schneider's pupil W. F. G. Nicolai.

106. Spitta 1873–79, vol. 2, 689. Emphasis added.

107. On this point, see Keller 1967, 152.

considered the opera in general a "continuation of Bach."[108] As may be seen in example 7.2 and 7.3, the second and third bars of Wagner's opening theme bear a strong melodic and rhythmic similarity to Bach's fugue subject. Furthermore, both movements are in the key

EXAMPLE 7.2. Fugue in C Major, BWV 547/2, subject

EXAMPLE 7.3. Richard Wagner, Prelude to *Die Meistersinger von Nürnberg*, opening theme

of C major, which is also the overall tonality of Wagner's opera. More significantly, Wagner in the middle of the *Meistersinger* prelude (mm. 138–56) condenses his theme down to two bars, with the rhythmic values cut in half, and places it in the woodwinds as the subject of a three-voice fugal exposition. Shortly after this passage, the low brass and strings proclaim the theme in its original guise, which is roughly analogous to how Bach in his fugue delays the entrance of the pedals until about three-fourths of the way through, where the subject appears for the first time in augmentation. On the basis of these admittedly loose connections, various late nineteenth- and early-twentieth-century commentators argued that Bach's fugue provided Wagner with a specific exemplar. Read, for instance, this excerpt from André Pirro's monograph on Bach's organ music: "It is curious to observe that this fugue…played a part in the inspiration of *Die Meistersinger*, in its analogous figures and in resuming the subject at the close, this time in augmentation, like a chorale melody."[109] Even today there are organists in Germany who know Bach's movement as the "*Meistersinger*-fuge."

The Prelude and Fugue in E Minor ("Wedge"), BWV 548

Both Hans von Bülow and Clara Schumann also concertized with this piece, the longest and most virtuosic of the Six Great, again with Bülow performing Liszt's transcription and Clara evidently her own.[110] She played it at least five times in London from 1873 to 1884, where, twelve years later, one disgruntled critic would write about the "perfect

---

108. Gregor-Dellin and Mack 1978–80, vol. 2, 232 and 229, respectively.

109. Pirro 1902, 57. See also D'Indy 1903–50, vol. 2, *Première Partie*, 85; and Grace 1922b, 241.

110. On Bülow and this work, see Hinrichsen and Sackmann 2004, 41. The collection of Clara's concert programs housed at the Robert-Schumann-Haus documents eight performances by her from 1872 to 1884 of both the prelude and fugue.

mania" there for "playing Bach's organ works on the pianoforte."[111] Her audience at one of these performances included Schneider's pupil Herbert Oakeley, and it is noteworthy that Oakeley defended Clara's *"organ-playing* on the piano" against those who found this a "decadent" practice.[112] In 1880, three years after Clara's performance, Guilmant rendered both movements in Paris on the gigantic Cavaillé-Coll organ at the Trocadéro, but whether to popular acclaim is doubtful, given the public's aversion there to "serious" organ music.[113]

In terms of compositional borrowing, Mendelssohn seems to have modeled his Prelude in C Minor for organ after this Bach prelude, and this is definitely the case with the opening movement of Rheinberger's first organ sonata.[114] Wilhelm Middelschulte's *Perpetuum mobile,* conversely, is indebted to Bach's scissors-like fugue subject.[115] This work originally comprised the fourth of a five-movement concerto for organ and orchestra, all movements of which are based on Bach's theme. Completed in 1903, the concerto was arranged for organ solo by Middelschulte the following year. Almost forty years later, he realized the potential of the fourth movement—the only one in either version for feet alone—as an independent pedal showpiece, changing its name from Intermezzo to *Perpetuum mobile* and dedicating it to his student Virgil Fox. Fox, in turn, made the work famous by regularly featuring it in concert and by editing it for performance as an "Etude for pedals alone on the Wedge Fugue subject by J. S. Bach." Suffice it to say that this may be the most difficult bit of music ever conceived for the organ pedalboard.

THE PRELUDE AND FUGUE IN E-FLAT MAJOR, BWV 552

The first point to be made about this glorious work is that it may have inspired one of Mozart's most famous melodies, that which opens the second thematic group of the first movement of *Eine kleine Nachtmusik.* At issue is the relationship between Mozart's theme, specifically its first two bars, and the theme that commences the first episode of Bach's prelude (see exx. 7.4 and 7.5). For starters, the themes themselves are analogous. Each begins or nearly begins with a descending stepwise flourish of three sixteenth notes, then proceeds with a series of eighth notes separated by eighth rests (virtually rendered by Bach's staccato markings) that rise to the sixth degree of the scale, fall to the fourth degree, and fall again to the second or third. Each theme, moreover, occurs at the first main formal juncture of its respective movement—in Bach's case after the opening ritornello statement, in Mozart's after the first thematic group in what is a sonata form—along

111. Scholes 1947, vol. 1, 309.

112. Oakeley 1904, 56–57 and 98; and Stinson 2006, 83.

113. Smith 1995, 302.

114. See, respectively, Stinson 2006, 41–43; and Steger 2001, 152–53.

115. Meyer 2007, 332–40, 367, and 369–71

EXAMPLE 7.4. Prelude in E-flat Major, BWV 552/1, mm. 32–34

EXAMPLE 7.5. W. A. Mozart, *Eine kleine Nachtmusik*, K. 525, first movement, theme beginning in m. 28 (transposed to E-flat)

with a significant reduction in texture. With respect to the latter, each theme is unaccompanied until the sixth degree of the scale is reached, at which point homorhythmic accompanimental voices are added beneath. Mozart appears to have expanded Bach's theme from a mere two bars to a full-blown eight-bar phrase period.

This theory is corroborated by external evidence. By the time Mozart composed his serenade, in 1787, he was a card-carrying member of Baron van Swieten's Bach and Handel cult, and it is an established fact that the baron owned a copy of Part 3 of Bach's *Clavierübung*, the collection in which this prelude was originally published.[116] Furthermore, scholars have long assumed that the French-overturish ritornello of the Fantasy in F Minor for mechanical clock, K. 608, composed in 1791, is derived from that of Bach's prelude. Mozart, then, seems to have been rewarded not once but twice by his perusal of this movement.

The E-flat was also greatly favored by English organists of the early nineteenth century.[117] For example, Vincent Novello saw fit to arrange the prelude for organ and orchestra for a performance in 1812 at London's Hanover Square, with the organ part rendered as a duet by Novello and Samuel Wesley. Both the event and the arrangement are historically important, for no Bach organ work had ever been placed before the English public and none evidently had ever been orchestrated anywhere. Two years later, Novello adapted the fugue as an organ duet, which he and Wesley played along with a prelude composed by the latter. When Wesley and Charles Smith performed this arrangement in 1815, the audience responded, in Wesley's words, "with the same kind of Wonder that people express when they see an Air Balloon ascend for the first Time." Surely their

116. Marshall 1998, 61 and 74–78.

117. Riethmüller 1990, 38–39; Thistlethwaite 1990, 172–73; McCrea 1998, 283–84; Olleson 2001, 163, 197, 201, 223, 226, and 244; and Olleson 2003, 302–3.

enthusiasm owed something to the fact that Bach's fugue subject is melodically identical to the first phrase of the Anglican hymn tune "St. Anne." Indeed, this coincidence would seem to be the main reason for the fugue's phenomenal popularity within the British organ community during this era. Twelve years later, the fugue received its first solo readings in England, when both Henry John Gauntlett and Samuel Sebastian Wesley (Samuel Wesley's son) played it at the audition for the organist's post at St. Stephen's, Coleman Street. Both candidates performed "extraordinarily" and to their "greatest credit," but the job went to the otherwise unknown Miss Sarah Alder Bradfield.[118]

On the Continent, the earliest documented performances of the work took place somewhat later in Germany and the Netherlands, courtesy of Fritz Schlemmer, Felix Mendelssohn, Eduard Krüger, C. F. Becker, and J. A. van Eijken (see chaps. 3 and 4). This list continues with Mendelssohn's and Becker's pupil J. G. Bastiaans, who on July 28, 1850—the centennial of Bach's death—offered the citizens of Amsterdam a commemorative all-Bach organ recital that included three of the same pieces played by Mendelssohn a decade earlier on his all-Bach program in Leipzig, namely, the Fugue in E-flat, the Toccata and Fugue in D Minor (BWV 565), and the Great Eighteen setting of "Schmücke dich."[119] We learn from the biography of Herbert Oakeley, apropos of his pilgrimage in 1863 to the great Müller organ at St. Bavo's, Haarlem, that one of Bastiaans's children also played the E-flat: "The organist (Bastiaans) and his clever daughter of fifteen played everything asked for, including—from the latter [!]—Bach's A-minor and E-flat fugues and Mendelssohn's sixth sonata."[120] And yet, upon his death in 1875, Bastiaans was succeeded as the church's organist not by this daughter but by his son of the same name.[121]

There is no evidence that French organists began to play the E-flat until 1862, when Camille Saint-Saëns chose the prelude for the inauguration of a three-manual instrument just rebuilt by Cavaillé-Coll in the town of Saint-Dizier.[122] In 1878, and in a much more public place, Saint-Saëns served up both the prelude and fugue at the Trocadéro.[123] His audience included fellow organist Eugène Gigout, who sensed in the "vast proportions" of the piece—it lasts about fifteen minutes, making it Bach's longest prelude-fugue pair by far—that "the hand of a giant had passed through it." Another of the work's proponents was Alexandre Guilmant, who in 1904 introduced throngs of Americans to it through his forty recitals at the St. Louis World's Fair.[124] Of the fugue he reportedly said: "I want it played when my soul goes to heaven." Seven years later, however, it was to the

---

118. Horton 2004, 19.

119. Bokum 2000, 57–61.

120. Oakeley 1904, 74. The "A-minor fugue" cited by Oakeley was presumably BWV 543, the first of the Six Great Preludes and Fugues. According to Nieuwkoop 1988, 418, Bastiaans and his daughter (Maria) played a memorial recital for his first wife on this organ in 1860.

121. Nieuwkoop 1988, 419–21; and Bokum 1971, 30.

122. Smith 1992, 73.

123. Smith 1992, 116–17; Smith 1995, 294–95; and Fauquet and Hennion 2000, 143.

plaintive sounds of a different Bach organ work, the double-pedal setting of "Aus tiefer Not schrei ich zu dir," that Guilmant's body was transported from his home to his final resting place, as per his instructions.

THE TOCCATA, ADAGIO, AND FUGUE IN C MAJOR, BWV 564

The "T A F," as it is affectionately known, is associated in various ways with several of the most prominent organists, American as well as European, of the late nineteenth and early twentieth centuries. For example, Charles Ives's encounter with this technically formidable work launched his career as a professional church musician at the tender age of fourteen.[125] In turn-of-the-century London, the piece was a favorite in Hubert Parry's organ studio at the Royal College of Music. As William Henry Harris reminisced:

> The things Parry liked most in Bach's organ works were those which the organ could do best and no other instrument quite so well, as, for instance, the great, massive chords and suspensions in the Toccata and Fugue in C Major.... His favourite organ work was undoubtedly the Toccata and Fugue in C. How he delighted in the big pedal solo of the Toccata—regarding the whole thing as a huge joke! On one occasion he showed me (mainly on my shoulder!) how to play that pedal solo so that it should not sound "stiff" or "like an exercise." He quoted the verse in the Psalms [Psalm 19:5] about the "giant rejoicing to run his course," and wished that glorious music to run its course in the manner of a splendid care-free improvisation.[126]

The "chords and suspensions" cited by Harris are obviously the suspended diminished-seventh chords from the thickly textured *grave* section that occurs between the Adagio and the Fugue. Parry himself rather emphatically described this music as follows: "The beautiful air ends with a short transition through one of the typical passages of truly tremendous suspensions which are so ideally fitted for the organ to display its remorseless persistence of tone, into the singularly gay and genial fugue which constitutes the finale."[127]

For Bruckner and Guilmant, we know about certain details of performance practice.[128] Bruckner's still extant copy of the score prescribes three different manuals for both the

---

124. Zimmerman and Archbold 1995, 202; Hinrichsen 1952, 276; and Hielscher 1987, 85. The enormous, six-manual organ played by Guilmant is the same known today as the "Wanamaker organ." Designed by G. A. Audsley and built for the St. Louis World's Fair in 1904, the instrument currently stands in the great hall at Macy's (previously Wanamaker's) department store in Philadelphia.

125. Burkholder 2002, 264.

126. Graves 1926, vol. 2, 188–89. It is clear from this source that Parry enjoyed calling Bach "the old man."

127. Parry 1909, 509.

128. Busch 1975, 13; Carragan 2001, 83 and 90; and Busch 2003, 126.

toccata and the fugue, with regular manual changes in the former aimed primarily at clarifying the concerto-like dialogue. These markings probably stem from Bruckner's performance of the piece in 1873 on the new three-manual Ladegast organ at the Vienna Musikverein, and on a program featuring the premiere of his Second Symphony. It has even been suggested that this symphony bears the stamp of Bach's toccata in its use of extremely low trombone notes. Guilmant's edition of Bach's work, published in 1890, calls for three manuals, with manual changes for the *manualiter* episodes in the fugue. This was presumably how he had performed the piece a year earlier at the Paris Exposition—where Claude Debussy famously heard a gamelan for the first time—on the four-manual Cavaillé-Coll at the Trocadéro.[129]

Both Bruckner's score and Guilmant's edition indicate that the work is to conclude *fortissimo*. But other players of that era felt just the opposite, owing to the absence of a pedal part for the last two measures and probably also because of the exceedingly brief final chord. In the words of Harvey Grace, writing in 1922, "The [fugue] ends, curiously, without pedals, a fact which leads most players to decide that the close must therefore be quiet."[130] Ten years earlier, this practice had been condemned by Widor and Schweitzer: "An organist who lets this grand piece dribble away to a *pianissimo* finish, instead of closing in a majestic *forte*, is guilty of an offense against the spirit of J. S. Bach."[131] Certainly, Ferruccio Busoni would have agreed with this verdict, for his piano transcription, published in 1900, ends at a volume level well in excess of *fortissimo*. For good measure, Busoni affixed four bars of his own fashioning—one C-major triad after the next—which are as bombastic as they are offensive. This codetta, though, absolutely pales in comparison to how the young Olivier Messiaen once played the fugue at the church of La Trinité, Paris, in the winter of 1932: "Messiaen's offerings on January 31 were a Bach chorale using a solo cornet or reed painfully off pitch, and the long C-major fugue in six-eight time, which he took in needlessly slow tempo, but accelerated somewhat as he progressed, *holding the final chord a full minute by the watch and reducing stop by stop down to the eight-foot bourdon*."[132] What was the man thinking?

To return to Bruckner's score, he heavily annotated the toccata and fugue but made no markings in either the Adagio or the *grave* section, which implies that he played only the outer two movements. If so, Bruckner jettisoned the movement that, due to its technical ease as well as its lyricism, has most often been performed by organists.[133] This movement has also been transcribed far more times than the other two—of the twenty-four surviving

129. Eleven years earlier, the work had been played at the Trocadéro by the Dutch virtuoso Samuel de Lange. See Smith 1995, 287.

130. Grace 1922b, 70.

131. Widor and Schweitzer 1912, xiv. According to Hiemke 1994, 263–64, the opening movement of Widor's Sixth Symphony for organ may be influenced by the pizzicato-like pedal part of Bach's Adagio.

132. Bingham 1932. Emphasis added. I would like to thank Lawrence Archbold for bringing this item to my attention.

133. This statement is especially true of Albert Schweitzer. See Schützeichel 1991, p. 164.

transcriptions, fourteen are of the Adagio alone—in part because the melody line can so conveniently be adapted to a string or woodwind instrument.[134] Pablo Casals played (and recorded) an arrangement for cello and piano accompaniment.[135] Still, Busoni's transcription of the piece is the most popular, thanks to Vladimir Horowitz's "return-to-the-concert-stage" recital in 1965 at Carnegie Hall.[136] As any serious Horowitz fan knows, that concert began with Busoni's arrangement—minus its codetta—in a performance, wrong notes and all, that remains the most famous of any version of the work. Horowitz's choice of Busoni's arrangement to open the first recital he had played in twelve years was a symbolic gesture of sorts, because forty years earlier it had opened his first recital since defecting from the USSR.

THE TOCCATA AND FUGUE IN D MINOR, BWV 565

As the best known of all organ compositions, this piece is represented not only by countless organ recordings, including the first one of a Bach organ work ever made, but also by forty-nine piano transcriptions and at least eleven for orchestra.[137] It survives in relatively few manuscripts, which suggests that it did not widely circulate before being published in 1833 by Mendelssohn and A. B. Marx. By the turn of the twentieth century, though, the piece had established itself as a perennial favorite, both on the organ and the piano. Pianists preferred Carl Tausig's overblown arrangement, to the degree that "it seemed to be against the law" not to open a recital with it.[138] The earliest orchestral transcription, that of Leopold Stokowski (who was an organist as well as a conductor), was premiered in 1925 by the Philadelphia Orchestra and first recorded by that ensemble two years later. Its success quickly inspired orchestrations by rival conductors, starting with one of monstrous proportions by Henry Wood, who, fearing yet another backlash from the Bach purists of the day, initially attributed his arrangement to the fictitious "Paul Klenovsky." Stokowski, a prolific orchestrator of Bach's oeuvre, was hardly immune to such attacks himself, as Paul Hindemith's derisive term "Bachowski" proves.

No other piece of organ music has been so exploited by the mass media for its "scary" sounds. By 1940, for instance, when Stokowski's transcription was used for the opening

---

134. The various transcriptions of BWV 564 are cited in Schanz 2000, 59–60 and 494; Hull 1929, 183–86; Smith 2004, 176–77; and Murray 1985, 103 and 131.

135. Kirk 1974, 582–83. According to 575 and 577 of this source, Casals performed two additional slow movements from organ works by Bach: the third movement of the Pastorale in F Major and the second movement of the Concerto in C Major after Vivaldi.

136. Schonberg 1992, 76–77 and 214–16. For a live recording, see *Horowitz Live and Unedited: The Historic 1965 Carnegie Hall Return Concert* (Sony Classical Legacy S2K 93023).

137. On these transcriptions, see Schanz 2000, 47–49 and 494; Smith 2004, 161–70; A. Krause 2007, 398; Stinson 2006, 120–23; Jacobs 1994, 231–32; and Prieberg 1982, 126–27. On the initial recording of BWV 565, made in 1910 by John J. McClellan on the Kimball organ of the Mormon Tabernacle, see Smith 2005, 234–39.

138. Schonberg 1963, 245.

scene of Walt Disney's *Fantasia*, the toccata had already been heard as an organ solo in the horror films *Dr. Jekyll and Mr. Hyde* and *The Raven*, where it is "played" by Fredric March and Béla Lugosi, respectively.[139] This trend continued at least into the 1970s, whether the organist-villain was Captain Nemo (James Mason, then Herbert Lom), the Phantom of the Opera (Lom again), or Dr. Phibes (the inimitable Vincent Price).[140] The horror trope still exists, but mainly as parody, as in the case of the nightly cable-television news program *Countdown with Keith Olbermann*, whose every broadcast, more or less, features the toccata in the segment known as "Worst Person in the World." Mass media or not, it is also worth pointing out the fugue subject has emerged today as a popular ringtone on cellular telephones, a fact charmingly alluded to by The King's Singers whenever they perform "Deconstructing Johann."

Other recent developments in this work's reception have come from the violin world, for various baroque violinists now play it, in response to Peter Williams's hypothesis that solo violin was the original instrumentation (see chap. 1). Alas, the best known violin adaptation of the piece is Vanessa-Mae's techno remix, which made the artist a teen sensation in 1995 when she released a sexy video of her performance.[141] Is this "offense against the spirit of J. S. Bach" also indebted to Williams's theory?

The new millennium has spawned two new organ versions, Enjott Schneider's *Ataccot* (Schott, 2006), whose preface promises that even when the toccata is played backwards, "its bold and distinctive qualities" are retained, and Cameron Carpenter's "evolutionary" account of both the toccata and fugue, from his Grammy-nominated album *Revolutionary* (Telarc CD-80711). The latter is a brilliant concept based on how the piece has "evolved" throughout history in the form of transcriptions. Carpenter explains his methodology as follows: "I'm simply seeking to give this warhorse, which the world knows not from the original organ version but from more widely heard instrumental and orchestral arrangements, a new life on the organ. To do so I've freely borrowed aspects of many non-organ versions, which makes it a remix—except that it was remixed in my brain, rather than in an audio mixer." In this endeavor, he admirably succeeds, despite his erroneous claim that the "original organ version" is relatively unknown to the musical public.

As an antidote to all this commercialization, enter the great German writer Hermann Hesse. Raised by Pietist missionaries and introduced to Bach's sacred vocal works at a young age, Hesse approached the composer in the spirit of mystical reverence. Bach also figures in Hesse's literary output, for example, in the novel *Demian*, whose protagonist is mentored in theology and philosophy by a Bach-playing organist. In 1913, a few years before *Demian* was written, Hesse attended an organ recital, and he was sufficiently enraptured by one of the selections to pen some detailed remarks on it. He did not identify this work by name, but there can be little doubt that it was the piece presently under

---

139. For a detailed analysis of the soundtrack of *Dr. Jekyll and Mr. Hyde*, see Lerner 2010.

140. On this topos, see J. Brown 2010, 5–10.

141. For a recording, see *The Violin Player* (EMI Records 7243 5 55089 2 8).

consideration (which, after all, has always dominated organ recitals). Observe, in particular, how closely the first five sentences of Hesse's commentary match the first seven measures of the toccata:

> Here, a high, powerful organ sound. Ever growing, it fills the huge space; it becomes the space itself, surrounding us totally. It surges, then retreats, and other sounds accompany it, and suddenly they all plunge into the depths in a mad rush, then bow, pray, defy, and persist, bound together in the harmonic bass. And now they become quiet, a pause wafts like the breeze before a storm through the vaulted space. And now again: powerful sounds rise from the depths, glorious passion, surge, storming, upward, howl high and low their plaint to God, howl once again and more urgently, louder, and then become silent. Yet again they rise up, again this bold master, lost in thought, raises his mighty voice to God, laments and pleads, cries out his sorrow in a series of powerful, stormy sounds, and rests, and wraps himself in his thoughts, and praises God in a chorale of awe and devotion, forges golden bows through the lofty twilight, causes pillars and bundles of musical pillars to rise up and erect the cathedral of his adoration, until he stands and takes pause, and still he stands and rests and envelops us all, as the sounds die away.[142]

According to this interpretation:

(1) The "high, powerful organ sound" is the very first note, which, like so much of the toccata's figuration, is played in octaves. Hesse describes this note as "high" because its upper octave contains the second highest pitch (a'') in the entire composition. The note is "ever growing" due to the two fermatas.

(2) This sound "surges" and "retreats," respectively, by means of the thirty-second notes and the two sets of rests that immediately follow.

(3) The "other sounds" that are "bound together" are the tied notes of the diminished-seventh chord in mm. 2–3; the "harmonic bass" is the pedal point at this juncture.

(4) A "breeze-like pause" is provided by the three sets of rests in m. 3; the "powerful sounds" that "rise from the depths" are the statements in mm. 3–7 of the new triplet figure. This figure rises via stepwise sequences in mm. 4–5; then the whole passage is transposed up an octave.

More than twenty years later, Hesse authored the poem "Zu einer Toccata von Bach." The title alone suggests that he turned his attention once again to the Toccata in D Minor, and his use of many of the same concepts as in the prose passage confirms this assumption.

---

142. For the original German, see Heinemann 2000, 450. For the English translation I thank Wm. A. Little.

These concepts include, in addition to the images of a wafting breeze and a vaulted cathedral, the idea of praising God and the dichotomies of sound versus silence, darkness versus light, and high versus low. Hesse, then, is depicting the same music as in the prose passage, again with an emphasis on its remarkable dramaturgy but in a far more abstract manner. The complete text appears below:

"On a Toccata by Bach"
Locked in primeval silence…darkness reigns…
Now a beam of light breaks through [the] jagged rent of clouds,
Tears worldly depths out from blind nothingness,
Raises up spaces, permeates the night with light,
Lets ridge and summit, slope and chasm, divine,
Lets airy breezes blue, lets earth be sealed.

The beam [of light] splits asunder the budding significance
Creatively to deed and conflict:
Sunbeams ignite the startled world;
Wherever the seeds of light fall, it is transformed,
Order is shaped and splendor rings
Praise to life, light and victory to the Creator.

And onward rolls the mighty impulse, toward God,
The great drive presses through the hustle of all creatures,
To the spirit of the Father.
He becomes pleasure and poverty, language, image, song.
World upon world vaults upward to the triumphal arch of the cathedral,
Is drive, is spirit, is struggle and good fortune, is love.[143]

THE FANTASY IN G MAJOR (*PIÈCE D'ORGUE*), BWV 572

The three main sections of this piece—they are not, strictly speaking, movements—are a study in dissimilitude, if not incompatibility. In the first, *perpetuum mobile* figuration in a single voice prevails, while the stately middle section is characterized by thick five-part texture and some of the composer's most sublime counterpoint. The last section is essentially a series of broken chords above a chromatically descending bass line. Because of this incongruity, various "receptors" of the work have focused on one section to the exclusion of the other two (although never, it seems, on the last section, which can be thought of as a glorified cadenza).

---

143. For the original German, see Heinemann 2000, 452. This translation is also Prof. Little's.

For example, the prelude of Max Reger's Prelude and Fugue in G Major for solo violin, op. 117, no. 5, a work dating from 1911, constitutes a transcription of just the first section of the fantasy.[144] (The fugue is newly composed, except that its subject is taken from Bach's G-major organ fugue, BWV 541/2.) In undertaking this exercise, Reger managed to simulate those movements from Bach's sonatas and partitas for solo violin—especially the finales of the A-minor and C-major sonatas—that likewise display fast perpetual motion, monophonic texture, and highly repetitive figuration. His methodology was to vary the repeated material with respect to phrasing, articulation, and/or dynamics (thereby creating numerous echo effects); to transpose mm. 18–28 up an octave, rather than rewrite the seven bars here that dip beneath the violin's range; and to add a cadence of his own composition.

Most of the other receptors who have chosen to dismember the fantasy have treated the middle section, which is by far the longest and most substantial of the three, as an independent work, changing its final sonority from a jarring diminished-seventh chord to a tonic triad. Two of the surviving manuscripts, for instance, contain only this section, transcribed for two violins, two violas, and double bass.[145] One is a score prepared in the 1830s by the Viennese scholar and collector Aloys Fuchs (1799–1853), who scribbled on the source that his master copy had been a set of printed parts. No such parts are extant, but Fuchs wrote elsewhere on this manuscript that "Herr J. B. Cramer in London" had arranged the music for string quintet. Therefore, it is likely that Fuchs copied a transcription by Johann Baptist Cramer (1771–1858), a German-born composer and pianist who lived in London for most of his life. Cramer, in turn, presumably gained access to the fantasy through his teacher Muzio Clementi, who, in the first volume of his anthology, *Clementi's Selection of Practical Harmony*, published in 1801, was the first to print the work (and in its entirety). Evidence of a contemporaneous performance of Cramer's arrangement comes from the diary of Mary Novello (Vincent's wife), where we read that at a soirée in London during the Christmas season of 1829–30, Cramer and four other musicians, including the double-bassist Dragonetti, "played exquisitely several quartets of Mozart and quintets of Bach."[146] Since Cramer is known to have played the violin, he probably took one of the parts for that instrument.

Among the many organists over the years who have championed the middle section of the fantasy at the expense of the other two, surely the most notorious was Herbert Haag,

---

144. Stein 1953, 285–86. See also the recording by Mateja Marinković, *Max Reger: Preludes and Fugues for Solo Violin*, vol. 2 (ASV Digital CD DCA 876).

145. Kilian 1988, 192–93. In this regard, see also the transcriptions by Arnold Bax (piano), Richard Franko Goldman (wind band), and, very recently, the viol ensemble "Fretwork." On Bax's arrangement, see Schanz 2000, 57 and 499. For recordings of the other two, see *Frederick Fennell: The Cleveland Symphonic Winds* (Telarc CD-80038); and Fretwork's *J. S. Bach: Alio modo* (harmonia mundi usa 907395). The latter disc contains disconcertingly effective performances as well of the Passacaglia in C Minor, the "St. Anne" fugue, and various organ chorales.

146. Palmer 1997, 32.

one of the leading musicians of the Nazi Confessionalist church as well as the chief ideo-
logue of the "organ-workshop" component of the Hitler Youth organization.[147] Haag's
activities as a Nazi organist need to be understood within the context of that party's
adoption of the organ as its symbolic instrument of choice, something that occurred with
the construction of a gigantic five-manual instrument, complete with loudspeakers, for
the 1936 Nazi rally in Nuremburg. As Haag's colleague Josef Müller-Blattau described
this phenomenon, the organ was "the total instrument of the total state," and Adolf
Hitler was the state's "omnipotent organist." In other words, the most powerful musical
instrument known to the world became linked to the most powerful politician in its history. Haag, for his part, opined that the organ was "the symbolic instrument of the [Nazi]
community" and ideally equipped to "serve a total weltanschauung and the will expressed
in its festivities."

Apropos of these festivals, which were basically celebrations of Nazi doctrine and
which featured organ music exclusively by "Aryan" composers, Haag was both an active
participant and an advisor. He wrote in 1939 that

> Most of Bach's [free] organ works easily lend themselves to festival planning. One
> thinks, say, of the middle part of the G-major fantasy, the introduction of the E-flat-
> major prelude, the C-minor [prelude], the D-major prelude, and many of the other
> large preludes, fugues, toccatas, and fantasies of the master....All these...pieces
> have their place as an introduction to a festival or as an interlude, say, between two
> speakers or between a speaker and a choir, etc., and at the end...[148]

Haag was therefore advocating those works, or just those sections of works, that are both
inherently "powerful" and that would traditionally have been played with a full registration, to glorify the totalitarianism of the Nazi regime. The relatively genteel-sounding
trio sonatas would hardly have accomplished this purpose, nor would the first section of
the G-major fantasy or the lightly textured episodes of the E-flat prelude (for Haag was
recommending that only the opening ritornello of the latter work be played).[149]

When he played the organ himself at these gatherings, Haag practiced what he
preached—and dressed in his storm trooper's uniform, he looked every bit the part. Just
consider the program for a Hitler Youth *Abendmusik* event in 1937 that showcased the
choir of Bach's own church (St. Thomas, Leipzig) and Haag as the organ soloist: limiting

---

147. Kater 1997, 171–76; and Kaufmann 1997, 131.

148. "Die meisten Orgelwerke Bachs sind für die Feiergestaltung ohne weiteres verwendbar, man denke etwa an
   den Mittelteil der G-Dur-Fantasie, die Einleitung des Es-Dur-Präludiums, das C-Moll-, das D-Dur-
   Präludium und vieles andere aus den grossen Präludien, Fugen, Toccaten und Fantasien des Meisters....Alle
   diesen...Stücke haben ihren Platz als Einleitung der Feier, als Zwischenspiele etwa zwischen zwei Sprechern
   oder Sprecher und Chor usw. und am Schluss..." See Kaufmann 1997, 190.

149. According to Reichling 2004, 434 n. 49, the E-flat prelude and fugue was commonly used to open those
   Nazi festivals where an organ was present.

himself to the music of Bach, Haag performed the G-major fantasy, the E-flat prelude and fugue, and the Toccata and Fugue in F Major. Perhaps his rendering of the fantasy was met with the same adulation as when the piece was heard in 1936 at another Nazi-sponsored concert, this one taking place at the Haus der deutschen Erziehung (House of German Education) in Bayreuth.[150] To quote a local critic, "Bach's Fantasy in G Major, which Karl August von Kotzebue consummately played on the organ, constituted the end [of the concert]. In the powerful second part, the organ sounded under his hands like a thunderstorm rumbling in the distance."[151] Predictably, that evening's entertainment ended with "Deutschland über alles," played as an organ solo by Kotzebue with all the might the instrument could muster.

THE PASSACAGLIA IN C MINOR, BWV 582

With the exception of the Toccata and Fugue in D Minor, no organ work composed by or attributed to Bach has achieved the level of popularity enjoyed by this piece. Outside the organ community, this popularity is due less to the thirty-three piano arrangements that have been made than to the orchestral transcriptions by Heinrich Esser, Leopold Stokowski, and Ottorino Respighi.[152]

Published around 1850, Esser's orchestration seems to have been regularly heard across Europe and in the United States well into the twentieth century. I am aware of performances from 1855 to 1886 in Prague, New York, Leipzig, and Vienna,[153] and a systematic investigation would undoubtedly uncover many others. According to a diary kept by Sergey Prokofiev while a student in Nikolay Tcherepnin's conducting class at the St. Petersburg Conservatory, Esser's transcription was also played there in 1913 (Esser is not named as the arranger, but no other orchestral transcription was in existence). We learn from this source that Prokofiev thought highly of Bach's work and that Tcherepnin was planning to have it performed twice on the same concert, once in Esser's transcription and once in the original version for organ. The pertinent entries are reproduced below:

(1) 26 September. Today I looked through Bach's organ *Passacaglia* in someone's orchestral version, which the small orchestra is going to do. A wonderful work; however, to judge from the score it is painfully long and will be exhausting to play.

---

150. Constructed in 1933–36 and substantially damaged by Allied bombing in 1945, this structure housed in its "Consecration Hall" a massive three-manual Steinmeyer organ. The building was privately described by Nazi propaganda minister Joseph Goebbels as a "collection of kitsch." See Reichling 2004, 434–35.

151. "Den Schluss bildete Bachs Fantasie in G-Dur, die Karl August von Kotzebue auf der Orgel vollendet spielte. In dem gewaltigen zweiten Teil erklang die Orgel unter seinen Händen wie ein ferngrollendes Gewitter." See Reichling 2004, 436.

152. On the piano arrangements, see Schanz 2000, 70–74 and 496.

153. See, respectively, Oakeley 1904, 50; Greer 2003, 72, 74, 107–8, and 111; the November 14, 1866, issue of the *Allgemeine musikalische Zeitung*, "Berichte" section; and Haselböck 2003, 100.

(2) 27 September. Tcherepnin's class in the Conservatoire went through the magnificent *Passacaglia* of Bach; it will be a real pleasure to learn it with the
orchestra.

(3) 4 October. In the class we rehearsed the Bach *Passacaglia* and a Handel organ
concerto. I enjoy very much working on the "old masters."

(4) 6 November. I have not been into the small orchestra class for some time, but
today I came in to conduct Bach's *Passacaglia*. The orchestra had forgotten
what they ever knew about the piece, and conducting it was torture. All the
same, Tcherepnin is proposing that the orchestra should appear in a concert on
22 November, and that the *Passacaglia* should also be played in its original form
on the organ by a student from the organ class. This will be very interesting.

(5) 9 November. I had myself woken at half past seven, as by nine I must be at
rehearsal, which today looked like being a complicated one. It began with the
Bach *Passacaglia* played by the small orchestra that we were preparing for the
student concert at the end of November. The organ professor [Jacques
Handschin] also attended, and we repeated the performance, this time with
him playing the organ. However, he played very quietly and without making
any changes in registration, so the performance did not produce any particularly impressive highlights.[154]

The closest Stokowski ever got to such a "comparative" performance of the passacaglia was
late in 1922, when it was played "as an organ and orchestra work" at Philadelphia's Wanamaker
department store, with Stokowski conducting the Philadelphia Orchestra and Charles
Courboin as the organ soloist.[155] It is unclear from this description exactly how the organ
and orchestra interfaced, but one assumes that Stokowski's own orchestration was used for
certain variations and Bach's original organ version for others, whereas during the fugue
there was much more in the way of simultaneous performance. Premiered in February of
that year and played seven more times that spring, this transcription quickly became one of
the most acclaimed numbers in the orchestra's repertory. In addition, the passacaglia was
the first large-scale Bach work ever orchestrated by Stokowski, who considered it the composer's greatest opus for the organ. When, in 1941, Stokowski conducted his arrangement
while touring with the All-American Youth Orchestra—an ensemble created by him in
response to Hitler Youth propaganda—he argued in a program note that the passacaglia
was a timeless masterpiece that transcended its original performance medium:

Bach's *Passacaglia* is in music what a great Gothic cathedral is in architecture—the
same vast conception—the same soaring mysticism given eternal form.... The

---

154. Phillips 2006, 516–17, 523, 535, and 538.

155. Smith 2004, 154–56 (see 117–43 for a discussion of Stokowski's Aeolian Duo-Art player pipe organ roll
recording of the work).

Passacaglia is one of those works whose content is so full and significant that its medium of expression is of relative unimportance; whether played on the organ, or on the greatest of all instruments—the orchestra—it is one of the most divinely inspired contrapuntal works ever conceived.

Respighi's orchestration, whose score includes an organ pedal part for the beginning and end of the passacaglia proper as well as for the end of the fugue, was commissioned in 1929 by legendary conductor (and Respighi's paisano) Arturo Toscanini.[156] Working like a man possessed to meet the maestro's demands, Respighi knocked off the transcription—which is by no means lacking in material of his own composition—in only nine days. After Toscanini premiered it with the New York Philharmonic at Carnegie Hall in April 1930, he cabled his colleague with the good news: "Passacaglia huge success: masterly orchestration. Bravo Respighi!" The orchestra's European tour during May and June of that year boasted five additional performances, including one at La Scala in Respighi's presence, and Toscanini continued with ten more over the next two seasons. It may be said that Respighi's transcription generated the same sort of excitement in New York that Stokowski's had in Philadelphia, which was surely one of Toscanini's goals in the first place.

Nowadays, Respighi's transcription is best known as the music to Roland Petit's ballet *Le jeune homme et la mort*.[157] According to Jean Cocteau's synopsis of the plot, "The young man is waiting for a young woman who does not love him. She arrives, he pleads with her, she insults him and leaves. He hangs himself. The room disappears. Death comes and tears off her mask: it is the girl. She puts the mask on the young man, then leads him over the rooftops." Since its premiere in 1946, this quintessential example of postwar existentialism has been interpreted by many of the world's leading male dancers, including Jean Babilée, Rudolf Nureyev, and Nicholas Le Riche. No doubt its most famous performance, albeit a drastically abbreviated one, is that by Mikhail Baryshnikov in the opening scene of Taylor Hackford's 1985 film *White Nights*. The orchestration heard there, which is restricted largely to the passacaglia proper, is by Michel Colombier.

Although he was one of the greatest French musicians of the nineteenth century, Camille Saint-Saëns's orchestration of the passacaglia languishes today in the archives of the Bibliothèque nationale, Paris.[158] Both the handwriting and paper of this autograph manuscript suggest a date of before 1855, which would mean that Saint-Saëns was no older than twenty when he inscribed it. The fugue is completely absent, but what is truly

---

156. Respighi 1962, 125–26; Erskine 1943, 113–30; Smith 2004, 156; and Guay 2008. Respighi also orchestrated Bach's Prelude and Fugue in D Major, BWV 532, and three of the composer's organ chorales (BWV 645, 648, and 659).

157. Koegler 2006; and Langer 2007, 210–11.

158. Ratner 2002, 431; and Fauquet and Hennion 2000, 86.

curious about the arrangement is the inclusion of an oboe da caccia and a tromba da tirarsi (slide trumpet), two Baroque instruments that had long since become obsolete. Otherwise, the scoring projects a distinctly French façade in its use of two harps but also a funereal ambience in its inclusion of three trombones. The editor or conductor to whom the manuscript was presented was probably voicing his dissatisfaction with this anachronistic and weirdly variegated instrumentation when he wrote on the source that "Saint-Saëns should review this transcription before any publication" (*S. S. doit revoir cette transcription avant toute publication*). In another hand is the more direct comment "*inutilisable.*"

In terms of overall popularity, Bach's passacaglia may rank behind the Toccata and Fugue in D Minor, but its influence on later composers has been infinitely greater. This comes as no surprise in view of the piece's superiority as a musical composition, for the passacaglia is an unequivocal masterwork and the most important set of variations above an ostinato bass ever written. Naturally, its imitators within the field of organ music are numerous, encompassing such names as Mendelssohn, Franck (see chap. 5), Middelschulte, Reger, Willan, Sowerby, and Shostakovitch.[159] Outside the organ world, Bach's passacaglia has inspired such talents as Brahms, D'Indy (see chap. 5), Holst, Schoenberg, Ravel, Webern, Berg, Hindemith, and Ligeti in the composition of orchestral, military band, and chamber pieces; harpsichord works; and even operas.

"ICH RUF ZU DIR, HERR JESU CHRIST," BWV 639

Of the roughly two hundred Bach organ chorales that exist today, this *Orgelbüchlein* setting is the most famous. Because the piece is short and dead easy to play, especially at the traditional slow tempo, and because it offers the bonus of playing on two different manuals, it is normally the first Bach organ chorale that any organist learns. Moreover, it has given birth to more transcriptions and adaptations than any organ work written by or ascribed to the composer save the Toccata and Fugue in D Minor. Indeed, with its trio-sonata texture and stringlike middle voice, "Ich ruf zu dir" may be a transcription itself. The work has also figured in two acclaimed films. Beyond these facts is the sheer beauty of the music, which seems perfectly suited to the hymn's plaintive text. A program note by the record producer Charles O'Connell seems to capture better than any other commentary the true essence of the piece: "One of the tenderest utterances in all the music of Bach is the infinitely touching, the emotionally searching, and yet resigned and complacent music of the chorale prelude "I Call Upon Thee, Lord Jesus Christ." Like so many works of consummate art, this is an utterance of the most profound simplicity, and therein lies its persuasiveness and its eloquence."[160]

---

159. See the recent recording by James Vivian, *Passacaglias from the Temple Church* (JAV Recordings 156).
160. O'Connell 1950, 13.

Some of these same attributes may have been recognized by the member of C. P. E. Bach's Hamburg circle (probably C. P. E. himself) who produced an organ arrangement of "Ich ruf zu dir" by adding to it an introduction, interludes between phrases, and a codetta, thereby expanding the original version by more than ten bars.[161] First edited for publication in 1996, this most appealing adaptation (BWV Anh. 73) is now the subject of three different editions and at least one recording.[162] Whatever Mendelssohn thought of the music, he realized the work's potential not only as a "strongly registered" organ solo but also as a transcription for solo piano—with the chorale tune played in octaves—or for violin with piano accompaniment. One can only imagine how Alkan interpreted the piece when he played it for his fellow Parisians on the pedal piano. Busoni's still-popular piano arrangement, published in 1898, involves doublings of various kinds as well as a host of performance instructions, all of which make for expressive and gorgeous piano writing.[163] He took bolder artistic license with the work's form, restating its last two phrases with the chorale melody transposed down an octave and tacking on three hokey chords at the end. It is no coincidence that Stokowski included this same repeat in his orchestration, first performed in 1926, but he had the good taste to ignore Busoni's codetta. Not to be outdone, however, Stokowski added three beats of his own at the beginning, thus complementing Bach's anacrusis. Stokowski's introduction, as we come full circle, was later appropriated by Virgil Fox.[164]

Writing in the late 1930s, the great American composer Aaron Copland in his book *What to Listen for in Music* presented this organ chorale as a kind of case study in polyphony.[165] He instructed his readers to listen to the work four times, first concentrating on each of the three individual voices and then focusing on how the three form a cohesive whole. For these purposes, he recommended Stokowski's orchestration, despite its lush texture. Today, Copland could choose from recordings of various transcriptions, whether for cello and piano (Pierre Fournier and Maurice Gendron); cello, lute, and continuo (Yo-Yo Ma and members of the Amsterdam Baroque Orchestra); classical guitar (Philip Hii); or viols with organ continuo (Ensemble Mare Nostrum).[166] An apparently unrecorded transcription for chamber ensemble comes from Harrison Birtwistle's *Bach Measures*, a set of *Orgelbüchlein* transcriptions first performed (with choreography) in 1996 and first published in 2001. With its tendency toward *Klangfarbenmelodie* (melody of tone colors, per Schoenberg), this arrangement looks like something out of the Second Viennese School.

161. Stinson 1996, 150–66; Stinson 2006, 32–34; Eddie 2007, 19–20; Ochse 1994, 67; and Smith 2004, 170–71.

162. See Stinson 1996, 169–73; Emans 2007; Richards and Yearsley 2008; and Kevin Bowyer's 2004 recording, *J. S. Bach: The Works for Organ, Volume 16* (Nimbus Records NI 5734/5).

163. Sixteen piano transcriptions of this work survive. See Schanz 2000, 113 and 529.

164. See *Virgil Fox: The Bach Gamut* (Reference Recordings RR-107).

165. Copland 1939, 106–7 (see 152–53 for a discussion of Bach's Passacaglia in C Minor, a work that certainly influenced Copland's own passacaglia for piano).

166. Using viols, lute, portative organ, and two different sopranos, the early-music group Ensemble Mare Nostrum has recently recorded a deeply affecting transcription of the entire *Orgelbüchlein* (MA Recordings M076A).

"Ich ruf zu dir" made its first appearance in a motion picture in 1931, in Rouben Mamoulian's *Dr. Jekyll and Mr. Hyde*.[167] Herman Hand's orchestration of the infamous Toccata and Fugue in D Minor runs through the opening title cards, and as the camera starts to roll we see and hear Jekyll playing a segment of the organ chorale, which has been transposed to D minor for the sake of a smooth transition from the D-minor cadence of the toccata.[168] The chorale prelude seems to have been chosen here for its vaguely "gloomy" nature (minor key, chromatic figuration, slow tempo), in accordance with the plot of this early horror film. Jekyll's other organ performance is of the same toccata and fugue heard at the beginning, as mentioned earlier in this chapter.

"Ich ruf zu dir" plays a far greater role in Andrei Tarkovsky's *Solaris*, an award-winning science-fiction film from 1972. The piece is heard there four times as a non-diegetic organ solo, although it is sometimes electronically enhanced. Selected by Tarkovsky himself in tribute to his favorite composer, the work symbolizes the earthly home of the film's protagonist, cosmonaut Kris Kelvin, and it possibly represents as well the earthly values of nature, art, and love. It is to planet Earth what Eduard Artemyev's electronic score is to the alien and dehumanized setting of outer space.

We first hear the work, in its entirety and exclusively as an organ solo, during the opening credits, which roll against a lifeless, solid black background. But when we next encounter it, the action has shifted to a space station on the planet Solaris, a once-thriving project now gone awry. With his materialized dead wife Hari at his side, and in a scene of nostalgic longing for Earth, Kris watches old home movies taken of his family in the beautiful forest surrounding their dacha. Again, the organ chorale is played complete, although it initially overlaps with Artemyev's score, which at that juncture is ominous noise accompanying a shot of the ocean that covers Solaris. The third hearing takes place inside the library of the space station in a segment dominated by Brueghel's *Hunters in the Snow*, a painting that bears an uncanny resemblance to one of the aforementioned home movies. Kris and Hari now float weightlessly to the music, which mixes the original organ version not only with the noise representing the Solaris Ocean but also with an ethereal, vibraphone-like countermelody courtesy of Artemyev. All of this before the scene is shattered, two phrases from the end of the work, with Hari's suicide. We hear the piece a fourth and final time, and again in its entirety, at the very end of the film, upon Kris's return to Earth. (Thus the work serves as a framing device.) Kris is again surrounded by the natural beauty of his childhood, and the organ chorale is again enhanced with Artemyev's vibraphone effects, along with what can be described as an electronic wordless

---

167. Lerner 2010, 57–61.

168. See J. Brown 2010, 9, for a still shot of this scene. It is clear from this photograph that Jekyll is playing from vol. 5 of the Peters edition of Bach's complete organ works, in which the chorale settings of the *Orgelbüchlein* are given in alphabetical order, rather than the familiar liturgical sequence of Bach's autograph. Thus the page from Jekyll's score facing "Ich ruf zu dir" contains "Hilf Gott, dass mir's gelinge," BWV 624, instead of "Es ist das Heil uns kommen her," BWV 638.

chorus and string orchestra.[169] As two experts on Tarkovsky have observed, "in space, the Bach music is gradually given subtle electronic enhancement, especially toward the end, as the settings of the dacha and the station seem to fuse, and when it occurs on Kris's (apparent) return to Earth it has become virtually a new, yet still recognizable piece—just as Kris himself is still the "same" person, yet utterly altered."[170]

The opening credits of the film identify the organ chorale not as "Ich ruf zu dir, Herr Jesu Christ" but as "BACH'S F MINOR CHORAL PRELUDE," thus divorcing the work from any religious connotations. Tarkovsky could scarcely have done otherwise, regardless of his motives for choosing a "sacred" work by Bach, for the Soviet censors demanded that he "remove the concept of God."[171] Due to the film's enduring popularity, it is by this generic title that the piece is known in Russia today, whether we mean the "Funky house / jazz remix" by techno artist Max Fomitchev (aka UltraMax), the microtonal synthesizer-duet arrangement by Mykhaylo Khramov, or the brass-choir transcription by members of the Novosibirsk State Philharmonic Society.

"HERZLICH TUT MICH VERLANGEN," BWV 727

Like "Ich ruf zu dir," this work is a brief, ostensibly slow, and relatively easy chorale setting for two manuals, and it too exemplifies Bach's ability to depict a poignant text—in this case, one that expresses a longing for death—with music of ravishing beauty. But "Herzlich tut" also owes its popularity, which is likewise attested to by all manner of transcriptions, to the extraordinarily beloved hymn tune on which it is based, that which since the 1829 revival of Bach's St. Matthew Passion has been associated with Paul Gerhardt's hymn "O Haupt voll Blut und Wunden." English speakers know this text as "O Sacred Head, Now Wounded."

The first indication of any sustained interest in the organ chorale emanates from the modern French organ school, starting with Théodore Dubois's rendition of it in 1878 at the Trocadéro.[172] Of the fifteen inaugural recitals played on that organ, this was the only one to include chorale preludes (Dubois performed as well the bicinium on "Allein Gott in der Höh sei Ehr," BWV 711). There is no evidence that the predominantly Catholic audience objected to this novelty, but by the same token the only review of the concert couched both works in wholly secular terms. Apropos of "Herzlich tut," the critic wrote that "a beautiful adagio in B minor, its theme simply stated, was easily grasped by the audience."

---

169. For a partial transcription, see Barham 2008, 267.

170. Johnson and Petrie 1994, 108.

171. Lopate 2002.

172. Smith 1995, 288–89. According to Bokum 1971, 113, Samuel de Lange had performed the work in concert already in 1870.

The evidence otherwise revolves around the figure of Charles-Marie Widor and his illustrious pupils Albert Schweitzer and Louis Vierne.[173] In his edition with Edouard Nies-Berger of "miscellaneous" organ chorales by Bach, published in 1954 by G. Schirmer, Schweitzer fondly remembered "Herzlich tut" as a piece performed by his maître at their very first lesson: "I shall never forget the plain manner in which Widor played this piece for me in 1893, in my first hour of organ lessons, which were such a joy to me." And from the start of Schweitzer's career as a concert organist to the end, this was one of five Bach works that he most often played (as was "Ich ruf zu dir"). He sometimes programmed the piece as "O Haupt voll Blut und Wunden."

According to Vierne, Widor once obtained permission, either in 1893 or 1894, for several "artists" to visit the organ loft at Notre Dame in order to hear Bach chorale preludes played by his students at the Paris Conservatory, for Widor treasured these pieces as much as Bach's free organ works, quite a revolutionary attitude for a French organist at that time. In Vierne's words, "Chance dealt me *Durch Adams Fall* [BWV 637], *Herzlich tut mich verlangen*, and *In dir ist Freude* [BWV 615]." All three works would remain in Vierne's repertoire for the rest of his professional life, evinced by his performances of all three on his tour of North America in 1927. His 1929 recording of "Herzlich tut" is distinguished by a slow tempo ($\flat$ = 50) and extremely long rallentando and diminuendo during the last phrase, which Bach concludes with an unnecessarily long inverted pedal point.

We must also mention two public performances in Paris that involved Widor and Vierne. One took place in 1932, at the dedication of the newly rebuilt organ at Notre Dame. To quote Vierne, "Herzlich tut" on that occasion was used "to show off the Récit solo Trompette." Both Vierne and Widor appeared on the bill, with the eighty-eight-year-old Widor flawlessly rendering his entire *Symphonie gothique* on the five-manual instrument, but which organist played the chorale prelude is unclear. The other performance dates back to 1899, when it was Widor's task to inaugurate the Merklin-Mutin organ at the Temple du Saint Esprit. His inclusion of "Herzlich tut" on that recital may be interpreted as a conciliatory gesture toward the church's Protestant congregation.

As early as 1844, when A. B. Marx published a piano arrangement of the work in his anthology *Auswahl aus Sebastian Bach's Kompositionen, zur ersten Bekanntschaft mit dem Meister am Pianoforte*, "Herzlich tut" has attracted the attention of transcribers. More than a dozen have chosen piano as their medium,[174] as did William Walton with his contribution to Harriet Cohen's "Bach Book" (Oxford University Press, 1932), a set of "transcriptions for pianoforte from the works of J. S. Bach" that involves practically every leading British composer of that era except for Elgar and Holst. Adhering strictly to the

173. Smith 1999, 208–9, 285, 379, 394, 417, 464, 504, 511–12; Schützeichel 1991, 19, 24, 27, 36, 46, 49–50, and 164; and Lueders 2000, 28.

174. Schanz 2000, 141 and 536.

length of his model and using a modicum of performance instructions, Walton's most substantial alteration here is the use of left-hand octaves for the pedal line. Around 1940 he orchestrated this same organ chorale, along with several other movements by Bach, for Frederick Ashton's ballet *The Wise Virgins*.[175] This is a finely nuanced affair, with the individual chorale phrases played by solo woodwinds and/or muted strings, and usually ending with a delicate timpani roll. Another notable arrangement is that "paraphrased for violin & pianoforte" by the English composer, conductor, and organist Fritz Bennicke Hart. Published in 1925, in a collection that also includes two chorales from the *Orgelbüchlein* ("Der Tag, der ist so freudenreich," and "Christ lag in Todesbanden") Hart's thoroughly romanticized adaptation combines a transcription proper (mm. 16–33) with a free paraphrase of essentially the same length. It is dedicated to and was performed by none other than Fritz Kreisler.

---

175. Boyd 1999, 528; Guay 2008; and Hull 1929, 181.

Appendix 1

EXPLANATORY NOTE

The data contained in this appendix are taken from the records of the Paris Conservatory during César Franck's tenure there as professor of organ. Housed today at the Archives Nationales, Paris, these documents preserve the progress reports drafted by Franck in conjunction with the semester examinations taken by his pupils (AJ^{37} 283–90) and the reports, which are not in Franck's hand, on the annual organ competitions at the school (AJ^{37} 251–52). While Franck's reports have survived complete, there are no extant competition reports for 1872, 1873, 1877, 1878, 1880, 1883, 1885, 1886, or 1887. For each exam or competition, the appendix lists the students in the same order found in the conservatory records.[1] Two students are known only by the surnames of "Rigaud" (January 1880) and "Fournier" (January 1887). The following commentary addresses, in roughly the order of performance, various issues surrounding the repertoire played by Franck's students at these events. Since chapter 5 of the present book covers the works by Bach that were played, the focus here will be on music by other composers.

1. MENDELSSOHN: SIX SONATAS FOR THE ORGAN, OP. 65

Within Franck's studio, the organ sonatas of Felix Mendelssohn were second in popularity only to the music of Bach. Franck taught these works to a total of nineteen pupils, literally from his first semester as organ professor to his last. (Only once, during the first semester of the 1886–87

---

1. For biographical information on these individuals, see Pierre 1900, 690–869; and Davies 1970, 320–21. See also Fauquet 1999a, 959–64; and Ochse 1994, 231–32.

academic year, did he teach from the other organ collection by Mendelssohn that would have been known in France at this time, namely, the Three Preludes and Fugues for the Organ, op. 37.) During the 1870s, the first, third, and sixth sonatas were played to the exclusion of the other three, but by the end of the 1887–88 year, all six sonatas had been performed by at least two different pupils. The conservatory records attest to almost thirty student performances altogether.

When citing his students' performances of these pieces, Franck often referred to a specific movement that was played, but in the case of Édouard Rouher's exam in January 1883 he referred to two movements from the sixth sonata, calling them *Andante et Fugue*. Rouher, therefore, essayed the fugue that concludes the variations on "Vater unser im Himmelreich" with which this work begins, and he most likely prefaced the fugue with the first variation in the set, marked by Mendelssohn as *Andante sostenuto*. Another possibility is that the fugue was coupled with the *Andante* that concludes the entire sonata, but this movement is not based on the "Vater unser" chorale, nor is it in the same key as the variations.

In his progress report on Henri Letocart in January 1889, Franck cited his pupil's repertory selection as the *1re partie de la sonate en ut min*. No composer is given, which is consistent with how Franck normally lists works by Bach in these sources (due to the multitude of Bach works played, Franck tended to give just the work title, along with the corresponding volume, number, and sometimes even page number from the Peters edition). Here, though, the only Bach work Franck can be referring to is the second of the six trio sonatas (BWV 525–30), a collection that was basically neglected by Franck as an organ pedagogue. It makes infinitely more sense that he is citing Mendelssohn's C-minor organ sonata (No. 2), which four other Franck students are documented to have played during the 1880s.

Franck's two progress reports on Édouard Bopp, which cite that pupil's performances in 1888 of the fourth and fifth Mendelssohn sonatas, corroborate Bopp's amusing claim that at one meeting of the conservatory organ class, Franck himself "pumped the bellows" while Bopp "played a piece by Mendelssohn."[2] By way of explanation, it seems that the staff member appointed to blow the organ was so often absent that his duties were regularly assumed by the first student to arrive—a tradition that may have discouraged punctuality. But on the morning described by Bopp, he was the only one of the eight or nine pupils in attendance. Another Franck student who comes to mind in the context of organ blowing is Jean Tolbecque, who during the first semester of the 1874–75 academic year happened to play the first movement of the first Mendelssohn sonata.[3] Tolbecque's habit, believe it or not, was to hide in the bellows chamber whenever he was unprepared to play, a tactic that accords with his mediocre record at the conservatory: Tolbecque studied with Franck for four whole years (1872–76)—twice as long as most students—yet he never advanced beyond first runner-up in any of the competitions that he entered, despite tackling several of Bach's most challenging pieces.

As someone who regularly taught the Mendelssohn sonatas (and who must also have played them), Franck was naturally influenced by these works in his own organ compositions. While this assertion has never before been made in either the Franck or Mendelssohn literature, it is quite incontestable in the case of Franck's *Choral No. 3*. Just consider how Franck prepares for

---

2. Smith 2002, 185.

3. Hinton, 7.

the beautiful Adagio section of this piece, first with a fermata-topped V⁷ chord and then, following a change of manual and registration, with a suspended treble pitch from that chord that begins the ornamental melody. The manner in which Mendelssohn introduces the *Adagio* section of the first movement of his second sonata is essentially the same in all respects. Furthermore, as Franck commences his melody line, he adopts the same basic contour as Mendelssohn (descending, stepwise motion) and, more tellingly, the same motivic pattern (four sixteenths followed by two eighth notes). Franck also borrows Mendelssohn's technique of immediately restating his opening phrase in a different key.

The slowly sustained and thickly textured arpeggiated seventh chords found throughout the first half of Franck's *Choral*, conversely, seem to be inspired by the third movement of Mendelssohn's first sonata. Similar material appears in certain works written by or attributed to Bach, most famously in mm. 2 and 10 of the Toccata and Fugue in D Minor, BWV 565,[4] but Franck's procedure, in the two such passages immediately before his Adagio, of chromatically altering the seventh chord exactly three-quarters of the way through has its precedent only in this movement by Mendelssohn. Moreover, Franck employs precisely the same texture: eight manual voices divided evenly between the two hands, with the lowest pitch duplicated in the middle of the pedalboard. Given the organ's ability to sustain pitches, the effect is both idiomatic and dramatic.

2. THE PRELUDE AND FUGUE IN C MAJOR, BWV 566

This early Bach work is known by various titles ("Prelude and Fugue," "Toccata and Fugue," and simply "Toccata") and is transmitted in two different keys (C major and E major). Franck and his pupils knew the piece, by virtue of its inclusion in volume 3 of the Peters edition of the complete Bach organ works, as a Prelude and Fugue in C Major. The work's popularity within the Franck circle, which is documented by approximately a dozen student performances, was surpassed only by the Fantasy and Fugue in C Minor, BWV 537.

According to Franck's progress reports, four different times (June 1874, January 1877, June 1879, and January 1880) his pupils played either the "first part" or "second part" of the fugue.[5] In making this distinction, Franck was alluding to the fact that this work actually contains two fugues, both of which are found in the section of the work marked *Fuga* (mm. 34–229). They correspond to mm. 34–122 (Peters edition, pp. 64–67) and measures 134–229 (Peters edition, pp. 68–71). One wonders whether Franck understood the "second part" of the fugue to include only the second fugue proper and not the brief toccata-like interlude that precedes it on the same page, for the latter seems too perfunctory to have served as an ersatz prelude. Whatever the answer, most of the student performances involved only the fugue and not the prelude, in accordance with Franck's general reliance on Bach fugues as teaching repertory.

---

4. See also m. 106 of the Fugue in C Minor on a Theme by Legrenzi, BWV 574, and m. 103 of "O Lamm Gottes, unschuldig," BWV 656.

5. For example, in his progress report on Joseph-Paul Humblot in June 1874, Franck designated the excerpt played as the *2e Partie de la fugue en ut. Livre* 3, *N°* 7. The book and number refer to the work's position in the Peters edition of Bach's complete organ works.

3. FRANCK'S OWN COMPOSITIONS

During the 1873–74 academic year, Franck began to teach his own organ works, and he would continue to do so until his final semester. He taught the *Six Pièces* throughout his tenure; starting in 1885, he also taught the *Trois Pièces* (the Fantasy in A Major, *Cantabile*, and *Pièce héroïque*), which were not published until 1883. The only one of these nine works not cited in the records is the *Pièce héroïque*, although we have it on good authority that Marie Prestat, one of Franck's favorite pupils, once brought this piece into class, much to her teacher's delight.[6] Twenty-two performances of these eight works are documented. Thus Franck's own music was almost as popular within his organ studio as the Mendelssohn sonatas were.

The various ways in which Franck's compositions are cited in the conservatory records are not without interest or, for that matter, without error. For example, Franck designated Jean-Jacques Jemain's repertoire selection for the June 1887 exam as the *commencement* or "beginning" of the *Grande Pièce symphonique*. By this, Franck must have meant the material that precedes the much longer sonata-form section beginning in m. 60, which in performance presumably would have extended only to m. 57, thereby avoiding the weak and transitional second-inversion F-sharp-minor chord in mm. 58–59. The next documented performance of this piece is that by Georges-Paul Bondon at the 1889 competition (implying that a piece of this length could be played in its entirety only at one of these events, rather than on a semester exam; see also Henri Kaiser in 1884). According to the staff member who quite carelessly prepared the report, Bondon performed the *Priere* [*sic*] *symphonique en fa # min.* by none other than *J. S. Bach* (!).

In his report on Anatole-Léon Grand-Jany in June 1883, Franck wrote that the repertory selection was his *Priere en si b*. It is by no means clear from this inscription whether Franck is referring to his *Prière*, which is in C-sharp minor, or his only organ work in B-flat, the *Final*. Happily, the matter is resolved by a recently published letter of May 14, 1883, from Franck to his pupil Gabriel Pierné:

> We speak of you often in class. It is going fairly well. I hope for a first prize for Grand-Jany. Kaiser works well; he could obtain a second prize. Jeannin does not progress much; for the moment he has been overtaken by Kaiser.... As for the new students, I cannot yet judge whether they will be ready to compete.... In next month's exam, Grand-Jany will play my piece in B-flat, [the one] with which you won your prize, and at the competition the Passacaglia of J. S. Bach.[7]

---

6. Smith 1999, 46 n. 14; and Smith 2002, 185.

7. "Nous parlons souvent de vous à la classe. Elle marche assez bien, j'espère un 1er prix pour Grand-Jany. Kaiser travaille bien il pourrait obtenir un 2d prix Jeannin n'avance pas beaucoup; pour le moment il est dépassé par Kaiser. Quant aux nouveaux je ne puis pas encore juger s'ils seront en état de concourir. A l'examen du mois prochain Grand-Jany jouera ma pièce en si b avec laquelle vous avez gagné votre prix et au concours la passa-caille de J. S. Bach." See Fauquet 1999b, 137–38.

The final paragraph of this excerpt shows conclusively—and this is corroborated by the data on Pierné's repertoire selection for the 1882 competition—that Grand-Jany played the *Final*, one of Franck's most virtuosic compositions for the organ. Significantly, it also reveals that Grand-Jany performed Bach's Passacaglia in C Minor at the competition in 1883, which is one of the nine years for which no official competition report has survived. Franck guessed correctly about his students' chances at the upcoming competition: Grand-Jany took first prize, and Henri Kaiser second prize.[8] There is no evidence that Paul-Joseph Jeannin, who placed higher at the 1882 competition than Kaiser (first runner-up versus second runner-up), or any other student took part. Jeannin was definitely allowed to compete in 1884 but continued his downward spiral by not even placing.

We also learn from this letter some interesting details, at least for the 1882–83 academic year, about Franck's timetable for selecting which pupils would enter the competitions. He probably never questioned that his two most advanced students would participate, but he was unsure of the beginners (which presumably included Édouard Rouher, Louis Landry, and Léon Honnoré, even though only Landry took the June exam). With only two months to go before the competition, these novices would have had relatively little time to learn a new piece, something that would have been expected of any competitor.[9] There is no way of knowing how long Grand-Jany had been preparing the Passacaglia, which he was learning at the same time as Franck's *Final*.

Franck was certainly proud of both Grand-Jany and Kaiser, but one senses that he was prouder still of Pierné, his star pupil from the previous year. According to Franck's final progress report on him in June 1882 (see app. 2), Pierné was that rare blend of talent and diligence, and Franck may regularly have lauded him ("We speak of you often in class") as a model student. Although Pierné was still a teenager at the time, Franck was already treating him less like a student than a colleague, as the disparaging remarks about poor Jeannin make all too clear.

4. LEMMENS: "PETITE PIÈCE"

The conservatory records document three student performances of music by the Belgian organist Jacques-Nicholas Lemmens, twice in January 1879 (Georges Marty and Lucien Hillemacher) and once in January 1885 (Jean-Jacques Jemain). In the first two instances, Franck cited the Lemmens work as "Petite Pièce," while in the last he merely wrote "Pièce." This is hardly enough information to identify the particular composition(s) played, especially considering the many organ works by Lemmens that could qualify as "petite pièces." All the students involved were in their first semester of study, which sug-

8. On these prizes, see Fauquet 1999a, 962; and Ochse 1994, 231–32.

9. Only in the case of Marie-Léonie Renaud and Jean Tolbecque in 1875, and of Samuel Rousseau in 1876, do we see that a student played the same work for both the June exam and the competition.

gests that Franck was referring to the same trifling work, perhaps one taken from Lemmens's *École d'orgue*.

5. HANDEL: CONCERTO IN B-FLAT MAJOR

One student performance of a work by George Frideric Handel is documented, that by Louis de Serres in June 1886 of a Concerto in B-flat Major. No fewer than five organ concertos in this key by Handel have survived, including two rather famous ones from his Opus 4. Most likely, de Serres played one of these two works. Whether he performed just the organ part, as opposed to a reduction of the entire score, is entirely conjectural. Franck himself, accompanied by an orchestra, played an F-major organ concerto by Handel on the first of his two concerts in Angers in December 1888.[10] It was presumably one of the two very popular concertos in this key from Opus 4.

6. SCHUMANN: STUDY IN A-FLAT MAJOR, OP. 56, NO. 4

The data attest to two student performances (Hedwige Chrétien in January 1887 and Georges Aubry in July 1889) of this piece from Robert Schumann's Six Studies for Pedal Piano. Given Franck's tendency toward canon in his own compositions, it is hardly surprising that he would have been attracted to this collection, which in fact is a set of canonic studies. Ironically, though, the only material from this opus appropriated by Franck in one of his organ works has nothing to do with this technique. Rather, in the Quasi allegretto section of his *Pastorale*, Franck simulates the accompaniment, and not the actual canon, of the fifth of Schumann's Studies. As one can tell by comparing mm. 45–56 of Franck's work to mm. 1–15 of Schumann's, Franck follows his model with respect to virtually all the elements of music: mode (minor), tempo (moderately fast), dynamics (soft), articulation (staccato), rhythm (constant eighth-note motion), harmony (minor triads and minor seventh chords), texture (four-voice chords in the hands supported by occasional "pizzicato" pedal notes), and melody (the first five chords in each section or work produce the same stepwise pattern in the top voice, beginning with the fifth degree of the scale, descending to the fourth, rising back to the fifth and then to the sixth, and falling back to the fifth). And lest there be any doubt about the matter, Franck even begins, like Schumann, not with a root-position chord but, most unusually, with one in second inversion.

---

10. Fauquet 1999a, 654.

Works Played by César Franck's Organ Students, 1872–90

Exam or Competition	Student	Work Played
Exam of June 1872	Georges Deslandres	Fugue in G Minor ("Little"), BWV 578
	Louis Benoit Bazile	Concerto in G Major after Prince Johann Ernst, BWV 592, first movement
	Paul Wachs	Mendelssohn: Sonata No. 3, first movement
	Samuel Rousseau	Fugue in B Minor on a Theme by Corelli, BWV 579
	Francis Thomé	minor-key fugue from vol. 3 of the Peters edition of Bach's organ works
Exam of January 1873	Louis Benoit Bazile	Fugue in G Minor ("Little"), BWV 578
	Samuel Rousseau	Fugue in C Minor, BWV 546/2
	Francis Thomé	Prelude and Fugue in C Major, BWV 566
	Jean Tolbecque	Fugue in G Minor, BWV 542/2
	Marie-Antoinette Gaillard	Fugue in F Minor from the Well-Tempered Clavier, BWV 857/2 or BWV 881/2
	Georges Verschneider	Canzona in D Minor, BWV 588
	Joseph-Paul Humblot	Fugue in E Minor, BWV 533/2
	Adèle Billault	Prelude in E Minor, BWV 533/1
Exam of June 1873	Louis Benoit Bazile	Fugue in A Major, BWV 536/2
	Samuel Rousseau	Prelude in C Minor, BWV 546/1
	Francis Thomé	Fugue in D Minor, BWV 539/2
	Jean Tolbecque	Concerto in A Minor after Vivaldi, BWV 593, first movement
	Georges Verschneider	Fugue in C Minor, BWV 546/2
	Joseph-Paul Humblot	Fantasy in C Minor, BWV 537/1
	Adèle Billault	Toccata in D Minor ("Dorian"), BWV 538/1

(*Continued*)

Works Played by César Franck's Organ Students, 1872–90   (Continued)

Exam or Competition	Student	Work Played
Exam of January 1874	Samuel Rousseau	Fugue in C Minor, BWV 537/2
	Jean Tolbecque	Fugue in G Minor ("Little"), BWV 578
	Georges Verschneider	Fugue in G Minor, BWV 542/2
	Joseph-Paul Humblot	Fugue in C Major, BWV 566/2, presumably the first fugue in the movement (pp. 64–67 of vol. 3 of the Peters edition)
	Adèle Billault	Concerto in A Minor after Vivaldi, BWV 593, first movement
Exam of June 1874	Samuel Rousseau	Fugue in G Minor, BWV 535/2
	Jean Tolbecque	Fugue in D Major, BWV 532/2
	Georges Verschneider	Franck: Fantasy in C Major; Bach: Trio Sonata No. 1, first movement
	Joseph-Paul Humblot	Fugue in C Major, BWV 566/2, "second part" (pp. 68–71 of vol. 3 of the Peters edition)
	Adèle Billault	Fantasy in G Minor, BWV 542/1
	Amédée-Jean Dutacq	Fantasy in C Minor, BWV 537/1
	Marie-Léonie Renaud	Canzona in D Minor, BWV 588
	Vincent D'Indy	Fugue in G Minor ("Little"), BWV 578
Competition of July 1874	Samuel Rousseau	Fugue in C Major, BWV 566/2
	Vincent D'Indy	Concerto in A Minor after Vivaldi, BWV 593
	Joseph-Paul Humblot	Fugue in C Minor, BWV 546/2
	Georges Verschneider	Prelude in B Minor, BWV 544/1

(Continued)

Exam or Competition	Student	Work Played
Exam of January 1875	Samuel Rousseau	Fugue in F Minor, BWV 534/2
	Jean Tolbecque	Mendelssohn: Sonata No. 1, first movement
	Georges Verschneider	Fugue in B Minor, BWV 544/2
	Adèle Billault	Franck: *Prélude, Fugue et Variation*
	Marie-Léonie Renaud	Fugue in C Minor, BWV 537/2
	Vincent D'Indy	Fugue in C Minor on a Theme by Legrenzi, BWV 574
Exam of June 1875	Samuel Rousseau	Fugue in C Major, BWV 545/2
	Jean Tolbecque	Prelude in D Major, BWV 532/1
	Georges Verschneider	Mendelssohn: Sonata No. 6
	Adèle Billault	Fugue in G Minor, BWV 535/2
	Marie-Léonie Renaud	Fugue in C Major, BWV 566/2
	Vincent D'Indy	Concerto in A Minor after Vivaldi, BWV 593, last movement
	Marie-Louise Genty	Fugue in B Minor on a Theme by Corelli, BWV 579
	Camille Benoit	Fugue in G Minor ("Little"), BWV 578
Competition of July 1875	Marie-Louise Genty	Concerto in G Major after Prince Johann Ernst, BWV 592
	Marie-Léonie Renaud	Fugue in C Major, BWV 566/2
	Samuel Rousseau	Prelude in E-flat Major, BWV 552/1
	Jean Tolbecque	Concerto in A Minor after Vivaldi, BWV 593
	Vincent D'Indy	Passacaglia in C Minor, BWV 582
	Georges Verschneider	Toccata in F Major, BWV 540/1

(Continued)

Works Played by César Franck's Organ Students, 1872–90   (Continued)

Exam or Competition	Student	Work Played
Exam of January 1876	Samuel Rousseau	Prelude in G Major, BWV 541/1
	Jean Tolbecque	Fugue in A Minor, BWV 543/2
	Georges Verschneider	Fantasy in G Minor, BWV 542/1
	Marie-Léonie Renaud	Fugue in D Minor, BWV 539/2
	Marie-Louise Genty	Fugue in G Minor ("Little"), BWV 578
	Camille Benoit	"O Mensch, bewein dein Sünde gross," BWV 622
Exam of June 1876	Jean Tolbecque	Toccata, Adagio, and Fugue in C Major, BWV 564, last two movements
	Georges Verschneider	"O Lamm Gottes, unschuldig," BWV 656
	Marie-Léonie Renaud	Fugue in C Minor on a Theme by Legrenzi, BWV 574
	Marie-Louise Genty	Fugue in F Minor, BWV 534/2
	Camille Benoit	Prelude and Fugue in C Minor, BWV 549
	Marie-Anna Papot	Fantasy in C Minor, BWV 537/1
Competition of July 1876	Marie-Louise Genty	Toccata and Fugue in D Minor, BWV 565
	Marie-Léonie Renaud	Franck: *Prélude, Fugue et Variation*
	Georges Verschneider	Mendelssohn: Sonata No. 3
	Samuel Rousseau	Fugue in C Minor, BWV 537/2
	Marie-Anna Papot	Fugue in B Minor on a Theme by Corelli, BWV 579
	Camille Benoit	Concerto in A Minor after Vivaldi, BWV 593
	Jean Tolbecque	Fugue in E Minor ("Wedge"), BWV 548/2

(Continued)

Exam or Competition	Student	Work Played
Exam of January 1877	Samuel Rousseau	Mendelssohn: Sonata No. 1, first movement
	Georges Verschneider	Franck: *Pastorale*
	Marie-Léonie Renaud	Fugue in A Major, BWV 536/2
	Marie-Anna Papot	Fugue in C Major, BWV 566/2, "second part"
	Clément-Jules Broutin	Fugue in C Minor, BWV 537/2
Exam of June 1877	Georges Verschneider	Franck: *Prière*
	Marie-Léonie Renaud	Fugue in C Minor, BWV 546/2
	Marie-Anna Papot	Fugue in F Major, BWV 540/2
Exam of January 1878	Marie-Anna Papot	Fugue in C Minor on a Theme by Legrenzi, BWV 574
	Clément-Jules Broutin	Mendelssohn: Sonata No. 6
	Henri Dallier	Fugue in C Minor, BWV 537/2
Exam of June 1878	Marie-Anna Papot	Fantasy in G Minor, BWV 542/1
	Henri Dallier	Franck: Fantasy in C Major
Exam of January 1879	Marie-Anna Papot	Bach: Fugue in C Major, either BWV 545/2 or BWV 547/2
	Auguste Chapuis	Pastorale in F Major, BWV 590
	Jean Lapuchin	Fugue in E Minor, BWV 533/2
	Georges Marty	Lemmens: "Petite Pièce"
	Lucien Hillemacher	Lemmens: "Petite Pièce"
Exam of June 1879	Marie-Anna Papot	Fugue in A Major, BWV 536/2
	Auguste Chapuis	Fugue in G Minor, BWV 535/2
	Jean Lapuchin	Fugue in C Major, BWV 566/2, "second part"
Competition of July 1879	Auguste Chapuis	Fugue in C Minor, BWV 546/2
	Marie-Anna Papot	Bach: Fugue in C Minor, either BWV 549/2 or BWV 574
Exam of January 1880	Marie-Anna Papot	Mendelssohn: Sonata No. 2
	Auguste Chapuis	Bach: Fugue in D Minor, either BWV 538/2 ("Dorian") or BWV 539/2
	Lucien Hillemacher	Fugue in C Major, BWV 566/2, "first part" (pp. 64–67 of vol. 3 of the Peters edition)
	"Rigaud"	Prelude and Fugue in G Major, BWV 541
	Pierre Sourilas	Fugue in G Minor, BWV 535/2

(Continued)

Works Played by César Franck's Organ Students, 1872–90   (Continued)

Exam or Competition	Student	Work Played
Exam of June 1880	Marie-Anna Papot	Mendelssohn: Sonata No. 2
	Auguste Chapuis	Toccata in D Minor ("Dorian"), BWV 538/1
	Pierre Sourilas	Toccata in F Major, BWV 540/1
Exam of January 1881	Auguste Chapuis	Prelude in E-flat Major, BWV 552/1
	Pierre Sourilas	Toccata in D Minor ("Dorian"), BWV 538/1
	Gabriel Pierné	Fantasy in C Minor, BWV 537/1
	Louis Ganne	Bach: Fugue in E Major from the Well-Tempered Clavier, BWV 854/2 or BWV 878/2
Exam of June 1881	Auguste Chapuis	Fugue in E-flat Major, BWV 552/2
	Pierre Sourilas	Fugue in D Minor, BWV 539/2
	Gabriel Pierné	Fugue in G Minor ("Little"), BWV 578
	Louis Ganne	Prelude and Fugue in E Minor, BWV 533
Competition of July 1881	Gabriel Pierné	Concerto in A Minor after Vivaldi, BWV 593, last movement
	Pierre Sourilas	Fugue in A Minor, BWV 543/2
	Auguste Chapuis	Fantasy in C Minor, BWV 537/1, or Fantasy in G Minor, BWV 542/1
Exam of January 1882	Gabriel Pierné	Franck: Fantasy in C Major
	Louis Ganne	Fugue in C Minor, BWV 537/2
	Paul-Joseph Jeannin	Prelude and Fugue in E Minor, BWV 533
	Henri Kaiser	Canzona in D Minor, BWV 588
	Anatole-Léon Grand-Jany	Bach: Fugue in D-sharp Minor from the Well-Tempered Clavier, BWV 853/2 or BWV 877/2
	Frédéric Duplessis	Bach: Fugue in E-flat Major from the Well-Tempered Clavier, BWV 852/2 or BWV 876/2

(Continued)

Exam or Competition	Student	Work Played
Exam of June 1882	Louis Ganne	Fugue in D Minor, BWV 539/2
	Paul-Joseph Jeannin	Fugue in G Minor, BWV 535/2
	Henri Kaiser	Fugue in G Major, BWV 550/2
	Anatole-Léon Grand-Jany	Fantasy in C Minor, BWV 537/1
Competition of July 1882	Louis Ganne	Fugue in F Major, BWV 540/2
	Paul-Joseph Jeannin	Bach: Fugue in C Major, either BWV 564/3 or BWV 566/2
	Anatole-Léon Grand-Jany	Fugue in C Minor, BWV 537/2
	Gabriel Pierné	Franck: *Final*
	Henri Kaiser	Bach: Fugue in C Minor, either BWV 549/2 or BWV 574
Exam of January 1883	Paul-Joseph Jeannin	Fugue in C Major, BWV 545/2
	Henri Kaiser	Prelude in A Minor, BWV 543/1
	Anatole-Léon Grand-Jany	Fugue in D Minor, BWV 539/2
	Édouard Rouher	Mendelssohn: Sonata No. 6, excerpts
	Louis Landry	Prelude and Fugue in G Major, BWV 557 (Eight Little Preludes and Fugues)
	Léon Honnoré	Fugue in E Minor, BWV 555/2 (Eight Little Preludes and Fugues)
Exam of June 1883	Paul-Joseph Jeannin	Fugue in C Minor, BWV 537/2
	Henri Kaiser	Prelude in C Minor, BWV 546/1
	Anatole-Léon Grand-Jany	Franck: *Final*
	Louis Landry	Concerto in G Major after Prince Johann Ernst, BWV 592
Exam of January 1884	Paul-Joseph Jeannin	Mendelssohn: Sonata No. 2
	Henri Kaiser	Mendelssohn: Sonata No. 4, second and third movements
	Édouard Rouher	"O Mensch, bewein dein Sünde gross," BWV 622
	Louis Landry	Concerto in A Minor after Vivaldi, BWV 593
	Léonie Guintrange	Mendelssohn: Sonata No. 1, third movement
	Carlos Mesquita	Canzona in D Minor, BWV 588

(*Continued*)

Works Played by César Franck's Organ Students, 1872–90   (Continued)

Exam or Competition	Student	Work Played
Exam of June 1884	Paul-Joseph Jeannin	Mendelssohn: Sonata No. 3
	Édouard Rouher	Mendelssohn: Sonata No. 2, last movement
	Louis Landry	Fugue in D Minor, BWV 539/2
	Carlos Mesquita	Fugue in G Minor ("Little"), BWV 578
	Léonie Guintrange	Prelude in C Minor, BWV 546/1
Competition of July 1884	Carlos Mesquita	Mendelssohn: Sonata No. 1
	Paul-Joseph Jeannin	unspecified Fugue in C Minor by Bach
	Henri Kaiser	Franck: *Grande Pièce symphonique*
	Louis Landry	Mendelssohn: Sonata No. 6
Exam of January 1885	Louis Landry	Concerto in A Minor after Vivaldi, BWV 593, last movement
	Carlos Mesquita	Toccata and Fugue in D Minor, BWV 565
	Léonie Guintrange	"O Mensch, bewein dein Sünde gross," BWV 622
	Henri Pinot	Fugue in G Minor, BWV 542/2
	Jean-Jacques Jemain	Lemmens: "Pièce"
Exam of June 1885	Louis Landry	Prelude and Fugue in A Minor, BWV 543
	Carlos Mesquita	Mendelssohn: Sonata No. 6
	Henri Pinot	Franck: Fantasy in A Major
	Jean-Jacques Jemain	Fugue in C Minor, BWV 537/2
Exam of January 1886	Louis Landry	Mendelssohn: Sonata No. 1
	Carlos Mesquita	Mendelssohn: Sonata No. 4, third movement
	Adolphe Marty	Fugue in A Minor, BWV 543/2

(Continued)

Exam or Competition	Student	Work Played
Exam of January 1886 (*contd.*)	Georges-Paul Bondon	Fugue in E Major from Book 2 of the Well-Tempered Clavier, BWV 878/2
	Louis de Serres	Fugue in G Minor ("Little"), BWV 578
	Dynam-Victor Fumet	Fugue in E Minor, BWV 533/2
	Alfred Bachelet	Fugue in F Minor from Book 1 of the Well-Tempered Clavier, BWV 857/2
	Georges Aubry	Fugue in B-flat Minor from Book 1 of the Well-Tempered Clavier, BWV 867/2
	Cesarino Galeotti	Prelude and Fugue in G Minor, BWV 558 (Eight Little Preludes and Fugues)
	Louis-André Frémaux	Prelude and Fugue in A Major from Book 2 of the Well-Tempered Clavier, BWV 888
	Henri Letocart	Fugue in C Minor, BWV 537/2
	Aimé Féry	Fugue in D Major from Book 2 of the Well-Tempered Clavier, BWV 874/2
Exam of June 1886	Louis Landry	Fugue in B Minor on a Theme by Corelli, BWV 579
	Jean-Jacques Jemain	"O Lamm Gottes, unschuldig," BWV 656
	Adolphe Marty	Fugue in D Major, BWV 532/2; Franck: Fantasy in C Major
	Georges-Paul Bondon	Prelude and Fugue in E Minor, BWV 555 (Eight Little Preludes and Fugues)
	Louis de Serres	Handel: Concerto in B-flat Major

(*Continued*)

Works Played by César Franck's Organ Students, 1872–90   (Continued)

Exam or Competition	Student	Work Played
Exam of June 1886 (*contd.*)	Dynam-Victor Fumet	Fugue in G Minor, BWV 535/2
	Georges Aubry	Fugue in C-sharp Minor from Book 1 of the Well-Tempered Clavier, BWV 849/2
	Louis-André Frémaux	Fugue in B-flat Minor from Book 2 of the Well-Tempered Clavier, BWV 891/2
	Aimé Féry	Fugue in C Minor from Book 2 of the Well-Tempered Clavier, BWV 871/2
Exam of January 1887	Jean-Jacques Jemain	Franck: *Cantabile*
	Georges-Paul Bondon	Concerto in G Major after Prince Johann Ernst, BWV 592
	Louis de Serres	Prelude in A Minor, BWV 543/1
	Dynam-Victor Fumet	Mendelssohn: Fugue in C Minor from *Three Preludes and Fugues for the Organ*, op. 37
	Alfred Bachelet	Prelude and Fugue in E Minor, BWV 555 (Eight Little Preludes and Fugues)
	Georges Aubry	Fugue in G Minor, BWV 131a
	Cesarino Galeotti	Prelude and Fugue in B-flat Major, BWV 560 (Eight Little Preludes and Fugues)
	Louis-André Frémaux	Prelude and Fugue in E Minor, BWV 533
	Aimé Féry	Fugue in D-sharp Minor from Book 2 of the Well-Tempered Clavier, BWV 877/2
	Henri Letocart	Fantasy in G Minor, BWV 542/1

(Continued)

Exam or Competition	Student	Work Played
Exam of January 1887 (*contd.*)	"Fournier"	Mendelssohn: Sonata No. 6
	Hedwige Chrétien	Schumann: Study in A-flat Major, op. 56, no. 4
	Paul-Albert Pillard	Fugue in B-flat Minor from Book 1 of the Well-Tempered Clavier, BWV 867/2
Exam of June 1887	Jean-Jacques Jemain	Franck: "beginning of" the *Grande Pièce symphonique* (presumably mm. 1-57)
	Georges-Paul Bondon	Fugue in C Minor, BWV 537/2
	Georges Aubry	Concerto in A Minor after Vivaldi, BWV 593
	Cesarino Galeotti	Toccata in D Minor, BWV 565/1
	Louis-André Frémaux	Fantasy in C Minor, BWV 537/1
	Aimé Féry	Fugue in A-flat Major from the Well-Tempered Clavier, BWV 862/2 or BWV 886/2
	Henri Letocart	Prelude in B Minor, BWV 544/1
	Hedwige Chrétien	Prelude in A Minor, BWV 543/1
	Paul-Albert Pillard	Prelude and Fugue in G Major, BWV 557 (Eight Little Preludes and Fugues)
Exam of January 1888	Jean-Jacques Jemain	Fugue in E Minor ("Wedge"), BWV 548/2
	Georges Aubry	Toccata in D Minor ("Dorian"), BWV 538/1
	Georges-Paul Bondon	Fugue in F Major, BWV 540/2
	Paul-Albert Pillard	Fugue in E Minor, BWV 555/2 (Eight Little Preludes and Fugues)

(*Continued*)

Works Played by César Franck's Organ Students, 1872–90   (Continued)

Exam or Competition	Student	Work Played
Exam of January 1888 (*contd.*)	Marie Prestat	Prelude and Fugue in C Major, BWV 566
	Joséphine Boulay	Toccata and Fugue in D Minor, BWV 565
	Jean-Ferdinand Schneider	Prelude and Fugue in B-flat Major, BWV 560 (Eight Little Preludes and Fugues)
	Bruno-Marius Maurel	Mendelssohn: Sonata No. 2
	Édouard Bopp	Mendelssohn: Sonata No. 5
Exam of June 1888	Georges-Paul Bondon	Prelude and Fugue in C Minor, BWV 546
	Georges Aubry	Franck: *Cantabile*
	Marie Prestat	Toccata in D Minor, BWV 565/1
	Joséphine Boulay	Fugue in C Minor on a Theme by Legrenzi, BWV 574
	Jean-Ferdinand Schneider	Prelude and Fugue in E Minor, BWV 533
	Bruno-Marius Maurel	Mendelssohn: Sonata No. 5, second movement
	Édouard Bopp	Mendelssohn: Sonata No. 4, first movement
Competition of July 1888	Georges-Paul Bondon	Franck: *Prière*
	Joséphine Boulay	Fugue in E Minor ("Wedge"), BWV 548/2
	Marie Prestat	Mendelssohn: Sonata No. 4
	Georges Aubry	Fugue in C Minor, BWV 546/2
Exam of January 1889	Georges-Paul Bondon	"O Lamm Gottes, unschuldig," BWV 656
	Georges Aubry	Bach: Prelude in A Minor, presumably BWV 543/1
	Henri Letocart	Mendelssohn: Sonata No. 3
	Marie Prestat	Toccata in F Major, BWV 540/1
	Bruno-Marius Maurel	Mendelssohn: Sonata No. 5, first movement

(Continued)

Exam or Competition	Student	Work Played
Exam of January 1889 (*contd.*)	Albert Mahaut	Fugue in D Major, BWV 532/2
	Paul Ternisien	Prelude and Fugue in G Minor, BWV 558 (Eight Little Preludes and Fugues)
	Achille Runner	Prelude and Fugue in E Minor, BWV 555 (Eight Little Preludes and Fugues)
Exam of June 1889	Georges-Paul Bondon	Prelude in B Minor, BWV 544/1
	Georges Aubry	Fugue in B Minor, BWV 544/2
	Henri Letocart	presumably Mendelssohn's Sonata No. 2, first movement
	Marie Prestat	Fugue in A Minor, BWV 543/2
	Albert Mahaut	Franck: *Prière*
	Paul Ternisien	Fugue in C Minor, BWV 537/2
	Achille Runner	Fantasy in C Minor, BWV 537/1
Competition of July 1889	Marie Prestat	Franck: *Prélude, Fugue et Variation*
	Albert Mahaut	Fantasy and Fugue in G Minor, BWV 542
	Georges Aubry	Schumann: Study in A-flat Major, op. 56, no. 4
	Georges-Paul Bondon	Franck: *Grande Pièce symphonique*
	Henri Letocart	Prelude in E-flat Major, BWV 552/1
Exam of January 1890	Henri Letocart	Prelude in G Major, BWV 541/1
	Marie Prestat	Franck: Fantasy in A Major
	Paul Ternisien	Prelude and Fugue in C Major, BWV 566
	Achille Runner	Toccata, Adagio, and Fugue in C Major, BWV 564, first movement
	Henri Libert	Prelude in G Major, BWV 568; Fugue in G Minor, BWV 131a

(*Continued*)

Works Played by César Franck's Organ Students, 1872–90   (Continued)

Exam or Competition	Student	Work Played
Exam of January 1890 (*contd.*)	Jules Bouval	Prelude and Fugue in E Minor, BWV 555 (Eight Little Preludes and Fugues)
	Henri Busser	Fugue in C Minor on a Theme by Legrenzi, BWV 574
	Georges Guiraud	Toccata, Adagio, and Fugue in C Major, BWV 564, last movement
	Charles Tournemire	Concerto in A Minor after Vivaldi, BWV 593
Exam of June 1890	Henri Letocart	Passacaglia in C Minor, BWV 582
	Marie Prestat	Passacaglia in C Minor, BWV 582, concluding fugue
	Paul Ternisien	Fantasy in C Minor, BWV 562/1
	Achille Runner	Mendelssohn: Sonata No. 4
	Henri Libert	Concerto in C Major after Prince Johann Ernst, BWV 595
	Henri Busser	Aria in F Major, BWV 587
	Charles Tournemire	Fugue in G Minor, BWV 542/2
Competition of July 1890	Henri Letocart	Franck: *Pastorale*
	Marie Prestat	Franck: *Prière*
	Charles Tournemire	Mendelssohn: Sonata No. 6
	Henri Libert	Bach: Prelude and Fugue in A Minor, presumably BWV 543
	Achille Runner	Bach: Prelude and Fugue in C Minor, presumably BWV 546

Appendix 2

EXPLANATORY NOTE

This appendix contains, in English translation, Franck's progress reports on twelve of his students, as found in the records of the Paris Conservatory (Archives Nationales, Paris, AJ[37] 283–90) and as transcribed by Marcelle Benoit in his article "César Franck et ses élèves" (*L'Orgue*, vol. 83). Although this material is discussed in chapter 5, certain comments made by Franck deserve to be elaborated on here.

Starting with Franck's remark that Gabriel Pierné was "still a little too much of a pianist and not enough of an organist" (June 1881), it bears pointing out that in the same letter discussed in appendix 1, Franck urged Pierné to "continue to play the organ."[1] Continue he did, even to the point of succeeding Franck at Sainte-Clotilde. In the same year as Franck's letter to him, 1883, the young Pierné published a piano transcription of Bach's F-major organ toccata.[2] Franck might have preferred for his erstwhile pupil simply to play the work on the organ—if only because of its demanding pedal part—but we should not forget that Franck himself enjoyed playing Bach's organ music at the piano. Indeed, according to Henri Duparc, some of his piano lessons with Franck "were entirely taken up by the master's enthusiastic reading of an act from [Gluck's] '*Iphigénie en Tauride*,' organ works by Bach, and certain passages from Weber's '*Euryanthe*.'"[3] Duparc was hardly immune to this practice either, as demonstrated by his transcriptions for two pianos of the Preludes and Fugues in A Minor and E Minor, BWV 543 and 548.[4] These arrange-

---

1. "Puisque vous le pouvez continuez aussi à jouer de l'orgue; vous ne le regretterez pas non plus." Fauquet 1999b, 138.
2. Fauquet and Hennion 2000, 218.
3. D'Indy 1910, 94.
4. Fauquet and Hennion 200, 218.

ments date from around 1880, when Duparc was no longer a Franck pupil, but they may well have resulted directly or indirectly from piano lessons at which Duparc and Franck played such pieces together, probably with the student taking the pedal line.

Franck's comments on two other students deserve mention as well. His last two reports on Louis de Serres imply that this pupil left the organ class because of physical ailments, and this suspicion is confirmed by de Serres's reminiscences of Franck: "That class, so interesting, I had to give up prematurely because of troublesome pains in my hands that made all playing difficult. I soon regretted it."[5] Finally, Franck's use of the word *Clavecin* (French for "harpsichord") in his first report on Alfred Bachelet constitutes a reference to Bach's Well-Tempered Clavier, known in France as *Le Clavecin bien tempéré*.

César Franck's Progress Reports on Twelve of His Organ Students, 1874–90

Student	Date of Report	Franck's Comments
Vincent D'Indy	June 1874	"Excellent pupil, fine musical intelligence, great worker. Nevertheless had difficulty with improvisation. Still has some. Excellent execution. Fugue in G Minor, book 4, number 7 [BWV 578]."
Vincent D'Indy	January 1875	"Excellent and hard-working pupil. He still lacks facility but will acquire it with work. Fugue in C Minor, book 4, number 6 [BWV 574]."
Vincent D'Indy	June 1875	"Excellent pupil. Great worker. Finale of the Concerto in A Minor, book 8, page 16 [BWV 593/3]."
Henri Dallier	January 1878	"Very good pupil who can be brilliant by the end of the year. Fugue in C Minor, third book [BWV 537/2]."
Henri Dallier	June 1878	"Very capable and distinguished pupil. Has worked much and has borne fruit. Piece in C, César Franck [Franck: Fantasy in C Major]."
Auguste Chapuis	January 1879	"Much inclination. A little soft. Pastorale of Bach, first book [BWV 590]."
Auguste Chapuis	June 1879	"Pupil gifted for the organ, but whose work could have been more regular. Fugue in G Minor, book 3 [BWV 535/2]."

---

5. Smith 2002, 182.

(Continued)

Student	Date of Report	Franck's Comments
Auguste Chapuis	January 1880	"This pupil is gifted for the organ. He should work more and be more exact. Fugue in D Minor, Bach, third book [BWV 538/2 or BWV 539/2]."
Auguste Chapuis	June 1880	"Does not work sufficiently. Toccata in D Minor, Bach, third book [BWV 538/1]."
Auguste Chapuis	January 1881	"Has worked well since the start of the new school year. An execution that was very defective has become much better. Prelude in E-flat, number 1, book 3 [BWV 552/1]."
Auguste Chapuis	June 1881	"Very distinguished pupil who truly has the makings of an organist. Bach, Fugue in E-flat, number 1, book 3 [BWV 552/2]."
Gabriel Pierné	January 1881	"Pleasing intelligence. Lively and sharp mind. Will be a very good pupil and will succeed, I hope. Fantasy in C Minor, book 3 [BWV 537/1]."
Gabriel Pierné	June 1881	"Charming pupil, worker. Open and quick intelligence. Is still a little too much of a pianist and not enough of an organist. Fugue in G Minor, book 4 [BWV 578]."
Gabriel Pierné	January 1882	"Always an excellent pupil. Fantasy in C [Major], Franck."
Gabriel Pierné	June 1882	"A pupil such as one has all too seldom, gifted and hard-working."
Adolphe Marty	January 1886	"Remarkable pupil and great worker. Fugue in A Minor, Bach, second book [BWV 543/2]."
Adolphe Marty	June 1886	"Excellent pupil who has worked much. Fugue in D, Bach, book 4 [BWV 532/2]. Piece in C, César Franck [Franck: Fantasy in C Major]."
Louis de Serres	January 1886	"A good pupil. Fugue in G Minor, fourth book [BWV 578]."
Louis de Serres	June 1886	"Good pupil. Concerto by Handel in B-flat."

(*Continued*)

César Franck's Progress Reports on Twelve of His Organ Students, 1874–90   (Continued)

Student	Date of Report	Franck's Comments
Louis de Serres	January 1887	"Conscientious pupil whose musical studies are not yet very advanced, which at the moment is hampering his organ studies. Prelude of the Fugue in A Minor, book 2, number 8 [BWV 543/1]."
Louis de Serres	June 1887	"Suffers pains in his hands and arms, which has often prevented him from working."
Louis de Serres	January 1888	"Resigned his seat."
Alfred Bachelet	January 1886	"Gifted pupil, but since the start of the new school year has often been indisposed. Fugue in F Minor, *Clavecin*, first book [BWV 857/2]."
Alfred Bachelet	June 1886	"A very good pupil. Has worked very little this year but has promised to work well next year. Will not take the exam."
Alfred Bachelet	January 1887	"Very gifted pupil but also as inexact as possible. Prelude and Fugue in E Minor, book 8, number 3 [BWV 555]."
Alfred Bachelet	June 1887	"In residence. Has done nothing all year."
Alfred Bachelet	January 1888	"Always promises me to come and work, but never comes."
Henri Letocart	January 1886	"A good pupil. Fugue in C Minor, book 3 [BWV 537/2]."
Henri Letocart	June 1886	"Exact pupil. Does his work, but not too bright. Has difficulty."
Henri Letocart	January 1887	"This pupil passionately loves the organ. He works, and is making progress, but still has difficulty. Fantasy in G Minor, book 2, number 4 [BWV 542/1]."
Henri Letocart	June 1887	"Very good pupil. Has progressed much during the year. Prelude in B Minor, book 2 [BWV 544/1]."
Henri Letocart	January 1888	"Doing his military service."
Henri Letocart	January 1889	"Has returned in good shape from his military service. Good pupil. Third sonata of Mendelssohn."

(Continued)

Student	Date of Report	Franck's Comments
Henri Letocart	June 1889	"Good pupil; works. Always has a fair amount of difficulty with fugue. First part of the Sonata in C Minor [presumably Mendelssohn's first organ Sonata]."
Henri Letocart	January 1890	"Good pupil always. Prelude in G Major, book 2, number 2 [BWV 541/1]."
Henri Letocart	June 1890	"Good pupil. Always has a little difficulty with fugue. Passacaglia, book 1 [BWV 582]."
Albert Mahaut	January 1889	"Excellent pupil. Fugue in D Major, number 3, book 4 [BWV 532/2]."
Albert Mahaut	June 1889	"Perfect pupil. *Prière* in C-sharp Minor by César Franck."
Henri Libert	January 1890	"A very good pupil. Serious and exact. Prelude in G Major and Fugue in G Minor, book 8, numbers 11 and 12 [BWV 568 and BWV 131a, respectively]."
Henri Libert	June 1890	"Good pupil. Fourth concerto, book 8 [BWV 595]."
Henri Busser	January 1890	"Will be a very good pupil. Quite gifted. Fugue in C Minor, book 4, number 6 [BWV 574]."
Henri Busser	June 1890	"Good pupil. Aria, book 9 [BWV 587]."
Charles Tournemire	January 1890	"Will be an excellent pupil. Very gifted. Concerto in A Minor, eighth book [BWV 593]."
Charles Tournemire	June 1890	"Excellent pupil. Gifted and hard-working. Fugue in G Minor, second book [BWV 542/2]."

LITERATURE CITED

Albrecht, Christoph, ed. *Gottfried August Homilius: Choralvorspiele für Orgel.* Leipzig: VEB Breitkopf & Härtel, 1988.

Anderson, Robert. *Elgar in Manuscript.* London: The British Library, 1990.

Anderson, Robert, and Christopher Kent, eds. *Edward Elgar: Music for Organ.* Elgar Complete Edition, 36. London: Novello, 1987.

Atkins, E. Wulstan. *The Elgar-Atkins Friendship.* London: David & Charles, 1984.

Barger, Judith. *Elizabeth Stirling and the Musical Life of Female Organists in Nineteenth-Century England.* Aldershot: Ashgate, 2007.

Barham, Jeremy. "Scoring Incredible Futures: Science-Fiction Screen Music, and 'Postmodernism' as Romantic Epiphany." *Musical Quarterly* 91 (2008): 240–74.

Bartels, Ulrich, and Peter Wollny, eds. *Johann Sebastian Bach: Freie Orgelwerke und Choralpartiten aus unterschiedlicher Überlieferung.* (*Neue Bach-Ausgabe,* ser. 4, vol. 11.) Kassel: Bärenreiter, 2003.

——. *Kritischer Bericht* to *Neue Bach-Ausgabe,* ser. 4, vol. 11 (*Freie Orgelwerke und Choralpartiten aus unterschiedlicher Überlieferung*). Kassel: Bärenreiter, 2004.

Bates, William H. "J. S. Bach's Fantasy and Fugue in G Minor, BWV 542: A Source Study for Organists." *Bach: Journal of the Riemenschneider Bach Institute* 39, no. 2 (2008): 1–88.

Becker, Carl Ferdinand. "Zur Geschichte der Hausmusik in früheren Jahrhunderten." *Neue Zeitschrift für Musik* 12, nos. 7 and 8 (January 21 and 24, 1840): 25–26 and 29–30.

Beckmann, Klaus, ed. *Georg Böhm: Sämtliche Orgelwerke.* Wiesbaden: Breitkopf & Härtel, 1986.

——. *Johann Gottfried Walther: Sämtliche Orgelwerke,* vol. 2. Wiesbaden: Breitkopf & Härtel, 1998.

Bennett, James Robert Sterndale. *The Life of William Sterndale Bennett.* Cambridge: Cambridge University Press, 1907.

Benoit, Marcelle. "César Franck et ses élèves." *L'Orgue* 83 (April-September 1957): 76–78.

Biba, Otto. "Bach-Pflege in Wien von Gottlieb Muffat bis Johann Georg Albrechtsberger." In *Mundus Organorum: Festschrift Walter Supper zum 70. Geburtstag*, edited by Alfred Reichling, 21–33. Berlin: Verlag Merseburger, 1978.

Bingham, Seth. "Old and New in French Organ Field Seen by New York Musician." *Diapason* 23, no. 11 (October 1932): 8.

Bird, Arthur. "German, French and English Interpretation of Bach's Organ Music." *Etude* 33 (1915): 140–41.

Blanken, Christine. "Zwischen Improvisation, Repertoire und Verlag—Bach und die Wiener Orgelpraxis in der ersten Hälfte des 19. Jahrhunderts." In *"Diess herrliche, imponirende Instrument": Die Orgel im Zeitalter Felix Mendelssohn Bartholdys*. Beiträge zur Geschichte der Bach-Rezeption 3, edited by Anselm Hartinger et al., 343–68. Wiesbaden: Breitkopf & Härtel, 2011.

Blaut, Stephan, and Michael Pacholke, eds. *Johann Sebastian Bach: Choralfantasie für Orgel über Wo Gott der Herr nicht bei uns hält, BWV 1128*. Ortus Organum, 1. Beeskow: Ortus Musikverlag, 2008.

Blaut, Stephan, and Hans-Joachim Schulze. "'Wo Gott der Herr nicht bei uns hält' BWV 1128: Quellenkundliche und stilistische Überlegungen." *Bach-Jahrbuch* 94 (2008): 11–32.

Boetticher, Wolfgang. *Briefe und Gedichte aus dem Album Robert und Clara Schumanns*. Leipzig: VEB Deutscher Verlag für Musik, 1979.

———. *Robert Schumann: Einführung in Persönlichkeit und Werk*. Berlin: Bernhard Hahnefeld Verlag, 1941.

Böhme, Ullrich. Liner notes to *Johann Sebastian Bach: Wo Gott der Herr nicht bei uns hält*. Rondeau Production ROP6023 (2008).

Bokum, Jan ten. "Die Beschäftigung niederländischer Organisten mit der Musik Johann Sebastian Bachs im 19. Jahrhundert." *Tijdschrift van de Koninklijke Vereniging voor Nederlandse Muziekgeschiedenis* 50, no. 1/2 (2000): 52–73.

———. *Johannes Gijsbertus Bastiaans (1812–1875)*. Utrecht: A. Oosthoek's Uitgeversmaatschappij, 1971.

Bormann, Oskar. "Johann Nepomuk Schelble: Sein Leben, sein Wirken und seine Werke." Ph.D. diss., University of Frankfurt, 1926.

Boyd, Malcolm, ed. *J. S. Bach*. Oxford Composer Companions. Oxford: Oxford University Press, 1999.

Breig, Werner. "The Musical Works." In *Wagner Handbook*, edited by Ulrich Müller and Peter Wapnewski, 397–484. Cambridge, MA: Harvard University Press, 1992.

Bréville, Pierre de. "Les Fioretti du père Franck." *Mercure de France* 281 (1938): 81–98.

Brown, Julie. "Carnival of Souls and the Organs of Horror." In *Music in the Horror Film: Listening to Fear*, edited by Neil Lerner, 1–20. New York: Routledge, 2010.

Brown, Royal S. *Overtones and Undertones: Reading Film Music*. Berkeley: University of California Press, 1994.

Buckley, Robert J. *Sir Edward Elgar*. Living Masters of Music, 2. London: John Lane, 1905.

Buitenen, Bart van. "Jan Albert van Eyken (1823–1868)." *De Orgelvriend* 40, no. 7/8 (July/August 1998): 20–25.

Burkholder, J. Peter. "The Organist in Ives." *Journal of the American Musicological Society* 55 (2002): 255–310.

Busch, Hermann J. "Anton Bruckner spielt Johann Sebastian Bach." *Internationale Bruckner-Gesellschaft Mitteilungsblatt* 8 (December 1975): 11–16.

——. "Organisten an St. Nikolai." In *Die Nikolaikirche zu Leipzig und ihre Orgel*, edited by Hermann J. Busch, 29–36. Leipzig: Evangelische Verlagsanstalt, 2004.

——. "Orgelbau und Bach-Interpretation in Frankreich und Deutschland im 19. Jahrhundert." In *Bach-Interpretation und -Rezeption seit dem 18. Jahrhundert*, edited by Raliza Nikolov, 123–35. Schneverdingen: Karl Dieter Wagner, 2003.

——. "Sächsische Bach-Tradition im Rheinland: Eine Quelle zur Interpretationsgeschichte der Orgelmusik Johann Sebastian Bachs aus der Mitte des 19. Jahrhunderts." *Freiberger Studien zur Orgel* 7 (2002): 111–19.

Butler, Gregory G. *Bach's Clavier-Übung III: The Making of a Print*. (Sources of Music and Their Interpretation.) Durham, NC: Duke University Press, 1990.

Cantagrel, Gilles. *Le moulin et la rivière: Air et variations sur BACH*. Paris: Fayard, 1998.

Cantoni, Angelo. *La référence à Bach dans les oeuvres néo-classiques de Stravinsky*. Musikwissenschaftliche Publikationen, 8. Hildesheim: Georg Olms, 1998.

Carragan, William. "The Early Version of the Second Symphony." In *Perspectives on Anton Bruckner*, edited by Crawford Howie et al., 69–92. Aldershot: Ashgate, 2001.

Chorley, Henry F. *Modern German Music*. 2 vols. London, 1854.

Clark, Relf. *Elgar and the Three Cathedral Organists and Other Essays*. Oxford: Positif Press, 2002.

Cooke, Mervyn. *A History of Film Music*. Cambridge: Cambridge University Press. 2008.

Copland, Aaron. *What to Listen for in Music*. New York: McGraw-Hill, 1939.

Crum, Margaret, and Peter Ward Jones. *Catalogue of the Mendelssohn Papers in the Bodleian Library, Oxford*. 3 vols. Musikbibliographische Arbeiten, 7–9. Tutzing: Hans Schneider, 1980–89.

Curley, Carlo. *In the Pipeline: Memoirs of an International Concert Organist*. London: HarperCollins, 1998.

Dahlhaus, Carl. "Wagner und Bach." In *Klassische und romantische Musikästhetik*, edited by Carl Dahlhaus, 440–58. Laaber: Laaber-Verlag, 1988.

Daverio, John. *Robert Schumann: Herald of a "New Poetic Age"*. New York: Oxford University Press, 1997.

Davies, Laurence. *César Franck and His Circle*. Boston: Houghton Mifflin, 1970.

David, Hans T., and Arthur Mendel, eds. *The New Bach Reader: A Life of Johann Sebastian Bach in Letters and Documents*. Revised by Christoph Wolff. New York: W. W. Norton, 1998.

D'Indy, Vincent. *César Franck*. Translated by Rosa Newmarch. London: John Lane, 1910.

——. *Cours de composition musicale*. 4 vols. Paris: A. Durand, 1903–50.

Dirksen, Pieter. "Bach's 'Acht Choralfughetten': Ein unbeachtetes Leipziger Sammelwerk?" In *Bach in Leipzig—Bach und Leipzig* (Konferenzbericht Leipzig 2000), edited by Ulrich Leisinger, 155–82. Leipziger Beiträge zur Bach-Forschung 5. Hildesheim: Georg Olms, 2002.

Douglass, Fenner. *Cavaillé-Coll and the Musicians*. 2 vols. Raleigh, NC: Sunbury Press, 1980.

Dunham, Rowland W. "From Yesterday, No. 2: Franck, Libert, Widor." *American Organist* 37 (1954): 402–03.

Dürr, Alfred, ed. *Acht kleine Präludien und Fugen BWV 553–560 für Orgel früher Johann Sebastian Bach zugeschrieben*. Kassel: Bärenreiter, 1987.

———. *The Cantatas of J. S. Bach.* Translated by Richard D. P. Jones. Oxford: Oxford University Press, 2005.

Dürr, Alfred, and Marianne Helms. *Kritischer Bericht to Neue Bach-Ausgabe*, ser. 5, vol. 7 (*Die sechs Englischen Suiten*). Kassel: Bärenreiter/Leipzig: VEB Deutscher Verlag für Musik, 1981.

Eddie, William Alexander. *Charles Valentin Alkan: His Life and His Music.* Aldershot: Ashgate, 2007.

Eismann, Georg, ed. *Erinnerungen an Felix Mendelssohn Bartholdy: Nachgelassene Aufzeichnungen von Robert Schumann.* Zwickau: Predella-Verlag, 1948.

Eismann, Georg, and Gerd Nauhaus, eds. *Robert Schumann: Tagebücher.* 3 vols. Leipzig: VEB Deutscher Verlag für Musik, 1971–82.

Ellis, Katherine. *Interpreting the Musical Past: Early Music in Nineteenth-Century France.* New York: Oxford University Press, 2005.

Elvers, Rudolf, ed. *Felix Mendelssohn Bartholdy: Briefe an deutsche Verleger.* Berlin: Walter de Gruyter, 1968.

Emans, Reinmar, ed. *Johann Sebastian Bach: Orgelchoräle aus unterschiedlicher Überlieferung.* Neue Bach-Ausgabe, ser. 4, vol. 10. Kassel: Bärenreiter, 2007.

———. *Johann Sebastian Bach. Orgelchoräle zweifelhafter Echtheit: Thematischer Katalog.* Göttingen: Johann-Sebastian-Bach-Institut Göttingen, 1997.

Emerson, Keith. *Pictures of an Exhibitionist.* London: John Blake, 2004.

Emery, Walter. "Organ Music: 1700–1750." In *Concert Music: 1630–1750.* New Oxford History of Music, 6, edited by Gerald Abraham, 650–93. Oxford: Oxford University Press, 1986.

Erskine, John. *The Philharmonic-Symphony Society of New York: Its First Hundred Years.* New York: Macmillan, 1943.

Fauquet, Joël Marie. *César Franck.* Paris: Fayard, 1999a.

———, ed. *César Franck: Correspondance.* Sprimont: Mardaga, 1999b.

Fauquet, Joël Marie, and Antoine Hennion. *La grandeur de Bach: L'amour de la musique en France au XIXe siècle.* Paris: Fayard, 2000.

Ferrard, Jean. "L'oeuvre pour orgue de César Franck: Sources et editions." *Revue belge de musicologie* 45 (1991): 163–80.

Föller, Helmut. *BACH: Verarbeitungen eines Motivs in der Orgelmusik des 19. Jahrhunderts.* Kirchenmusikalische Studien 8. Sinzig: Studio, 2004.

Foster, Myles Birket. *History of the Philharmonic Soceity of London: 1813–1912.* London: John Lane, 1912.

Friedrich, Felix. "Johann Ludwig Krebs als Vertreter einer frühen Bach-Rezeption? Grundlegende Gedanken zum Symposium am 15. April 2000 in Altenburg." *Freiberger Studien zur Orgel* 7 (2002): 5–9.

Frith, Michael. "'…Des Chorals d'orgue, ainsi qu'a fait Bach, mais sur un autre plan': César Franck's *Trois Chorals* Reconsidered." *British Institute of Organ Studies Journal* 30 (2006): 30–39.

Frotscher, Gotthold. *Geschichte des Orgelspiels und der Orgelkomposition.* Berlin: Max Hesse, 1935.

Fuchs, Ingrid. "Bach-Aufführungen im Spiegel der Berichterstattung der *Neuen Zeitschrift für Musik* unter der Redaktion Robert Schumanns von 1834 bis 1844." In *Festschrift Othmar Wessely*, edited by Manfred Angerer et al., 207–36. Tutzing: Hans Schneider, 1982.

Geck, Martin. *"Es ist wie die Stimme des Ding an sich*: Wagners 'Bach.'" In Geck, *"Denn alles findet bei Bach statt": Erforschtes und Erfahrenes*, 170–90. Stuttgart: J. B. Metzler, 2000.

——. "Richard Wagner und die ältere Musik." In *Die Ausbreitung des Historismus über die Musik*, edited by Walter Wiora, 123–46. Studien zur Musikgeschichte des 19. Jahrhunderts 14. Regensburg: Gustav Bosse, 1969.

Glöckner, Andreas, et al., eds. *Ausgewählte Dokumente zum Nachwirken Johann Sebastian Bachs 1801–1850*. Bach-Dokumente 6. Kassel: Bärenreiter, 2007.

Goossens, Eugene. *Overture and Beginners: A Musical Autobiography*. London: Methuen, 1951.

Grace, Harvey. "The Bach-Elgar Fugue." *Musical Times* 63 (1922a): 21–23.

——. *The Organ Works of Bach*. Handbooks for Musicians. London: Novello, 1922b.

Graves, Charles L. *Hubert Parry: His Life and Works*. 2 vols. London: Macmillan, 1926.

Greer, Mary J. "'The Public … Would Probably Prefer Something that Appeals Less to the Brain and More to the Senses': The Reception of Bach's Music in New York City, 1855–1900." *Bach Perspectives* 5 (2003): 57–114.

Gregor-Dellin, Martin, and Dietrich Mack, eds. *Cosima Wagner's Diaries*. 2 vols. Translated by Geoffrey Skelton. New York: Harcourt Brace Jovanovich, 1977–80.

Grossmann-Vendrey, Susanna. *Felix Mendelssohn Bartholdy und die Musik der Vergangenheit*. Studien zur Musikgeschichte des 19. Jahrhunderts 17. Regensburg: Gustav Bosse, 1969.

Guay, Bertrand. Liner notes to *Bach Métamorphoses (Orchestre symphonique de Québec)*. ATMA Classique ACD2 2570 (2008).

Haag, Herbert. *César Franck als Orgelkomponist*. Heidelberger Studien zur Musikwissenschaft 4. Kassel: Bärenreiter, 1936.

Haselböck, Martin. "Wiener Bachpflege: Zur Aufführungsgeschichte der Vokalwerke 1770–1908." *Freiberger Studien zur Orgel* 7 (2002): 52–110.

Hastings, Karen. "New Franck Fingerings Brought to Light," *American Organist* 24, no. 12 (December 1990): 92–101.

Heinemann, Michael. *Die Bach-Rezeption von Franz Liszt*. Musik und Musikanschauung im 19. Jahrhundert 1. Cologne: Studio, 1995.

——. "Worte der Mahnung: Bach als Thema deutschsprachiger Literatur." In *Bach und die Nachwelt*, vol. 3: 1900–1950, edited by Michael Heinemann and Hans-Joachim Hinrichsen, 427–69. Laaber: Laaber-Verlag, 2000.

Hielscher, Hans Uwe. *Alexandre Guilmant (1837–1911): Leben und Werk*. 2nd ed. Cologne: Christoph Dohr, 1987.

Hiemke, Sven. *Die Bach-Rezeption Charles-Marie Widors*. Frankfurt: Peter Lang, 1994.

——, ed. *Johann Sebastian Bach: Orgelbüchlein (BWV 599–644)*. Meisterwerke der Musik im Faksimile 6. Laaber: Laaber-Verlag, 2004.

Hill, Robert, ed. *Keyboard Music from the Andreas Bach Book and the Möller Manuscript*. Cambridge, MA: Harvard University Press, 1991.

Hinrichsen, Hans-Joachim, and Dominik Sackmann. *Bach-Rezeption im Umkreis Franz Liszts: Joseph Joachim Raff und Hans von Bülow*. Stuttgart: Carus-Verlag, 2004.

Hinrichsen, Max, ed. *Music Book: Volume VII of Hinrichsen's Musical Year Book*. London: Hinrichsen Edition, 1952.

Hinton, John W. *César Franck: Some Personal Reminiscences*. London: William Reeves, n.d.

Hofmann, Renate. *Clara Schumanns Briefe an Theodor Kirchner*. Tutzing: Hans Schneider, 1996.

Hofmann, Renate, and Kurt. *Johannes Brahms als Pianist und Dirigent*. Veröffentlichungen des Archivs der Gesellschaft der Musikfreunde in Wien 8. Tutzing: Hans Schneider, 2006.

Holmes, Edward. *A Ranble Among the Musicians of Germany*. London: Hunt and Clarke, 1828.

Honegger, Arthur. *I am a Composer*. Translated by Wilson O. Clough. New York: St. Martin's Press, 1966.

Horn, Erwin. "Zwischen Interpretation und Improvisation: Anton Bruckner als Organist." In *Bruckner-Symposion Bericht 1995*, edited by Othmar Wessely et al., 111–39. Linz: Anton Bruckner Institut, 1997.

Horton, Peter. *Samuel Sebastian Wesley: A Life*. Oxford: Oxford University Press, 2004.

Howie, Crawford. "Bruckner—the Travelling Virtuoso." In *Perspectives on Anton Bruckner*, edited by Crawford Howie et al., 299–316. Aldershot: Ashgate, 2001.

Hull, A. Eaglefield. *Bach's Organ Works*. London: Office of *Musical Opinion*, 1929.

Jacobs, Arthur. *Henry J. Wood: Maker of the Proms*. London: Methuen, 1994.

Jander, Owen. "J. S. Bach's 'Gradus Ad Parnassum' in the Realm of Meter and Tempo: The Six Sonatas for Two Manuals and Pedal." *Keyboard Perspectives* 1 (2007): 73–85.

Jansen, Friedrich Gustav. *Robert Schumanns Briefe: Neue Folge*. 2nd ed. Leipzig: Breitkopf & Härtel, 1904. (English translation of first edition, *The Life of Robert Schumann Told in His Letters*. London: Richard Bentley and Son, 1890.)

Johnson, Vida T., and Graham Petrie. *The Films of Andrei Tarkovsky: A Visual Fugue*. Bloomington, IN: Indiana University Press, 1994.

Joy, Charles R. *Music in the Life of Albert Schweitzer*. Freeport, NY: Books for Libraries Press, 1951.

Kassler, Michael, ed. *The English Bach Awakening: Knowledge of J. S. Bach and his Music in England* 1750–1830. Aldershot: Ashgate, 2004.

Kater, Michael H. *The Twisted Muse: Musicians and Their Music in the Third Reich*. New York: Oxford University Press, 1997.

Kaufmann, Michael Gerhard. *Orgel und Nationalsozialismus: Die ideologische Vereinnahmung des Instruments im "Dritten Reich"*. Schriftenreihe der Walcker-Stiftung für orgelwissenschaftliche Forschung 5. Kleinblittersdorf: Musikwissenschaftliche Verlags-Gesellschaft MBH, 1997.

Kehler, George. *The Piano in Concert*. 2 vols. Metuchen, NJ: Scarecrow Press, 1982.

Keller, Hermann. *The Organ Works of Bach: A Contribution to Their History, Form, Interpretation and Performance*. Translated by Helen Hewitt. New York: C. F. Peters, 1967.

Kent, Christopher. *Edward Elgar: A Guide to Research*. Garland Composer Resource Manuals 37. New York: Garland Publishing, 1993.

——. "Elgar and J. S. Bach: A Wider Perspective." "The Maynooth International Musicological Conference 1995 Selected Proceedings: Part 2," edited by Patrick F. Devine and Harry White, 179–90. Irish Musical Studies 5. Dublin: Four Courts Press, 1996.

——. "The Organ of St. George's Church, Worcester, in the Early Life of Edward Elgar." *British Institute of Organ Studies Journal* 18 (1994): 92–107.

Kilian, Dietrich. *Kritischer Bericht to Neue Bach-Ausgabe*, ser. 4, vols. 5 and 6 (*Präludien, Toccaten, Fantasien und Fugen für Orgel*). Kassel: Bärenreiter; Leipzig: VEB Deutscher Verlag für Musik, 1978–79.

——. *Kritischer Bericht to Neue Bach-Ausgabe*, ser. 4, vol. 7 (*Sechs Sonaten und verschiedene Einzelwerke*). Kassel: Bärenreiter; Leipzig: VEB Deutscher Verlag für Musik, 1988.

Kinsky, Georg. *Manuskripte. Briefe. Dokumente von Scarlatti bis Stravinsky. Katalog der Musikautographen Sammlung Louis Koch*. Stuttgart: Hoffmannsche Buchdruckerei Felix Krais, 1953.

Kirk, Herbert L. *Pablo Casals*. New York: Holt, Rinehart and Winston, 1974.

Klingemann, Karl, ed. *Felix Mendelssohn-Bartholdys Briefwechsel mit Legationsrat Karl Klingemann*. Essen: G. D. Baedeker, 1909.

Klotz, Hans. *Kritischer Bericht to Neue Bach-Ausgabe*, ser. 4, vol. 2 (*Die Orgelchoräle aus der Leipziger Originalhandschrift*). Kassel: Bärenreiter; Leipzig: VEB Deutscher Verlag für Musik, 1957.

Kobayashi, Yoshitake. "Franz Hauser und seine Bach-Handschriftensammlung." Ph.D. diss., Georg-August-Universität, 1973.

Koegler, Horst. Liner notes to *Roland Petit: Le jeune homme et la mort—Carmen*. TDK Marketing Europe (2006).

Kossmaly, Carl. "Das Sängerfest in Frankfurt am Main." *Neue Zeitschrift für Musik* 9, nos. 21 and 24 (September 11 and 21, 1838): 83–84 and 96–98.

Krause, Andreas. "…und fliehet dem Bache zu…Kompositorische Bach-Rezeption 1950–2000." In *Johann Sebastian Bach und die Gegenwart: Beiträge zur Bach-Rezeption 1945–2005*, edited by Michael Heinemann and Hans-Joachim Hinrichsen, 307–403. Cologne: Verlag Dohr, 2007.

Krause, Peter. "Carl Ferdinand Beckers Wirken für das Werk Johann Sebastian Bachs." *Beiträge zur Bachforschung* 1 (1982): 85–95.

——. *Originalausgaben und ältere Drucke der Werke Johann Sebastian Bachs in der Musikbibliothek der Stadt Leipzig*. Bibliographische Veröffentlichungen der Musikbibliothek der Stadt Leipzig 5. Leipzig: Musikbibliothek der Stadt Leipzig, 1970.

Kube, Michael. "Modelle und Lösungen: Überlegungen zu den Choralbearbeitungen über 'Wie schön leuchtet der Morgenstern' von Pachelbel, Buttstett/Armsdorf und Bach." In *Bach und seine mitteldeutschen Zeitgenossen*, edited by Rainer Kaiser, 190–98. Schriften zur mitteldeutschen Musikgeschichte 4. Eisenach: Karl Dieter Wagner, 2001.

Langer, Arne. "Bach auf der Bühne—Ein Überblick." In *Johann Sebastian Bach und die Gegenwart: Beiträge zur Bach-Rezeption 1945–2005*, edited by Michael Heinemann and Hans-Joachim Hinrichsen, 201–29. Cologne: Verlag Dohr, 2007.

Leaver, Emmie Bowman. "Some Impressions of Sir Edward Elgar." *Musical Opinion*, July 1934, 869–70.

Leisinger, Ulrich. "Bachian Fugues in Mozart's Vienna." *Bach Notes: The Newsletter of the American Bach Society* 6 (Fall 2006): 1–7.

Leisinger, Ulrich, and Peter Wollny. "'Altes Zeug von mir': Carl Philipp Emanuel Bachs kompositorisches Schaffen vor 1740." *Bach-Jahrbuch* 79 (1993): 127–204.

——. *Die Bach-Quellen der Bibliotheken in Brüssel: Katalog*. Leipziger Beiträge zur Bach-Forschung 2. Hildesheim: Georg Olms, 1997.

Lerner, Neil. "The Strange Case of Rouben Mamoulian's Sound Stew: The Uncanny Soundtrack in *Dr. Jekyll and Mr. Hyde* (1931)." In *Music in the Horror Film: Listening to Fear*, edited by Neil Lerner, 55–79. New York: Routledge, 2010.

Leupold, Wayne, ed. *César Franck: The Complete Organ Works*. 2 vols. Colfax, NC: Wayne Leupold Editions, 2002.

Little, Wm. A. "Felix Mendelssohn and J. S. Bach's *Prelude and Fugue in E Minor* (BWV 533)." *American Organist* 39, no. 2 (February 2005): 73–83.

——. *Mendelssohn and the Organ*. New York: Oxford University Press, 2010.

——. "Mendelssohns Dilemma: Die Sammlung Choralvorspiele oder die Passecaille?" In *"Zu gross, zu unerreichbar"—Bach-Rezeption im Zeitalter Mendelssohns und Schumanns*. Beiträge zur Geschichte der Bach-Rezeption 1, edited by Anselm Hartinger et al., 381–93. Wiesbaden: Breitkopf & Härtel, 2007.

Löhlein, Heinz-Harald. *Kritischer Bericht to Neue Bach-Ausgabe*, ser. 4, vol. 1 *(Orgelbüchlein, Sechs Choräle von verschiedener Art [Schübler Choräle], Orgelpartiten)*. Kassel: Bärenreiter; Leipzig: VEB Deutscher Verlag für Musik, 1987.

Lopate, Phillip. Liner notes to *Andrei Tarkovsky's Solaris*. The Criterion Collection, 2002.

Lueders, Kurt. "Bach in Frankrijk rond 1900." *Het orgel* 96, no. 4 (2000): 26–34.

Lutz, Rudolf. "Eine Orgelsonate über den Choral 'O Haupt voll Blut und Wunden'? Zur Ergänzung von Mendelssohns Fragment GB-Ob, MS. M. Deneke Mendelssohn, b. 5, 28. Ein Arbeitsbericht." In *"Diess herrliche, imponirende Instrument": Die Orgel im Zeitalter Felix Mendelssohn Bartholdys*. Beiträge zur Geschichte der Bach-Rezeption 3), edited by Anselm Hartinger et al., 151–71. Wiesbaden: Breitkopf & Härtel, 2011.

Macan, Edward. *Endless Enigma: A Musical Biography of Emerson, Lake and Palmer*. Chicago: Open Court, 2006.

Marshall, Robert L. "Bach and Mozart's Artistic Maturity," *Bach Perspectives* 3 (1998): 47–79.

Martin, Uwe. "Ein unbekanntes Schumann-Autograph aus dem Nachlass Eduard Krügers." *Die Musikforschung* 12 (1959): 405–15.

Matthaei, Karl, ed. *Johann Pachelbel: Ausgewählte Orgelwerke*, vol. 3. Kassel: Bärenreiter, 1965.

Maul, Michael, and Peter Wollny, eds. *Weimarer Orgeltabulatur: Die frühesten Notenhandschriften Johann Sebastian Bachs sowie Abschriften seines Schülers Johann Martin Schubart*. Kassel: Bärenreiter, 2007.

McCrea, Andrew. "British Organ Music after 1800." In *The Cambridge Companion to the Organ*, edited by Nicholas Thistlethwaite and Geoffrey Webber, 279–98. Cambridge: Cambridge University Press, 1998.

Mendelssohn Bartholdy, Paul, ed. *Reisebriefe von Felix Mendelssohn Bartholdy aus den Jahren 1830 bis 1832*. Leipzig: Hermann Mendelssohn, 1861. (English translation, *Letters from Italy and Switzerland by Felix Mendelssohn Bartholdy*. London: Longmans, Green, Reader, and Dyer, 1863.)

Mendelssohn Bartholdy, Paul, and Carl Mendelssohn Bartholdy, eds. *Briefe aus den Jahren 1833 bis 1847 von Felix Mendelssohn Bartholdy*. Leipzig: Hermann Mendelssohn, 1863. (English translation, *Letters of Felix Mendelssohn Bartholdy, from 1833 to 1847*. London: Longmans, Green, Reader & Dyer, 1863.)

Meyer, Hans-Dieter. *"Wie aus einer anderen Welt:" Wilhelm Middelschulte, Leben und Werk*. Kassel: Bärenreiter, 2007.

Millington, Barry. "Who's Who of Wagner's Contemporaries." In *The Wagner Compendium: A Guide to Wagner's Life and Music*, edited by Barry Millington, 22–34. New York: Schirmer Books, 1992.

Miramon Fitz-James, Henri de. Obituary notice for Adolphe Marty. *L'Orgue* 44 (1947): 95–96.

Mohr, Wilhelm. *Cäsar Franck: Ein deutscher Musiker*. Stuttgart: J. G. Cotta, 1942.

Moore, Jerrold Northrop. *Edward Elgar: A Creative Life*. Oxford: Oxford University Press, 1984.

———. *Edward Elgar: Letters of a Lifetime*. Oxford: Clarendon Press, 1990.

———. *Edward Elgar: The Windflower Letters (Correspondence with Alice Caroline Stuart Wortley and her Family)*. Oxford: Clarendon Press, 1989.

———. *Elgar and his Publishers*. 2 vols. Oxford: Clarendon Press, 1987.

———. *Elgar on Record: The Composer and the Gramophone*. London: Oxford University Press, 1974.

Morana, Frank. "A New Bach Organ Chorale." *American Organist* 42, no. 12 (December 2008): 76–77.

Moser, Dietz-Rüdiger, ed. *Clara Schumann: Mein liebes Julchen (Briefe von Clara Schumann an ihre Enkeltochter Julie Schumann)*. Munich: Nymphenburger, 1990.

Murray, Michael. *Marcel Dupré: The Work of a Master Organist*. Boston: Northeastern University Press, 1985.

Musch, Hans. "Johann Sebastian Bachs Pastorella BWV 590." *Ars Organi* 55 (2007): 234–40.

Neubacher, Jürgen. "Der Hamburger St. Petri-Organist Johann Ernst Bernhard Pfeiffer (1703–1774) und die Organistenproben unter Mattheson (1725) und Telemann (1735)." In *"Critica musica": Studien zum 17. und 18. Jahrhundert. Festschrift Hans Joachim Marx zum 65. Geburtstag*, edited by Nicole Ristow et al., 221–32. Stuttgart: Metzler, 2001.

———. "Unbekannte Kompositionen Georg Philipp Telemanns in der wieder zugänglichen Musikhandschrift ND VI 81g:4 der Staats- und Universitätsbibliothek Hamburg." In *50 Jahre Musikwissenschaftliches Institut in Hamburg*, edited by Peter Petersen and Helmut Rösing, 385–404. *Hamburger Jahrbuch für Musikwissenschaft*, 16. Frankfurt: Peter Lang, 1999.

Newcomb, Anthony. "Ritornello Ritornato: A Variety of Wagnerian Refrain Form." In *Analyzing Opera: Verdi and Wagner*, edited by Carolyn Abbate and Roger Parker, 202–21. Berkeley: University of California Press, 1989.

New Grove Dictionary of Music and Musicians, 2nd ed., s.v. "Indy, (Paul Marie Théodore) Vincent d'." (by Andrew Thomson and Robert Orledge). Edited by Stanley Sadie. 12:370–75. London: Macmillan, 2001.

Nieuwkoop, Hans van. *Haarlemse orgelkunst van 1400 tot heden: orgels, organisten en orgelgebruik in de Grote of St.-Bavokerk te Haarlem. Muziekhistorische monografieën* 11. Utrecht: Vereniging voor Nederlandse Muziekgeschiedenis, 1988.

Oakeley, Edward Murray. *The Life of Sir Herbert Stanley Oakeley*. London: George Allen, 1904.

Ochse, Orpha. *Organists and Organ-Playing in Nineteenth-Century France and Belgium*. Bloomington: Indiana University Press, 1994.

O'Connell, Charles. *The Victor Book of Overtures, Tone Poems, and Other Orchestral Works*. New York: Simon & Schuster, 1950.

O'Donnell, John. "Mattheson, Bach, Krebs and the Fantasia & Fugue in C Minor BWV 537." *Organ Yearbook* 20 (1989): 88–95.

Olleson, Philip, ed. *The Letters of Samuel Wesley: Professional and Social Correspondence, 1797–1837*. Oxford: Oxford University Press, 2001.

———. *Samuel Wesley: The Man and his Music*. Woodbridge: The Boydell Press, 2003.

Owen, Barbara. "Bach Comes to America." *Bach Perspectives* 5 (2003): 1–14.

Palmer, Fiona M. *Domenico Dragonetti in England (1794–1846): The Career of a Double Bass Virtuoso*. Oxford: Clarendon Press, 1997.

Pape, Matthias. *Mendelssohns Leipziger Orgelkonzert 1840: Ein Beitrag zur Bach-Pflege im 19. Jahrhundert.* Wiesbaden: Breitkopf & Härtel, 1988.

Parrott, Ian. *Elgar.* London: J. M. Dent, 1971.

Parry, C. Hubert H. *Johann Sebastian Bach: The Story of the Development of a Great Personality.* New York: G. P. Putnam's Sons, 1909.

———. *The Life and Works of Edward John Hopkins.* London: Vincent, 1910.

Peterson, William J. "Lemmens, His *École d'orgue,* and Nineteenth-Century Organ Methods." In *French Organ Music from the Revolution to Franck and Widor,* edited by Lawrence Archbold and William J. Peterson, 51–100. Rochester: University of Rochester Press, 1995.

Phillips, Anthony, ed. *Sergey Prokofiev Diaries, 1907–1914: Prodigious Youth.* Ithaca, NY: Cornell University Press, 2006.

Pierre, Constant. *Le Conservatoire National de Musique et de Déclamation.* Paris: Imprimerie Nationale, 1900.

Pirro, André. *Johann Sebastian Bach: The Organist and His Works for the Organ.* Translated by Wallace Goodrich. New York: G. Schirmer, 1902.

Plath, Wolfgang. "Ein 'geistlicher' Sinfoniesatz Mozarts." *Die Musikforschung* 27 (1974): 93–95.

Pleasants, Henry, ed. *The Musical World of Robert Schumann: A Selection from His Own Writings.* London: Gollancz, 1965.

Prieberg, Fred K. *Musik im NS-Staat.* Frankfurt: Fischer Taschenbuch Verlag, 1982.

Rampe, Siegbert, ed. *Deutsche Orgel- und Claviermusik der Bach-Zeit: Werke in Erstausgaben.* Kassel: Bärenreiter, 2007.

Ratner, Sabina Teller. *Camille Saint-Saëns, 1835–1921: A Thematic Catalogue of His Complete Works.* Vol. 1, *The Instrumental Works.* New York: Oxford University Press, 2002.

Reed, William H. *Elgar as I Knew Him.* London: Victor Gollancz, 1936.

Reichling, Alfred. "Orgelklänge unter dem Hakenkreuz: Feiern–Feirräume–Feierorgeln." *Acta Organologica* 28 (2004): 411–44.

Respighi, Elsa. *Ottorino Respighi: His Life-Story.* London: Ricordi, 1962.

Richards, Annette, and David Yearsley, eds. *Carl Philipp Emanuel Bach: The Organ Works. Carl Philipp Emanuel Bach: The Complete Works,* ser. 1, vol. 9. Los Altos, CA: The Packard Humanities Institute, 2008.

Riethmüller, Albrecht. "Zur Geschichte eines Musikwerks: Die Interpretation von Präludium und Fuge ('St. Anne') für Orgel Es-Dur (BWV 552) zwischen Bach und Schönberg." In *Berliner Orgel-Colloquium,* edited by Hans Heinrich Eggebrecht, 31–44. Veröffentlichungen der Walcker-Stiftung 12. Kleinblittersdorf: Musikwissenschaftliche Verlags-Gesellschaft, 1990.

Rojsman, Leonid. *Die Orgel in der Geschichte der russischen Musikkultur.* Mettlach: Gesellschaft der Orgelfreunde, 2001.

Rosenmüller, Annegret. *Carl Ferdinand Becker (1804–1877): Studien zu Leben und Werk.* (*Musikstadt Leipzig* 4.) Hamburg: von Bockel Verlag, 2000.

———. "Carl Ferdinand Becker und die Organistenausbildung am Leipziger Konservatorium." In *"Diess herrliche, imponirende Instrument": Die Orgel im Zeitalter Felix Mendelssohn Bartholdys.* Beiträge zur Geschichte der Bach-Rezeption 3, edited by Anselm Hartinger et al., 285–301. Wiesbaden: Breitkopf & Härtel, 2011.

Rottermund, Krzysztof. "Chopin and Hesse: New Facts about their Artistic Acquaintance." *American Organist* 42, no. 3 (March 2008): 82–88.

Sabatier, Francois. *César Franck et l'orgue.* Paris: Presses Universitaires de France, 1982.

Schanz, Arthur. *Johann Sebastian Bach in der Klaviertranskription*. Eisenach: Karl Dieter Wagner, 2000.

Schmieder, Wolfgang. *Thematisch-systematisches Verzeichnis der musikalischen Werke von Johann Sebastian Bach*. Rev. ed. Wiesbaden: Breitkopf & Härtel, 1990.

Schneider, Max. "Verzeichnis der bis zum Jahre 1851 gedruckten (und der geschrieben im Handel gewesenen) Werke von Johann Sebastian Bach." *Bach-Jahrbuch* 3 (1906): 84–113.

Scholes, Percy A. *The Mirror of Music 1844–1944: A Century of Musical Life in Britain as Reflected in the Pages of the Musical Times*. 2 vols. London: Novello, 1947.

Schonberg, Harold C. *The Great Pianists*. New York: Simon & Schuster, 1963.

——. *Horowitz: His Life and Music*. New York: Simon & Schuster, 1992.

Schulenberg, David. *The Keyboard Music of J. S. Bach*. New York: Schirmer Books, 1992.

Schulze, Hans-Joachim. *Studien zur Bach-Überlieferung im 18. Jahrhundert*. Leipzig: Edition Peters, 1984.

Schumann, Eugenie. *Erinnerungen*. Stuttgart: Engelhorn, 1925.

Schumann, Robert. *Gesammelte Schriften*. 4 vols. Leipzig: Georg Wigand, 1854.

Schünemann, Georg. "Die Bachpflege der Berliner Singakademie." *Bach-Jahrbuch* 25 (1928): 138–71.

Schweitzer, Albert. *J. S. Bach*. 2 vols. Translated by Ernest Newman. Leipzig: Breitkopf & Härtel, 1911.

Schützeichel, Harald. *Die Konzerttätigkeit Albert Schweitzers*. Bern: Paul Haupt, 1991.

Setchell, Jenny. *Organ-isms: Anecdotes from the World of the King of Instruments*. Christchurch: Pipeline Press, 2008.

Seyfried, Hans Jürgen. *Adolph Friedrich Hesse als Orgelvirtuose und Orgelkomponist*. Forschungsbeiträge zur Musikwissenschaft 17. Regensburg: Gustav Bosse, 1965.

Shaw, (George) Bernard. *Music in London 1890–94*. 3 vols. London: Constable and Company, 1932.

Sieling, Andreas. "'Selbst den alten Vater Sebastian suchte man nicht mehr so langstielig abzu-haspeln': Zur Rezeptionsgeschichte der Orgelwerke Bachs." In *Bach und die Nachwelt*. Vol. 2, 1850–1900, edited by Michael Heinemann and Hans-Joachim Hinrichsen, 299–339. Laaber: Laaber-Verlag, 1999.

Smith, Rollin. "Early American Organ Recordings." In *Litterae Organi: Essays in Honor of Barbara Owen*, edited by John Ogasapian et al., 233–52. Richmond, VA: OHS Press, 2005.

——. *Louis Vierne: Organist of Notre-Dame Cathedral*. The Complete Organ 3. Stuyvesant, NY: Pendragon Press, 1999.

——. "The Organ of the Trocadéro and Its Players." In *French Organ Music from the Revolution to Franck and Widor*, edited by Lawrence Archbold and William J. Peterson, 275–308. Rochester: University of Rochester Press, 1995.

——. *Playing the Organ Works of César Franck*. The Complete Organ 1. Stuyvesant, NY: Pendragon Press, 1997.

——. *Saint-Saëns and the Organ*. Stuyvesant, NY: Pendragon Press, 1992.

——. *Stokowski and the Organ*. The Complete Organ 8. Hillsdale, NY: Pendragon Press, 2004.

——. *Toward an Authentic Interpretation of the Organ Works of César Franck*. Juilliard Performance Guide 1. New York: Pendragon Press, 1983.

——. *Toward an Authentic Interpretation of the Organ Works of César Franck*. Second edition. The Complete Organ 6. Hillsdale, NY: Pendragon Press, 2002.

Somfai, László. "Bartók's Transcription of J. S. Bach." In *Studien zur Musikgeschichte: Eine Festschrift für Ludwig Finscher,* edited by Annegrit Laubenthal, 689–96. Kassel: Bärenreiter, 1995.

Spitta, Philipp. *Johann Sebastian Bach.* 2 vols. Leipzig: Breitkopf & Härtel, 1873–79. (English translation, *Johann Sebastian Bach.* London: Novello, 1889.)

Sposato, Jeffrey S. "'For You Have Been Rebellious against the Lord': The Jewish Image in Mendelssohn's *Moses* and Marx's *Mose.*" In *Historical Musicology: Sources, Methods, Interpretations,* edited by Stephen A. Crist and Roberta Montemorra Marvin, 256–79. Rochester, NY: University of Rochester Press, 2004.

Statham, Heathcote. *The Organ and its Position in Musical Art.* London: Chapman and Hall, 1909.

Stauffer, George B. "Bach's Pastorale in F: A Closer Look at a Maligned Work." *Organ Yearbook* 14 (1983): 44–60.

———. "The Complete Organ Works of J. S. Bach: The Leupold Edition." *American Organist* 44, no. 9 (September 2010b): 40–43.

———. "Ein neuer Blick auf Bachs 'Handexemplare': Das Beispiel Clavier-Übung III." *Bach-Jahrbuch* 96 (2010a): 29–52.

———. *The Organ Preludes of Johann Sebastian Bach.* Studies in Musicology 27. Ann Arbor: UMI Research Press, 1980.

Steger, Hanns. *Vor allem Klangschönheit: Die Musikanschauung Josef Rheinbergers dargestellt an seinem Klavierschaffen.* Studien und Materialien zur Musikwissenschaft 23. Hildesheim: Georg Olms, 2001.

Stein, Fritz. *Thematisches Verzeichnis der im Druck erschienenen Werke von Max Reger.* Leipzig: VEB Breitkopf & Härtel, 1953.

Stinson, Russell. *Bach: The Orgelbüchlein.* Monuments of Western Music. New York: Schirmer Books, 1996.

———. "Bach's Earliest Autograph." *Musical Quarterly* 71 (1985): 235–63.

———. "Clara Schumann's Bach Book: A Neglected Document of the Bach Revival." *Bach: Journal of the Riemenschneider Bach Institute* 39, no. 1 (2008): 1–66.

———. *J. S. Bach's Great Eighteen Organ Chorales.* New York: Oxford University Press, 2001.

———. "Mendelssohns grosse Reise: Ein Beitrag zur Rezeption von Bachs Orgelwerken." *Bach-Jahrbuch* 88 (2002): 119–37.

———. *The Reception of Bach's Organ Works from Mendelssohn to Brahms.* New York: Oxford University Press, 2006.

———. "Some Thoughts on Bach's Neumeister Chorales." *Journal of Musicology* 11 (1993): 455–77.

———. "Toward a Chronology of Bach's Instrumental Music: Observations on Three Keyboard Works." *Journal of Musicology* 7 (1989): 440–70.

Synofzik, Thomas. "'Ich lasse mir alles von Bach gefallen': Robert Schumann als Bach-Herausgeber." In *"Diess herrliche, imponirende Instrument": Die Orgel im Zeitalter Felix Mendelssohn Bartholdys.* Beiträge zur Geschichte der Bach-Rezeption 3, edited by Anselm Hartinger et al., 369–88. Wiesbaden: Breitkopf & Härtel, 2011.

———. "Neues aus Bachs Werkstatt: Die Choralbearbeitung 'O Lamm Gottes unschuldig' aus der Sammlung Mempell-Preller." *Concerto* 155 (2000): 26–35.

Taille, Andrew. "Nürnberg, Darmstadt, Köthen–Neuerkenntnisse zur Bach-Überlieferung in der ersten Hälfte des 18. Jahrhunderts." *Bach-Jahrbuch* 89 (2003): 143–72.

Thistlethwaite, Nicholas. *The Making of the Victorian Organ*. Cambridge Musical Texts and Monographs. Cambridge: Cambridge University Press, 1990.

Thorau, Christian. "Richard Wagners Bach." In *Bach und die Nachwelt*. Vol. 2, 1850–1900, edited by Michael Heinemann and Hans-Joachim Hinrichsen, 163–99. Laaber: Laaber-Verlag, 1999.

Tielke, Martin. "Eduard Krüger als Wegbereiter der Bach- und Händelrenaissance." *Jahrbuch der Gesellschaft für bildende Kunst und vaterländische Altertümer zu Emden* 72 (1992): 170–206.

Todd, R. Larry. *Mendelssohn: A Life in Music*. New York: Oxford University Press, 2003.

——. "New Light on Mendelssohn's *Freie Phantasie* (1840)." In *Literary and Musical Notes: A Festschrift for Wm. A. Little*, edited by Geoffrey C. Orth, 205–18. Frankfurt: Peter Lang, 1995.

Torrence, Richard, and Marshall Yeager. *Virgil Fox (The Dish): An Irreverent Biography of the Great American Organist*. New York: Circles International, 2001.

Tournemire, Charles. *César Franck*. Les grands musiciens par les maitres d'aujourd'hui 5. Paris: Librairie Delagrave, 1931.

Vallas, Léon. *César Franck*. Translated by Hubert Foss. New York: Oxford University Press, 1951.

Verdin, Joris. "César Francks *L'Organiste*." In *César Franck: Werk und Rezeption*, edited by Peter Jost, 159–73. Stuttgart: Franz Steiner Verlag, 2004.

Walker, Alan. *Franz Liszt*. 3 vols. Ithaca, NY: Cornell University Press, 1988–97.

Ward Jones, Peter, ed. *The Mendelssohns on Honeymoon: The 1837 Diary of Felix and Cécile Mendelssohn Bartholdy Together with Letters to Their Families*. Oxford: Clarendon Press, 1997.

——. Review of organ editions in *Notes: Quarterly Journal of the Music Library Association* 65, no. 3 (March 2009): 577–81.

Weissweiler, Eva, ed. *Clara und Robert Schumann: Briefwechsel*. 3 vols. Basel and Frankfurt: Stroemfeld Verlag, 1984–2001.

Widor, Charles-Marie, and Albert Schweitzer, eds. *Johann Sebastian Bach: Complete Organ Works*. Vol. 2, *Preludes and Fugues of the First Master Period*. New York: G. Schirmer, 1912.

——. *Johann Sebastian Bach: Complete Organ Works*. Vol. 4, pt. 2, *Preludes and Fugues of the Mature Master Period*. New York: G. Schirmer, 1913.

Williams, Peter. *The Organ Music of J. S. Bach*. Cambridge Studies in Music. 3 vols. Cambridge: Cambridge University Press, 1980–84.

——. *The Organ Music of J. S. Bach*. 2nd ed. Cambridge: Cambridge University Press, 2003.

Wolff, Christoph. "Bach's Organ Toccata in D Minor and the Issue of its Authenticity." In *Perspectives on Organ Playing and Musical Interpretation: A Festschrift for Heinrich Fleischer at 90*. Veröffentlichung der Gesellschaft der Orgelfreunde 191, edited by Ames Anderson et al., 85–107. New Ulm, MN: Martin Luther College, 2002.

——. "Bach's Personal Copy of the Schübler Chorales." In *J. S. Bach as Organist: His Instruments, Music, and Performance Practices*, edited by George Stauffer and Ernest May, 121–32. Bloomington, IN: Indiana University Press, 1986a.

——. "The Deathbed Chorale: Exposing a Myth." In Wolff, *Bach: Essays on His Life and Music*, 282–94. Cambridge, MA: Harvard University Press, 1991.

——. "Die historischen Orgeln der Thomaskirche." In *Die Orgeln der Thomaskirche zu Leipzig*, edited by Christian Wolff, 9–20. Leipzig: Evangelische Verlagsanstalt, 2005.

——. *Johann Sebastian Bach: The Learned Musician*. New York: W. W. Norton, 2000.

——, ed. *The Neumeister Collection of Chorale Preludes from the Bach Circle*. New Haven: Yale University Press, 1986b.

Wolff, Christoph, and Markus Zepf. *Die Orgeln J. S. Bachs: Ein Handbuch*. Veröffentlichung der Gesellschaft der Orgelfreunde 216. Leipzig: Evangelische Verlagsanstalt, 2006.

Wollny, Peter. "Zur Bach-Rezeption in den Orgelwerken von Felix Mendelssohn Bartholdy." In *"Diess herrliche, imponirende Instrument": Die Orgel im Zeitalter Felix Mendelssohn Bartholdys*. Beiträge zur Geschichte der Bach-Rezeption 3, edited by Anselm Hartinger et al., 133–49. Wiesbaden: Breitkopf & Härtel, 2011.

Young, Percy M. *Elgar, O. M.: A Study of a Musician*. London: Collins, 1955.

Zászkaliczy, Támas, ed. *Johann Sebastian Bach: Sämtliche Orgelwerke*, vol. 4, Verschiedene Einzelwerke. Budapest: Editio Musica Budapest, 1990.

Zenck, Martin. *Die Bach-Rezeption des späten Beethoven*. Beihefte zum Archiv für Musikwissenschaft 24. Stuttgart: Franz Steiner Verlag, 1986.

Zimmerman, Edward, and Lawrence Archbold. "'Why Should We Not Do the Same with Our Catholic Melodies?': Guilmant's *L'Organiste liturgiste*, op. 65." In *French Organ Music from the Revolution to Franck and Widor*, edited by Lawrence Archbold and William J. Peterson, 201–47. Rochester: University of Rochester Press, 1995.

Zwetzschke, Jana. *"…ich bin sicher, dass ich ihn lieben lerne…" Studien zur Bach-Rezeption in Russland*. Studien und Materialien zur Musikwissenschaft 52. Hildesheim: Georg Olms, 2008.

INDEX

Lightning Source UK Ltd.
Milton Keynes UK
UKHW020801290520
363954UK00005B/452